THE OFPIS FILE

Books by Vernon Coleman include:

The Medicine Men (1975)
Paper Doctors (1976)
Stress Control (1978)
The Home Pharmacy (1980)
Aspirin or Ambulance (1980)
Face Values (1981)
The Good Medicine Guide (1982)
Bodypower (1983)
Thomas Winsden's Cricketing Almanack (1983)
Diary of a Cricket Lover (1984)
Bodysense (1984)
Life Without Tranquillisers (1985)
The Story Of Medicine (1985, 1998)
Mindpower (1986)
Addicts and Addictions (1986)
Dr Vernon Coleman's Guide To Alternative Medicine (1988)
Stress Management Techniques (1988)
Know Yourself (1988)
The Health Scandal (1988)
The 20 Minute Health Check (1989)
Sex For Everyone (1989)
Mind Over Body (1989)
Eat Green Lose Weight (1990)
How To Overcome Toxic Stress (1990)
Why Animal Experiments Must Stop (1991)
The Drugs Myth (1992)
Complete Guide To Sex (1993)
How to Conquer Backache (1993)
How to Conquer Pain (1993)
Betrayal of Trust (1994)
Know Your Drugs (1994, 1997)
Food for Thought (1994, revised edition 2000)
The Traditional Home Doctor (1994)
People Watching (1995)
Relief from IBS (1995)
The Parent's Handbook (1995)
Men in Dresses (1996)
Power over Cancer (1996)
Crossdressing (1996)

How to Conquer Arthritis (1996)
High Blood Pressure (1996)
How To Stop Your Doctor Killing You (1996, revised edition 2003)
Fighting For Animals (1996)
Alice and Other Friends (1996)
Spiritpower (1997)
How To Publish Your Own Book (1999)
How To Relax and Overcome Stress (1999)
Animal Rights – Human Wrongs (1999)
Superbody (1999)
Complete Guide to Life (2000)
Strange But True (2000)
Daily Inspirations (2000)
Stomach Problems: Relief At Last (2001)
How To Overcome Guilt (2001)
How To Live Longer (2001)
Sex (2001)
We Love Cats (2002)
England Our England (2002)
Rogue Nation (2003)
People Push Bottles Up Peaceniks (2003)
The Cats' Own Annual (2003)
Confronting The Global Bully (2004)
Saving England (2004)
Why Everything Is Going To Get Worse Before It Gets Better (2004)
The Secret Lives of Cats (2004)
The Cat Basket (2005)
The Truth They Won't Tell You (And Don't Want You To Know)
About The EU (2005)
Living in a Fascist Country (2006)
How To Protect and Preserve Your Freedom, Identity and Privacy
(2006)
The Cataholic's Handbook (2006)
Animal Experiments: Simple Truths (2006)
Coleman's Laws (2006)
Secrets of Paris (2007)
Cat Fables (2007)
Too Sexy To Print (2007)
Oil Apocalypse (2007)
Gordon is a Moron (2007)

novels
The Village Cricket Tour (1990)
The Bilbury Chronicles (1992)
Bilbury Grange (1993)
Mrs Caldicot's Cabbage War (1993)
Bilbury Revels (1994)
Deadline (1994)
The Man Who Inherited a Golf Course (1995)
Bilbury Pie (1995)
Bilbury Country (1996)
Second Innings (1999)
Around the Wicket (2000)
It's Never Too Late (2001)
Paris In My Springtime (2002)
Mrs Caldicot's Knickerbocker Glory (2003)
Too Many Clubs And Not Enough Balls (2005)
Tunnel (1980, 2005)
Mr Henry Mulligan (2007)
Bilbury Village (2008)

as Edward Vernon
Practice Makes Perfect (1977)
Practise What You Preach (1978)
Getting Into Practice (1979)
Aphrodisiacs – An Owner's Manual (1983)

with Alice
Alice's Diary (1989)
Alice's Adventures (1992)

with Donna Antoinette Coleman
How To Conquer Health Problems Between Ages 50 and 120 (2003)
Health Secrets Doctors Share With Their Families (2005)

THE OFPIS
FILE

The Organisation For The Preservation Of Individuality And Sovereignty

Vernon Coleman

Published by Blue Books, Publishing House, Trinity Place,
Barnstaple, Devon EX32 9HG, England.

First published in 2008
Reprinted 2008

ISBN: 978-1-899726-09-7

A catalogue record for this book is available from
the British Library.

Printed by CPI Antony Rowe, Chippenham

Dedication

To Donna Antoinette, all ways and forever; with all my love (as always) and with my thanks to her for her having the good sense to persuade me not to use the working title I had originally intended to adopt for this book. The abandoned title consisted of two words, the second of which was spelt EU and pronounced 'you'

Contents

Vernon Coleman

Acknowledgements

I owe a huge debt to the many readers who have helped me by sending in information. I am constantly amazed at (and grateful for) the variety of documents which I am sent. The trick, in political and investigative journalism is, of course, to be able to put news items into perspective and it seems to me that many of my readers are far more skilled at this than most professionals. Much reporting about the EU ends with vitally important developments, pronouncements and facts being relegated to a couple of lines on page 48; though it is always difficult to say whether this is a result of deliberate obfuscation or simple ignorance and incompetence. These are darker and more dangerous times than most people realise. Discovering and exposing the truth can be a strange, tiring, frustrating (and sometimes dangerous) business. I offer my heartfelt thanks to those readers who have overcome all these obstacles to continue to dig out nuggets of truth.

These days I rely very little on the mainstream media for news and information. Television, radio and newspapers rarely contain anything of value or significance. And most of what they do contain is spin – planted by lobbyists with a vested interest and a message to sell. Instead, I rely far more on books produced by small presses around the world, newsletters and documents which have been sent to me by readers. Occasionally, I obtain a small nugget of value from the Internet but, like the mainstream media, most of the so-called news and information on the Internet is contaminated

13

by vested interests, commercial lobbyists and prejudice. The Web is not a safe source of honest, unbiased information and is never to be relied upon unless you know (or trust and respect) the specific source, the creator(s) of the website you are using, and know whether or not they accept advertisements, subsidies and other financial inducements.

Special thanks to Thumper Robinson and Patchy Fogg (for providing security), Peter Marshall (for stationery supplies and general sustenance) and to all at the Duck and Puddle (especially Frank and Gilly) for providing moral and spiritual guidance and a torch and umbrella on dark and wet nights.

This book incorporates some material from two previous books of mine: *Saving England* and *The Truth They Won't Tell You (And Don't Want You To Know) About The EU*. But the vast majority of the material here is new. I have shown in detail how we have been deceived, betrayed and cheated by a ruthless bunch of lying fascists. And how we've paid them well to do it to us.

Finally, I am delighted to report that this book was written, published and printed in England.

Vernon Coleman, March 2008

1

Foreword

'One day the whole of Europe will be one vast socialist state...even England.'
LENIN

If you are over 30, you will have noticed some dramatic changes to just about every aspect of life in Britain. If you are under 30, you will just have to take my word for it: things weren't always this bad. There were times when you could walk through a provincial town centre at 11p.m., unarmed and unguarded, and stand an excellent chance of arriving at your destination with your skin and wallet intact.

This isn't a prelude to the usual, dreary things-were-better-in-my-day tirade. Statistics as well as abundant anecdotal evidence show that just about every aspect of life in Britain is deteriorating rapidly. Everything is getting worse. For example, private medical care in Britain is now about at the level that the NHS was at twenty years ago.

For decades I have campaigned about health care and food, and on behalf of people and animals. During recent years, I have noticed (I could hardly not) that the introduction of many new laws has seemed to coincide with the rapid deterioration in the quality of life in Britain. Most of these new laws seemed to remove the rights of individuals and increase the rights of bureaucrats, politicians and international corporations.

As a campaigning writer, I found life becoming increasingly difficult. Obtaining information has become considerably more difficult (despite the Government's inaccurately named Freedom of Information Act), and many of my books were very effectively banned – for no other reason than that they told the truth.

It didn't take long to discover that most of the new legislation eroding our freedom, destroying our culture and damaging our ability to speak out came not from Westminster but from our Masters in Brussels. It became clear that the EU was the reason for most of the bad things that were happening. At first glance, the EU is either a fascist organisation run by crooks or a crooked organisation run by fascists. On close examination, however, it becomes clear that it is a fascist and crooked organisation run by fascist crooks.

England, I realised, would be a better, happier, healthier, richer place if the EU had never been invented, the nation had never joined and the voters had never been tricked into keeping the country in.

It became clear that attempting to campaign on behalf of people and animals was unlikely to be of much use while the EU continued to exist, and continued to churn out thousands of new laws. I was reminded of the old tale of the man who spends his life fishing people out of the river and then, at the end of his life, realises that he would have been rather more effective if he'd walked up the bank and had a firm word with the chap who was throwing all the people in.

At this point I should, I think, make my personal position clear.

I am not so much 'for' anything as I am against totalitarianism and fascism. I don't want to convert the world to my way of thinking and I certainly don't want to rule the world. I don't even want to tell everyone else what to do.

What I do object to, is being hemmed in by rules and regulations which have nothing to do with protecting society as a whole but everything to do with protecting the interests (mainly financial) of a few people who, it seems to me, have helped themselves to enough of our money and are quite rich enough and powerful enough already.

Freedom isn't something we are given by politicians. It is one of our few basic rights. It is something we must value and protect when it is threatened. You and I have rights as individuals which are being eroded by the people who run the EU without our permission. I believe that our freedom is now under greater threat than it was at any time during the 20th century. The EU is quite clearly a fascist organisation, and I firmly believe that it is as much of a threat to our liberty and our way of life as were the Nazis of Hitler's national socialism party. Our fight against the European Union is a fight against totalitarianism, tyranny and fascism.

I value the history and culture of my country.

I don't think it is better than the history or culture of any other country, but it is different and it is worth protecting – I would, as a matter of record, also fight to defend the history and culture of other sovereign nations within the EU. That, after all, is what so many Englishmen and women fought for in the two World Wars of the twentieth century.

I would, I confess, much rather be writing about things other than the EU. But I have always been fired and motivated by the importance of personal freedom and by injustice, and have written much, over the years, about animal and human rights. There is, I believe, little point in campaigning about other issues without also attacking the existence of the EU. The EU reaches into all aspects of our personal and professional lives. The true story of the EU is one of corruption, fraud and deceit.

Millions of people ignore what is happening. They do and say nothing for a variety of reasons. Some don't think the EU really affects them. Others don't have the energy to fight, and to stand up for their freedom. They are beaten down by daily drudgery – much of it produced, perhaps, with that intention by the EU. Most do and say nothing because they don't understand what is going on. They don't realise that every time they turn on the television or open a newspaper they are being lied to.

I've written this book solely because I want to expose the lies told by those who support the EU and to give the truth a bit of an airing.

All books and articles take sides, though many writers pretend to be fair and balanced when they are not. Journalists are skilled at writing articles which appear to say one thing but which actually say another. They are also adept at writing articles which appear to be fair and balanced but which are, in fact, designed to propose the very specific political interests and concerns of their corporate paymasters.

The advantage of writing something which is not going to be published by a corporation with 'interests' and 'agendas' is that I can tell the truth and express my views.

★★★

'Follow the path of the unsafe, independent thinker. Expose your ideas to the danger of controversy. Speak your mind and fear less the label of 'crackpot' than the stigma of conformity. And on issues that seem important to you, stand up and be counted at any cost.'
THOMAS J WATSON

★★★

When I started to research this book, I began collecting evidence of deceit, misinformation, corruption and dishonesty by governments, large companies and the EU.

I was concerned, in particular, with deceits which affect our freedom.

After twelve months of research I had (almost literally) a room full of research notes. It is usually impossible to see the surface of my desk but it had become impossible to see the carpet. Cuttings, Internet print-outs, letters, documents, journals, books and videotapes were piled in perilously high stacks. There is so much corruption and deceit practised by and within the EU that it is impossible for one man to keep track of it all. The EU has made freedom a dirty word and has turned patriotism into a sin. When British MPs voted to approve the signing of the Treaty of Lisbon (which Gordon Brown had signed in December 2007) they signed the final death warrant for Britain and for England. I am certain now that it is no exaggeration to say that almost everything bad that has happened to Britain in the last few decades is the fault of the EU. (Starting wars and exposing ourselves to terrorist activity was, of course, the responsibility of Tony Blair and Gordon Brown.)

Within this book you will find many things you should know, and many things the Government, the BBC and the national press won't tell you (and don't want you to know).

Vernon Coleman   March 2008

2

The History of the EU

'Europe's nations should be guided towards the superstate without their people understanding what is happening. This can be accomplished by successive steps, each disguised as having an economic purpose, but which will eventually and irreversibly lead to federation.'
JEAN MONNET (A FRENCH FOUNDER OF THE EU)

'We are with Europe, but not of it. We are linked, but not combined. We are associated, but not absorbed. And should European statesmen address us and say, 'Shall we speak for thee?', we should reply, 'Nay, Sir, for we dwell amongst our own people.''
WINSTON CHURCHILL (CHURCHILL WAS A FIRM ADVOCATE OF A PAN EUROPEAN UNION OF STATES BUT HE PREFERRED BRITAIN TO BE ON THE OUTSIDE, AS AN INDEPENDENT, FREE MARKET PARTNER.

Forming a European superstate is not a new idea. In 800 AD, just three centuries after the fall of the Roman Empire, Charlemagne, King of the Franks, had himself crowned by the Pope in Rome. His imperial seal bore the words 'The Renewal of the Roman Empire'.

After his death, Charlemagne's empire fell apart but the idea didn't go away and was fondly remembered by Napoleon Bonaparte. A millennium or so later, in 1804, when Napoleon had himself crowned, he publicly called for the help and support of Charlemagne. In 1802, he created the Legion of Honour on the model of the Roman Legio Honoratorum.

Napoleon claimed that if he had won the siege of Moscow, Europe would have been: 'but one people, and anyone who travelled anywhere would have found himself always in the common fatherland.' But Napoleon, though born a Corsican, was the self-appointed protector of all things French, and couldn't help adding: 'Paris would have been the capital of the world, and the French the envy of the nations.'

★★★

A century and a half after the great days of Napoleon, supporters of Adolf Hitler gave their leader the Roman salute. The cry 'Heil Hitler!' was modelled on 'Hail Caesar'. When Hitler's army formed a new SS division for French volunteers, they called it the Charlemagne division. In 1936, Hitler told the Reichstag: 'It is not very intelligent to imagine that in such a cramped house like that of Europe, a community of peoples can maintain different legal systems and different concepts of law for long.' His pal Mussolini, the father of fascism, said in 1933 that: 'Europe may once again grasp the helm of world civilisation if it can develop a modicum of political unity.' Oswald Mosley, Britain's leading fascist in the 1930s, also supported the idea of a European Union.

★★★

In 1944, a conference was held in Berlin entitled 'How Will Germany Dominate The Peace When It Loses The War?' Powerful Germans decided to move a huge amount of money out of Germany, through Madrid, and to take it to America. The money stayed there until after the Nürnberg Trials when it came back to Europe. Some of the money was, allegedly, used to hold a series of conferences. The first was held at The Hague at the Bilderberg Hotel. And that was the beginning of the infamous Bilderberg Group. And a little later, Heidricht's 1942 Plan for the Domination of Europe was reworked a little and renamed the Treaty of Rome.

The blueprint for the New Europe uses many of Napoleon's ideas (federal law, the common economic market and the dismantling of frontiers for example). The EU's plan for a common legal code, a common currency as a symbol of imperial rule and the building of 'trans-European' roads linking the various parts of the empire was hardly new and would have been recognised by both Napoleon and Hitler.

In 1941, Walter Funk, Hitler's economics Minister, launched the Europaische Wirtschafts Gemeinschaft (European Economic Community) to establish a single European currency – the reichsmark. Hitler's plan was to integrate the European economy into a single market.

In 1945, Hitler's masterplan (captured by the allies) included a scheme to create an economic integration of Europe and to found a European Union on a federal basis. The Nazi plan for a federal Europe was based on Lenin's belief that: 'Federation is a transitional form towards complete union of all nations.'

I will send a case of good champagne to the first person who can define a noticeable difference between the design of Hitler's planned EU and the structure of the EU we have.

Oddly enough, however, it was neither the French nor the Germans who started off the plans for this latest superstate. It was the Americans who triggered the formation of the modern EU – a new European superstate destined to be run by a group of powerful, unelected bureaucrats.

The Americans encouraged the formation of the European superstate because they thought it would be easier to control and, therefore, to bring under the wing of their world government. They thought it would be much easier to take charge of the EU than to take charge of a bunch of scheming, jealous nations with a long, bad history together. And they thought that by building up the world's most powerful military machine and taking charge of the world's oil (a rapidly disappearing but essential resource) they would eventually be able to control everything. When they succeeded in breaking up the Soviet Union they thought they were well on the way to controlling the world.

But the American plan has been wrecked by two things that the Americans didn't foresee and didn't control.

The first thing they didn't foresee was that their hubris would lead to their downfall. America, of course, is now finished as an imperial nation. It has started on a rapid and unstoppable slide into chaos and penury.

And the second thing they missed was the rise of two hugely

populated countries which aren't particularly rich in natural resources and which they had previously thought were largely irrelevant: China and India.

However, as America has declined, their creation – the EU – has prospered.

★★★

The birth of the modern EU started at the end of the Second World War when USA President Truman's advisors warned him that European countries were so broke that they didn't have any money left with which to buy American exports. The Americans, ever conscious of their own wealth, were worried that their country would suffer if the Europeans cut back on their spending and so decided that Europe needed to be 'economically revived'.

(Naturally, there was a political purpose to this too. The Americans also believed that giving Europe a boost, and making European countries look more attractive, would attract parts of the communist world into the Western camp).

And so the Americans organised a meeting in Paris. To make things look good they invited the Russians (who had, after all, just played a major part in defeating Hitler) but laid down conditions (as Americans are prone to do) requiring the Russians to allow the Americans to have free access to Russian raw materials and to dictate Russian industrial targets. Naturally, as the Americans well knew, this ensured that the Russians walked out.

(The walk-out resulted in the creation of the Iron Curtain and the Eastern European trading bloc, and for decades gave the American Government an excuse to hand over huge amounts of tax payers' money to arms manufacturers.)

When the Russians had stomped off back home, the Americans laid down European targets for industrial output and gave various sectors of Europe different schedules. (The Americans have never really subscribed to the free market theory.) It was these targets which led first to the development of the European Coal and Steel Community, then to the Common Market and, eventually, to the birth of the European Union. Europe was effectively organised to suit the American economy.

Contrary to the view generally held by Americans, the Marshall

Plan (for thus it was) cost the Americans nothing but gave them a great deal. This was, perhaps, the first grand example of the Americans interfering with other nations in order to benefit their own economy.

Through their self-interest, the Americans changed the face of Europe for decades and created chaos and suspicion everywhere. Curiously, George Marshall (the man who gave his name to the 'Plan') was awarded the Nobel Peace Prize for his work in helping to create the Iron Curtain. There is a plaque remembering the Marshall Plan fixed to the wall at the join of the rue de Rivoli and the place de la Concorde (just a few yards away from the present site of the Paris branch of the English booksellers W.H.Smith). The survival of the plaque is a tribute to the ability of the Americans to con the French and make them believe that the whole Marshall Plan business was for their benefit.

★★★

Many people have written to me suggesting that we should support the EU in order to oppose and influence the growing strength and belligerence of the USA. Those who suggest this, claim that it is crucial that we help the EU become a powerful superstate as a counter-balance and opposition to the United States of America. What they perhaps do not realise is that the EU is very much a creation of the USA. The USA has been secretly funding and encouraging the growth of the EU since its very inception.

The Americans (with that peculiar brand of naivety which is going to cause them so much trouble) have always believed that a united Europe will be easier to deal with and easier to control. They even believe (and I know this is difficult to believe but please bear with me because it is true) that Britain will be able to persuade the rest of Europe to agree to join Britain in being a sort of American colony (and voting for America at the United Nations).

The USA has always supported the idea of a strong EU, with the UK as a member, and has constantly pushed the UK into becoming more closely integrated with the other members of the EU. They have done this, as always, out of self-interest. The Americans want a strong Europe which will buy large quantities of American goods

– particularly arms and aircraft – and be capable of paying for the policing of the European theatre. The Americans are unlikely to feel threatened by a strong Europe. They believe that they can always bully any group of countries and get their own way.

★★★

For decades now, the two fundamental pillars of British foreign policy have been the so-called 'special relationship' with the USA (we do what they want us to do and use what is left of our fading reputation to give their aggressive, imperialistic ambitions some credibility and, in return, they ignore us when we want anything) and our membership of the developing European Union.

The Americans have never hidden the fact that they see Britain's enthusiasm for what our politicians call the 'special relationship' as a rather pathetic allegiance. In a fit of honesty, the American Secretary of State, Dean Rusk once told Harold Wilson that 'the USA did not want to be the only country ready to intervene in any trouble spot in the world'. The Americans realised, many decades ago, that their plan to rule the world would arouse far less resentment among other nations if they were seen to have a sabre waving ally. And, in the most dangerous of their military adventures the Americans have used British troops as fodder.

Our 'special relationship' with the USA dates back to the 1940s when we were desperately trying to persuade the Americans to join in the Second World War.

(During the Second World War, the USA made no secret of the fact that it saw the conflict as an opportunity to take over the role as global superpower and to displace Britain from those parts of the world which had for some years been coloured pink on the old-fashioned atlases. The Americans had already started to plan control of the entire non-Soviet world.)

There is today absolutely no evidence that British politicians have any influence over the USA.

Our link with the EU is rather more recent but dates back to the 1960s when civil servants decided that Britain had no future unless it became part of the burgeoning European State. Back in 1968, the Foreign Office wrote that: 'If we want to exercise a major influence in shaping world events, and are prepared to meet the costs, we need to be influential with a much larger power system than we ourselves possess. The only practical possibilities open to us are to wield influence with Western Europe or the United States or both.'

But there is evidence that even the intellectually disadvantaged civil servants at the Foreign Office were aware of the dangers of this policy.

A Foreign Office paper published in 1958 warned that 'the United Kingdom is already greatly dependent upon US support' but that 'we must never allow this to develop to the point where we seem to be little more than an instrument of United States policy'.

Oh dear. Whoops.

It was this civil service policy which misled Wilson into trying to take Britain into the EU and encouraged the wretched, lying and treacherous Heath to succeed.

Back in the 1960s, Foreign Office civil servants regarded our membership of the Common Market as likely to enhance our 'special relationship' with the USA. And there is no doubt that it was to please America that Britain persisted in attempting to join the Common Market. In 1968, the Foreign Office warned that 'if we fail to become part of a more united Europe, Britain's links with the USA will not be enough to prevent us becoming increasingly peripheral to USA concerns.'

The Foreign Office believed that 'we can regain sufficient influence in world affairs to protect our interests overseas' by joining the EEC.

Bizarrely, and with an appalling lack of foresight and understanding, the Foreign Office stated that: 'it is the hope of bringing our economic influence to bear more effectively in the political field that constitutes the principle motive of our application to join the EEC'.

Who were these anonymous Foreign Office civil servants who got it so completely wrong? Who were the Foreign Office mandarins who betrayed their nation? How many of them supplemented their grotesquely over-generous, index-linked pensions with knighthoods in reward for their stupidity and treachery? They should have all been shot as traitors.

Right from the start, America saw Britain as a Trojan Horse within the Common Market.

In 1966, American President Johnson was told by his Undersecretary of State that Britain should be 'applying her talents and resources to the leadership of Western Europe'. Johnson was advised that the USA should be encouraging Britain's membership of the EEC because this would suit American interests by providing the balance in Europe that 'might tend to check the dangerous tendencies which French nationalism is already producing.'

In other words, the Americans wanted us to join the EEC so that we could push the EEC into behaving in a way which the Americans wanted. We were also expected to keep America up-to-date with what the EEC was planning.

By 1972, the bright boys and girls at the Foreign Office had spotted this and were reporting that: 'The UK will, in its own interests, take on at times the role of Trojan Horse (in the EEC)... but its effectiveness in this role will depend on...not appearing to act as a US stooge.'

Even today, on the rare occasions when the Labour Party opposes EU plans for the new federal state they do so not because they care about our disappearing culture and history but because some of the specific objectives (notably plans for EU military capability and plans to sell weapons to China) are seen as contrary to American interests. The Americans, having created the EU, are now terrified that if the EU becomes a truly powerful force there is a considerable risk that Germany will pull the strings.

★★★

'It (is) impossible for Britain to accept the principle, that the most economic forces of this country should be handed over to an authority that is utterly undemocratic and is responsible to nobody.'
CLEMENT ATTLEE, LABOUR PRIME MINISTER RESPONDING
TO THE SCHUMAN PLAN FOR THE EUROPEAN COAL AND STEEL
COMMUNITY IN 1950.

★★★

The European Union was created on 25th March 1957 when the leaders of Belgium, France, Germany, Italy, Luxembourg and the Netherlands gathered to sign the Treaty of Rome. The aim, they said, was to ensure the free movement of goods, labour and capital between their countries and to abolish trusts and cartels. They wanted reciprocal policies on labour, social welfare, transport, foreign trade and agriculture.

To begin with, Britain remained outside the original Common Market but when British Prime Minister Harold Macmillan visited America in 1961, he asked President Kennedy how America would react if Britain applied to join the EEC. The response was that the White House would support the application only if Britain accepted that the true goal of the Common Market was political integration.

From that moment on, successive British Governments knew (but didn't tell the people) that the aim of the Common Market was the formation of a new European state.

British politicians lied to disguise the damaging consequences to the Commonwealth – knowing that Britain would have to turn her back on her traditional long-established trusting trading partners.

★★★

It is perhaps not widely known but the British press helped trick the electorate into supporting Britain's entry into the Common Market. And once we had been taken in, it was the press which encouraged that Britons voted 'Yes' to stay in the Common Market.

By 1971, it was obvious that most British newspapers were wildly committed to Britain becoming a member of the EEC. Only the *Express* titles were not clamouring for membership.

The *Financial Times* and the *Daily Mirror* had both been strong advocates of membership from the early 1960s.

The first Prime Minister to try to lead Britain into the EEC was Harold Wilson who, from 1966, was convinced that Britain could not survive outside the EEC. His Government's application to join, in May 1967 was vetoed by General de Gaulle, the French president, whose life and career had been saved by the British during the Second World War. Actually, French President Charles de Gaulle rejected Britain's application to join the Common Market twice. In public he argued that Britain, a traditional island nation, was not suited to be part of a European superstate. That was just political flim-flam. In reality he rejected Britain (despite everything that Britain had done for him and France during the Second World War) because he wanted to delay Britain's entry until the Common Agricultural Policy (the CAP – designed to give huge subsidies to French peasant farmers) had been properly set up. Once the CAP was in place, the loathsome de Gaulle suddenly decided that Britain's island history no longer mattered and he became enthusiastic about Britain joining the Common Market. Naturally, he really wanted Britain to join the Market in order to help pay for the costs of running the CAP and keeping French farmers satisfied. Right from the start of the EU, Britain has been used by both America and France. And it is still happening.

Three years later, when the utterly foul and repulsive Ted Heath got into Number 10 Downing Street he began negotiations again and a treaty was agreed in January 1972. This was the infamous treaty in which the treasonous Heath lied to everyone and betrayed his country. Heath is the greatest traitor Britain has ever had. He has done more long-term damage to his country than any outsider – including Hitler.

Just in case any reader feels that I'm calling Edward Heath a traitor because he is dead and cannot sue me I should, perhaps, point out that I called this self-confessed liar a traitor when he was alive. (And dying didn't change his status as a traitor.)

★★★

'When Britain signed the Treaty of Rome and passed the European Communities Act 1972, the superiority of European Law was accepted, and Parliament was no longer sovereign (although the UK can leave the EU any time it wishes). As a result, British Courts have no power to review Acts of Parliament and in light of EU legislation, suspend Statute Law.'
JAMES COPELAND, WRITING FROM THE BRITISH GOVERNMENT'S DEPARTMENT FOR CONSTITUTIONAL AFFAIRS

★★★

In the months prior to Heath's betrayal, the British public had not been convinced that they wanted their country to enter the EEC. Many, perhaps, simply didn't trust the politicians' claims that membership would be merely a commercial convenience. One opinion poll in early 1971 showed that the British people were against entry by the astonishing ratio of three to one. This opposition came despite the expenditure by the European Commission Information Service of around £10 million on trying to persuade opinion formers of the benefits of membership of the EEC.

With it looking as though joining the EEC might be political suicide the Government became desperate. Heath's Government paid for the distribution of propaganda extolling the virtues of membership and produced a White Paper which was full of unsubstantiated claims for the EEC and which deliberately omitted any mention of the costs of membership or the fact that joining the EEC was the first step towards a United States of Europe.

Heath only got away with his Great Betrayal because the press had decided that entry was a 'good thing' (for them and their proprietors), and so did not question any of the claims made by Heath's Government.

Editors and columnists slavishly obeyed the dictates of their proprietors. If the press had done its job properly, Britain would have almost certainly never joined the EEC and would now be a considerably wealthier and more powerful nation.

The *Financial Times*, *The Times*, *The Guardian*, *The Daily Telegraph*, *The Sunday Times*, *The Observer*, the *Daily Mail*, *The Sun* and *The Economist* were all wildly enthusiastic about Britain joining the EEC. (As, indeed, most of them still are.) Throughout the run up to the day of our joining, the daily news in Britain was delivered with a preposterous pro-EEC slant designed to suppress the truth and to convince the public that without membership of the EEC neither they nor their country had much of a future. Only occasionally did the papers admit that the politicians were spinning like tops. *The Times* remarked that Geoffrey Rippon, the Cabinet Minister responsible for negotiating Britain's entry, was behaving 'almost as though he has something to hide'. (He certainly did.) The *Daily Mirror* (which, at the time, had by far the largest sale in England) was unrelenting in describing the prizes of membership as immense and warning readers that if they voted against membership of the EEC they would become 'mere lookers-on from an off-shore island of dwindling insignificance'.

When Prince Philip claimed that the EEC's Common

Agricultural Policy was an example of bad management the *Daily Mirror* called him a 'chump'. (So, now who's the chump?)

The pro-EEC line appeared on news and feature pages and was supplemented with huge numbers of full-page advertisements paid for by the European Movement.

Heath took Britain into the EEC with the help of the nation's press and without ever giving the electors a chance to say whether or not their country should become part of the European 'project'.

Only the *Daily Express* 'stood alone – with the people' against membership of the EEC. The paper praised Philip's scepticism about the Common Agricultural Policy, announcing that 'The people applaud his good sense...and wish it were more widely shared by our rulers.' But once the vote for membership had been won, even the *Daily Express* capitulated and accepted the verdict.

★★★

'A nation can survive its fools, and even the ambitious. But it cannot survive treason from within. An enemy at the gates is less formidable, for he is known and he carries his banners openly. But the traitor moves among those within the gate freely, his sly whispers rustling through all the alleys, heard in the very halls of government itself. For the traitor appears no traitor; he speaks in the accents familiar to his victims, and he wears their face and their garments, and he appeals to the baseness that lies deep in the hearts of all men. He rots the soul of a nation; he works secretly and unknown in the night to undermine the pillars of a city; he infects the body politic so that it can no longer resist.
A murderer is less to be feared.'
MARCUS TULLIUS CICERO

★★★

When, at the next election, Heath was thrown out by the British electorate the subsequent Prime Minister, crafty pipe sucking Harold Wilson, agreed to the unprecedented idea of asking the British people for their view on membership; he announced that there would be a referendum to decide whether or not Britain should remain in the EEC. (The referendum appeared in the Labour Party's 1974 election manifesto, and may well have been one of the reasons for Wilson's victory.)

This was the first and last chance the British people had to express their view on the EEC. (For the record, I am delighted to report that I voted 'No' – against the EEC. It seemed to me pretty obvious that the politicians were lying and planning something considerably more sinister than a trading partnership.) The question to be asked in the referendum was simple: 'Do you think that the United Kingdom should stay in the European Community (the Common Market)?'

The referendum vote took place in June 1975 and virtually the whole of the British press joined in to extol the virtues of membership of the EEC. Even the *Daily Express* now joined the other papers in support of the EEC. Of Britain's national press only the *Morning Star* campaigned against the EEC.

During the run up to the referendum, the press either supported the 'Yes' vote campaigners or ignored the campaign completely. When Tony Benn accurately revealed that almost half a million jobs had been lost in England since the country had entered the Common Market, and correctly predicted that many jobs would be lost if we stayed in, the papers dismissed his claim as nonsense. The *Daily Mirror*, for example, sneered about 'lies, more lies and those damned statistics'. *The Daily Telegraph* nauseatingly talked about 'an intellectual, moral and spiritual value' in the EEC. The *Financial Times* predictably quoted John Donne ('no man is an island') and argued that to leave the EEC 'would be a gratuitous act of irresponsible folly'. *The Guardian* described the referendum as 'a vote for the next century'. The *Daily Mail* told its readers to 'Vote YES for Britain'. The *Daily Express* announced: 'The Express is for the market'. *The Sun* told readers: 'Yes for a future together. No for a future alone.'

In the days before the crucial vote, the national papers had, between them, 188 front pages. Disgracefully, only 33 of those front pages were devoted to the most important vote in Britain's history.

On the day of the vote, the *Daily Mail* didn't even put the referendum on its front page. The *Daily Mirror*'s front page on polling day screamed: 'A Vote for the Future'. Inside the Mirror had a picture of nine pupils at an international school in Brussels, one child from each EEC country. Eight of the children stood together, cuddling and cosy. The ninth child stood alone, isolated and sad. 'He's the odd lad out,' said the *Mirror*. 'The boy beyond the fringe. The one whose country still has to make up its mind. For The Lad Outside, Vote Yes.'

The vast majority of the material printed in the national press was supportive of the EEC and dismissive of those who questioned the value of membership. There was no debate and the result, therefore, was a foregone conclusion. The political establishment, big business and the press conspired to suppress the truth and to 'sell' the electorate a ragbag of lies.

This was, in my view, the beginning of the end for the independence and integrity of the British press. Newspaper proprietors have always used their papers to promote their own views, often for their own commercial advantage, but this was I believe the first time that the British press had united to support such a sinister and dishonest purpose. If editors did not know that they were encouraging the British people to hand over their independence, they were incompetent and stupid. If they knew but did it anyway then they were as guilty of treason as Heath, Rippon and the long tawdry line of British Prime Ministers and Ministers who have followed them.

Conned, tricked, lied to and spun into a world which bore no resemblance to reality, the British people voted to stay in the Common Market. A total of 17.3 million voted 'yes' and 8.4 million voted 'no'. The establishment, aided and abetted by the press, had turned a massive suspicion and disapproval of the Common Market into a massive level of support.

It was the British press which helped lying, cheating, conniving politicians trick the electorate into accepting membership of the EEC. How many people would have voted for the EEC if they had known the truth?

★★★

It has been revealed that prior to the signing of the Treaty of Rome, England's Lord Chancellor wrote to Prime Minister Edward Heath with this warning: 'I must emphasise that in my view the surrenders of sovereignty involved are serious ones...these objections ought to be brought out into the open.'

Heath, who should have been hung as a traitor, assured the nation that there would be no loss of sovereignty.

★★★

'Better to lose a little sovereignty than to lose a son or daughter.'
A BIZARRE AND REVEALING SLOGAN FROM THE 1975 PRO-COMMON
MARKET CAMPAIGN. THE SLOGAN SHOWED THAT THE PROPONENTS OF
THE COMMON MARKET WERE ADMITTING THAT THERE WOULD BE A
LOSS OF SOVEREIGNTY IF WE STAYED IN THE COMMON MARKET. THE
REFERENCE TO LOSING 'A SON OR DAUGHTER' WAS INTENDED TO IMPLY
THAT IF WE DIDN'T STAY IN THE COMMON MARKET WE MIGHT SOMEHOW
FIND OURSELVES AT WAR WITH GERMANY OR FRANCE.

★★★

*'Britain could not be an ordinary member of a federal union limited to Europe
in any period which can...be foreseen.'*
WINSTON CHURCHILL

★★★

The EU has expanded a great deal in a relatively short period
of time. It started life as a simple coal-and-steel community in
the early 1950s. By the time England joined, it had become a
Common Market, designed to help encourage trade between
selected European countries. When Britons got a chance to vote
on whether or not the country should stay in the Common
Market there were no outward signs that the EEC was about to
metamorphose into a United States of Europe.

Today, bit by bit, the EU has acquired a currency, a central
bank, a parliament, a civil service, a supreme court, a military staff
and an army, its own police force, a flag, a diplomatic corps and
an anthem.

★★★

'What good fortune for governments that the people do not think.'
ADOLF HITLER

★★★

The changes have taken place with hardly a whimper of protest.
There have been very few electoral revolts against European
integration. Most taxpayers know very little of the EU or the
impact it is having on their lives. Most assume (erroneously) that
the new laws they dislike come from their own governments.
There are no mainstream political parties opposing or even
questioning the aims and targets of the EU.

But the number of people opposed to the EU is growing. In Germany, one of the founder members of the EU, around 40% think their country has benefited from EU membership but another 40% think it hasn't. The citizens of France are so unenthusiastic about the EU that huge numbers of shops still display prices in francs as well as euros, even though the French franc has been of only historical interest for some years now. A poll taken throughout Europe showed that around half of the electorate would be 'very relieved', or wouldn't mind, if the EU simply disappeared. Where governments have offered their citizens a referendum on EU issues the results have been largely negative. The people of Ireland have probably benefited more from the EU than the citizens of most other countries and yet when the Irish Government gave voters a chance to express their views on the Nice Treaty (a flawed attempt to modernise the EU, which paved the way for a recent EU expansion) the voters roundly rejected the Treaty. The Irish Government and the EU had to do some fancy dancing and have a second vote in order to get the Irish people to come up with the 'right' answer. Forcing a second vote when the first vote doesn't produce the right result is becoming increasingly common. When the Danes voted 'No' to the Maastricht Treaty in 1992, they were given a 'second chance' and duly voted 'Yes' in 1993.

The Swedes and the Danes both voted against adopting the euro. Three quarters of Britons dislike the EU, and in most other EU countries the EU has a positive image among less than half the electorate.

The EU has been foisted on us without our understanding and against our will. We have been lied to, deceived and cheated by whole generations of European and British politicians. Every British Minister from Ted Heath onwards should be locked in the Tower of London and charged with treason.

The EU simply isn't what they said it was going to be.

We were sold a trading partnership.

We've been given a federal Europe.

★★★

'Seven multinational companies or wealthy families own all the mass circulation newspapers in Britain. Generally speaking, they use their papers

*to campaign single-mindedly in defence of their commercial interests and the
political policies which will protect them.'*
Tony Benn, 1981

★★★

The European Commission helped to fund the YES campaign in 1975 when Britons voted on whether or not to stay in the Common Market. This was like allowing an accused man and his friends sit on the jury. More recently, when Britain was preparing for a referendum on the EU constitution, the European Commission once again provided funds to help the YES campaign. What can be more corrupt than a public body using taxpayers' funds to pay to influence a vote in its favour?

★★★

'The German is an expert on secret paths to chaos.'
Nietzsche

★★★

In 1776, Adam Waishaupt suggested that the 'elite' members of the population should take over the world.

His plan for world domination contained seven basic points:

1. Abolition of all individual governments.
2. Abolition of private property.
3. Abolition of inheritance.
4. Abolition of patriotism.
5. Abolition of religion.
6. Abolition of the idea of the family,
7. Creation of a World Government.

These plans have been adopted by many secret organisations now active in geopolitical affairs.

The EU's policies and aims seem to fit well into Waishaupt's plan.

★★★

'If you ask me to choose between Europe and the open sea, I choose the open sea.'
Winston Churchill

★★★

When the Single European Act was signed in the mid 1980s, it was sold by the British Government as nothing more than a removal of trade barriers – the development of a free trade area; a single market.

But the EU and its employees and bribees saw the Act as a major step towards a United States of Europe. They saw the single market as a chance to establish heavily regulated domestic markets and to protect them from globalisation. The single market was devised as a way to remove competitive advantages which individual countries might have and to smother every industry within the EU with bureaucracy intended to harmonise and standardise European industries.

The single market was devised with political ends. Working hours had to be regulated so that no country had any advantage over another because its people were prepared to work harder. Labour rules had to be regulated so that no country was at a disadvantage because its employers were more heavily controlled. Taxes had to be regulated and unified so that individuals and companies were all burdened in the same way.

The single market doesn't encourage competition. On the contrary, it stifles competition and works against free trade.

The irony is that none of this stifling comes cheap. One of the EU's own commissioners for enterprise and industry admitted that EU regulations cost the European economy 600 billion euros a year (about £450 billion in real money). Any benefits which the single market might theoretically bring are far, far outweighed by the bureaucratic costs. Europeans are a good deal poorer because of the EU. And because the world's expiring work horse (America) and the up and coming workhorses (China and India and other Asian countries) have none of these nonsensical regulations, Europeans are bound to get considerably poorer in the future.

Incidentally, the same EU commissioner who reported that EU regulations are costing so much also complained that attempts to get rid of regulations were thwarted by the powerful civil servants working for the EU. A plain example of the tail wagging the dog.

All things considered, it is hardly surprising that most British businesses now claim that the costs of the single market now far outweigh any benefits there may be.

A poll conducted by Open Europe showed that by a margin of two to one, British businesses want to reduce the UK's relationship with the EU to a free trade area. Clearly, the vast majority of British businesses want Britain to leave the European Union. So much for the oft-repeated claim that British business is enthusiastic about the EU and would hate Britain to leave.

It is clear that the vocal and powerful minority who want Britain to remain within the EU are locked in an outdated geopolitical paradigm.

★★★

When Britain joined the EU we knew we had to accept all the existing laws that the members had already set up. But even at the last minute we were stitched up. Just hours before Britain joined, the existing members suddenly agreed to the principle of equal access to 'community' fishing waters. This really should have been a deal-breaker for Britain which is, after all, an island with rather traditional reliance on its fishing waters.

But Edward Heath's Government was desperate to sign up, and regarded Britain's fishing industry as expendable. Having promoted the Common Market and won some sort of public support for joining it, the Government simply didn't have the courage to turn to the electors and admit that the deal had gone sour. So, like sad teenagers joining a club, we accepted this new agreement without a murmur. It was one of the most pathetic and dumb pieces of negotiating ever done.

Today, the EU's common fisheries policy, which sets maximum allowable catches, is a shambles. It has ruined the British fishing industry and created a social, economic and environmental disaster. A report by auditors confirms that the actual level of catches is unknown, that most rule-breakers are never caught and that the ones who are caught face only 'trifling' fines. As a result of the EU's common fisheries policy, 81% of north-east Atlantic fish stocks are dangerously over-exploited. The current quota system means that fishermen throw cheaper fish back into the sea and keep only the most valuable ones. Sadly, the cheaper fish are dead by the time they get back into the water. The only question remaining is: how long will it be before there are no fish at all left in European seas?

★★★

Heath and other British leaders knew that joining the EEC meant ultimately creating a European federal state, with monetary, political and military union. Moreover, Heath knew that the policy must be regarded as irreversible.

And yet in a White paper presented to Parliament, Heath promised that joining the EEC would involve no surrender of essential sovereignty.

It was, quite possibly, the biggest and most important lie ever told, and just why Heath did not die incarcerated in the Tower of London as a traitor is a mystery. (The dictionary definition of a traitor is someone who is disloyal to their country.)

An internal Government memorandum justified the deception by suggesting that the British people wouldn't notice what had happened until the end of the century by which time it would all be far too late. The anonymous writer of that memorandum was, of course, quite right. I believe that every politician who has served in a British Government since Edward Heath took England into the Common Market is a traitor. Some may not have known what was going on. They should have known. Some may now regret what they did. That doesn't alter the fact that they betrayed their country.

In retrospect, we would have been better off, and better able to recapture our freedom if the wretched Heath had tied us into the Soviet bloc.

The biggest threat to freedom always comes from a nation's own government. If criminality is the violation of individual rights then the British Government has done more to justify the label 'criminal' than any individual or organisation.

★★★

Since we joined the EEC, every British PM has been completely outfoxed by our negotiating 'partners'. The outfoxing has usually been done by the French.

Margaret Thatcher, a supporter of the Common Market ('It is a myth that the Community is simply a bureaucracy with no concern for the individual,' she is reported to have once said, though if she did say that then it was perhaps under the influence of some mind-expanding substance) tried to reduce our payments into the EU, and was jubilant when she got a rebate. But the small print attached to the deal she had done meant that Britain had to pay much of its rebate itself. Whenever Britain now applies for CAP funds to help our farmers, anything over an agreed threshold triggers a correction mechanism which allows the European Union to claw back a huge chunk of the money. This means that Britain has to try to avoid applying for Common Agricultural Policy funds from the EU funds, though other countries more or less help themselves. Much of the money in the EU's CAP fund is, of course, provided by, you've guessed it, British taxpayers.

Thatcher's next blunder occurred four years later when she insisted on big cuts being made in the subsidies paid by the EU to French farmers. While negotiating, she made a concession which allowed an increase in the EU budget for regional funds.

This was what is commonly known as a mistake. Or, given the French influence, a faux pas.

Thatcher's concession enabled the EC to deal directly with regional authorities, bypassing national governments completely. This was a masterstroke by the EC bureaucrats who wanted a Federal Europe because, from this moment on, Brussels was free to give £20 billion a year to the European regions for all sorts of bizarre regional projects.

Naturally each project has to show the ring of stars EU flag to make it clear that the money has been donated by the kindly and benevolent EU.

(As an aside, the EU flag is getting everywhere these days. If a garage sells you a car with number plates carrying the flag of the European Union ask them to replace the plates with ones carrying the cross of St George. If they won't do that tell them that you will accept plain plates. If they won't do that – take your business elsewhere.)

For every £1 the EU hands out to a British region (always with a great deal of back slapping about how generous the EU is) the British taxpayer has already paid £2 into the EU pot. Britain also has to add another £1 to match the regional donation.

We must, I suppose, be grateful that the British negotiators let us off this lightly.

I wonder if the British civil servants who were responsible for all this are so inept when they get around to spending their own money. I do hope so. Perhaps motorcar and electrical appliance salesmen hang around in Whitehall making deals on the pavement with buffoons from all the British Ministries.

★★★

'Europe is always blind, cowardly, ungrateful and incorrigible –
a continent without hope...'
MARGARET THATCHER

★★★

There were, from the early 1980s, active plans to continue the process of turning the EU into a federal state. To this end there were two crucial treaties. The first was the Single European Act, signed by Margaret Thatcher and the second was the Treaty of Maastricht, which was signed by John Major.

The act which was signed by Margaret Thatcher, included a commitment to 'the progressive realisation of economic and monetary union'.

I'm not convinced that the lady with the handbag entirely understood what was going on. In 1988, Thatcher told the House of Commons that monetary union would not 'necessarily involve a single currency'. Just how monetary union would work without a single currency wasn't explained.

(Enthusiasts for various European projects do have a wonderfully whimsical way of looking at things. One leading industrialist told me that he was for the euro but not for the EU. I'm still trying to work out just how that could be managed.)

In 1994, the European Commissioners (an unaccountable, unelected group of dictators) decided to scrap the EEC and create the single Nation State of Europe.

The runaway vehicle was now totally out of control.

And we had become mere passengers, being driven to our destiny by anonymous, unelected bureaucrats.

★★★

The EU treaties are:
1. The Paris Treaty (established the European Coal and Steel Community). Not signed by the UK.
2. The Rome Treaty (signed by Edward Heath)

3. The Single European Act 1986 (signed by Margaret Thatcher)
4. The Maastricht Treaty 1992 (signed by John Major)
5. The Amsterdam Treaty 1997 (signed by Tony Blair)
6. The Nice Treaty 2001 (signed by Tony Blair)
7. The Lisbon Treaty 2007 (signed by Gordon Brown)

All the Prime Ministers who signed these treaties betrayed their country and their people.

★★★

Totalitarianism can be defined as:
1. A single mass party which is intertwined with government bureaucracy.
2. A system of terror by the police and secret police which is directed against the real and imagined enemies of the regime
3. A monopolistic control of the mass media.
4. A near monopoly of weapons.
5. A central control of the economy.
6. An elaborate ideology which covers all aspects of existence.

3

The Structure Of The EU

'The coming of a world state is longed for, and confidently expected, by all the worst and most disordered elements. This state, based on the principles of absolute equality of men and a community of possessions, would banish all national loyalties. In it, no acknowledgement would be made of the authority of a father over his children, or of God over human society. If these ideas are put into practice, there will inevitably follow a reign of unheard of terror.'
POPE BENEDICT XV, SPEAKING IN 1920

The EU has a Parliament. (Actually, it has two. A palace in Brussels and another one in Strasbourg. This is an excellent way to double the costs of doing nothing much.) The MEPs who sit in the Parliament have about as much power as the cleaners who tidy up the two buildings. There is one MEP for every 600,000 citizens in the new EU. Few people have any idea who their representative is, fewer still have ever had any contact with him or her. Votes are invariably cast along party political lines. The only people with whom MEPs have regular contact are lobbyists, representing business interests, and bureaucrats. This is the way fascism works in practice.

And then there is the European Council. This is a bizarre body which is made up of the heads of government of the 27 member countries. The Council meets every three months.

In practice, the EU is effectively run by 27 European Commissioners. These are unelected people who are nominated by their Governments. Each country has a commissioner. Britain's recent nominees include such luminaries as Neil Kinnock and Peter Mandelson. (Mandelson, of course, had to resign twice from Government in disgrace. It takes quite a lot for a Labour Minister to resign. He is currently the EU's man in charge of trade though precisely what qualifications he has for the job are being kept secret.)

Most of these commissioners have pretty pointless jobs which are created merely to give jobs for the boys. There is, for example, a Multilingualism Commissioner who is paid 18,200 euros a month to ensure that all EU documents are translated into the EU's 23 languages (including Irish Gaelic).

Labour's decision to appoint Peter Mandelson as England's EU commissioner accurately sums up the Government's contempt for the electorate and their fundamental lack of moral direction. The fact that the slimy Mandelson was readily accepted as a Commissioner, and seems to have fitted well into the EU bureaucracy, tells us more than we want to know about the nature of the EU. Mandelson and the EU go together well.

The European Commissioners have the exclusive right to put forward new legislation, to decide on priorities and to decide how EU members are to be integrated. Just about everything the commissioners do is designed to guard and protect their own power, to boost the power of the EU and to speed up the rate at which the federal state is developed. All powers which are surrendered by individual nations are quickly grabbed by the EC – never to be returned.

The EU is quango heaven and now provides huge salaries and pensions for a rapidly growing eurocracy. A bewildering array of agencies and organisations has been quietly created. There are now thousands of jobs for the boys and girls.

Here's a list of some of the EU's vast variety of quangos:

- The EU Fundamental Rights Agency
- The EU institute for Gender Equality
- The Translation Centre for the Bodies of the European Union
- The European Monitoring Centre on Racism and Xenophobia

- The Community Plant Variety Office
- The European Chemicals Agency
- The EU Food Safety Agency

There are many more. You are unlikely to have heard of most of them, though they will undoubtedly have a huge influence on your life.

The ability to place 'friends' and relatives (and, when they are contemplating retirement, themselves) on these quangos (and on the 7,000 quangos which now exist in England), ensures that politicians and bureaucrats and their associates remain loyal to the EU.

The original creators of the EU knew that once you create a bureaucracy it will quickly become self-sustaining. It was, of course, the French who invented the word 'bureaucrat'. Those who have experience of bureaucracy (there are few bigger and more bureaucratic organisations in the world than the National Health Service) will know that bureaucracy is self-sustaining, self-perpetuating and self-protecting. Bureaucrats always exist primarily to exist. Their primary responsibility is to themselves, their jobs, their status and their security. They will never admit to mistakes. They never resign. And if they are attacked they group together and defend themselves.

★★★

The enlarging of the EU benefits no one as much as the European Commission itself – the little band of unelected commissars whose decisions affect our lives but who are unregulated and uncontrolled.

Back in 1960, the EU budget was around £330,000,000 a year. That was equivalent to 0.03% of the national income of the EU's member states.

By 1985, the EU budget had risen to £30,000,000,000. A total of 0.93% of the EU's gross domestic product (GDP).

And by 1998, the EU's spending money had gone up to £60,000,000,000 a year, or 1.14% of the EU's GDP.

The plans now are to increase it to 1.24% of EU GDP.

This means that the financial burden on Britain must rise dramatically.

The countries which most recently joined the EU were mainly

former members of the Soviet bloc and are, therefore, quite poor. Their entry into the EU will raise the GDP of the EU as a whole by a mere 4% overall.

But as more and more poor nations join so the enthusiasm for a rising budget will go up. Turkey is due to be the next member of the EU. Turkey will have more votes than any other country (it's bigger) and will doubtless want a bigger-than-ever budget.

Inevitably, therefore, existing members of the EU will have to bear most of the burden of the higher budget. And since England is the EU's main contributor, it will be England which will have to find the extra cash. A few more NHS hospitals will have to close and a few more motorways will have to remain unbuilt.

The plan is that by 2013 the EU will be spending £110 billion a year. Precisely what our contribution will then be is anybody's guess.

All I can tell you is that if we are still in the EU it will be a lot. A hell of a lot.

And we will all be a lot poorer than we are now.

The EU has over 3,000 secret working groups. None of these groups is answerable to the public. All are staffed with people who suffer from delusions of adequacy.

★★★

Apart from the crooks who have found ways to take millions out of the EU, the main beneficiaries of the EU are the bureaucrats who work for it. (Actually, some of the crooks are also paid as bureaucrats and so use two shovels to help themselves to money from the EU money mountain.) EU bureaucrats aren't as bright as they think they are and are more crooked than we feared them to be. The vast majority of those working for the EU have no experience whatsoever of what it is like to run a business or to try to survive in the real world.

Thousands and thousands of the best paid, most mollycoddled administrators in the world sit in the Belgian capital running what will soon be the richest state in the world. They run the EU without interference from electors or taxpayers. They have massive expense accounts and many of them are adding to their huge salaries with kickbacks and fraud.

In 1999, the European Commission collapsed after charges of misconduct. In 2002, the EU's Court of Auditors refused to approve the 2002 $119 billion budget because of 'ineffective spending controls and financial irregularities'.

It isn't difficult to see why the EU exists.

But it's difficult to see why Britain is still a member.

★★★

The European Parliament exists as a rubber stamp for the EC, and to give the commission an appearance of respectability. Members of the European Parliament are there to 'serve' the commissioners, to pass the new legislation which has been decided by the commission. Individual MEPs are allowed to speak but never for more than 90 seconds at a time.

Today, the vast majority of the new laws which affect us come from unelected bureaucrats in Brussels. We have no opportunity to say 'no'. Most of this new legislation may, it is true, be discussed by the European Parliament but debating isn't allowed in the European Parliament. And decisions are made by majority voting. Even if we say no, no, a thousand times no, it will make no difference. It really will be a case of no meaning yes.

When you hear people talk about democracy in Europe, remember that the European Parliament exists only to rubber stamp new laws made up by the unelected European Commission and its bureaucrats. Members of the EU Parliament cannot veto the work of the European Commission.

★★★

The Members of the European Parliament get perks worth £140 million a year. That works out at a little over £175,000 a year per MEP.

Naturally, MEPs also receive a substantial salary.

The EU is the very antithesis of democracy; it is a perfect example of practical fascism in action. Those who support the EU do so either because they approve of the version of totalitarianism, statism and fascism purveyed by the EU or because they simply don't understand what has happened, what is happening and what is due to happen.

We are no longer in control of our lives or of our destinies.

The EU is as democratic as Nazi Germany under Hitler. The police forces and prisons of individual nations now exist to support the EU.

(I would remind any readers who think that I am exaggerating by comparing the EU with Germany under Hitler that it was George Orwell who pointed out that Hitler's Germany, in the guise of the Nazi Party, controlled investment, raw materials, rates of interest, working hours and wages and that although the factory owner still owned his factory he was for practical purposes reduced to the status of a manager. What difference is there between the EU and the Nazi Party?)

★★★

There are many EU supporters around who claim that the EU is democratically run, and that the European Parliament ensures that the wishes of the people of Europe are respected.

That is, to put it politely, a lie.

It isn't a teeny weeny little white lie.

It's a massive, twenty mile wide, five mile high, stinking, dirty black lie.

And here's a simple, single, specific example which shows that it is the unelected bureaucrats – not the political representatives – who have the power in the EU.

The people of Europe have, in numerous opinion polls, shown that they do not want to eat genetically modified food. And, in response to this feeling, the EU had planned to introduce strict regulations which would have protected European citizens from this threat.

But, just weeks before the stricter regulations were due to come into force, the unelected European Commission overruled the European Council of Ministers and the European Parliament (the one which is full of elected MEPs) and authorised the import of genetically modified maize for the manufacture of human food – either as whole sweet corn or as tinned sweet corn.

Why did they do this?

Simple.

The USA was putting a lot of pressure on the Commission.

And so the Commission caved in.

(You might now understand why the Labour Government

has shocked even its own supporters by ignoring public protests and insisting that we accept genetically modified food. The Government had no alternative. Once again, the EU bureaucrats had spoken.)

There have been no tests on the long-term effects of eating genetically modified food. There have been too few tests on the possibility of consumers developing allergy reactions. There has been no adequate toxicological testing.

But, even though we have made it perfectly clear that we are opposed to it, we now eat genetically modified food.

And we have to hope that nothing terrible happens.

Because no one knows whether it will or not.

The only thing I can tell you for certain is that the bureaucrats who made this decision are, like all EU employees, immune from prosecution for life. They cannot be prosecuted, whatever they have done. Even if they can be shown to have broken the law they are still immune.

The EU bureaucrats are untouchable and above the law.

If you care about justice, liberty, truth, humanity and your health then the EU and the Government are your enemy.

★★★

The EU has become a self-serving industry which now needs to continue to exist simply in order to satisfy the employment needs of the over-paid, over-fed people who work for it. It is difficult to find an accurate figure for the tens of thousands of people whose monthly salary cheques, hefty expenses and huge pensions are paid by the EU (the total figure seems to be in excess of 39,000) but, to put the whole thing in perspective, it is worth noting that there are 20,000 registered lobbyists in Brussels. There are also 2,600 registered 'interest groups' promoting the needs of their branch of industry, and countless thousands of journalists both writing pamphlets for the EU and then rewriting the pamphlets for public consumption.

★★★

A few years ago, I was invited to be patron of a charity called 'Transform' which was founded to campaign towards better drug control laws. (I have, for several decades, written extensively about the benefits of decriminalising drugs which are currently illegal). I helped the organisation as much as I could and gave them a large quantity of copies of my book *The Drugs Myth* to sell to raise funds.

Then, by accident, I discovered that my name had been taken off the charity's notepaper and website. Puzzled by the fact that this had happened and the fact that I had never been told, I wrote to them asking for an explanation. But I never received a reply.

However, I'm pleased to report that the organisation seems to be doing well. I have discovered that it has received funding from the European Commission.

How wise they were to have removed my name as a patron. I can't believe that having the author of *England Our England* on their masthead would have done much for the charity's chances of receiving an EU grant.

★★★

Every year the European Commission pays out around 800 million euros of our money to lobby groups. (That's around £600 million in real money.) Approximately 10,000 pressure groups receive funding from the EU this way. There is, of course, no link between this largesse and the fact that very few lobby groups have a bad word to say about the European Union.

Naturally, the lobby groups (who receive their funding from the EU) then lobby the EU (the only game in town if you're a lobbyist) to get what the companies they represent want.

Their effectiveness is readily shown.

So, for example, although the consumption of meat is as certain and as significant a cause of cancer as the smoking of tobacco, and although smoking is banned in public places, the consumption of meat is actively and openly encouraged. Television chefs, butchers shops and food corporations are all allowed to promote the eating of meat. When they tell lies and promote meat as an essential food no one tells them off.

The tobacco companies, whose lobbyists have been far less effective, have to concentrate on selling their products to Third World countries. And tobacco companies have now been banned from sponsoring sporting events within the EU. A good thing too, you might agree.

But for decades, the EU has paid out the best part of £1 billion a year in subsidies to European tobacco farmers. The subsidies were authorised so that farmers within the EU could grow cheaper tobacco.

Much of the tobacco the EU farmers grow is of poor quality; being so rich in tar and nicotine that it is unsuitable for sale within the EU.

So what happens to the particularly dangerous type of tobacco which the EU encourages farmers to grow?

You're not going to like this.

This tobacco, is dumped on poor Third World and Eastern block countries. It's relatively cheap for them to buy because (wait for it) it is subsidised by European taxpayers (that's you and me) through the EU.

Makes you proud to be a European, doesn't it?

★★★

Daft as they may seem to us, the constant storm of new laws produced by the EU are not without their raison d'être.

As one MP said recently: 'Whenever you see an apparently insane Brussels directive, someone, somewhere stands to gain'.

For example, the EU Food Supplements Directive effectively bans 300 nutrients included in 5,000 health products. This directive takes free choice and responsibility away from ordinary citizens and puts pressure on GPs who will have to deal with more patients wanting prescriptions.

Who stood to benefit from this directive?

That's easy to see: the international pharmaceutical industry.

Who lobbied for the directive?

There's no mystery about that: the international pharmaceutical industry.

When examining any EU directive, one only has to remember Lenin: to find the reason for a decision, simply find who benefits.

The EU and the Labour Government clearly care far more for the pharmaceutical industry than they do for the freedom, health and welfare of the British people.

EU regulators have decided that food from cloned animals is safe to eat. Eurocrats at the European Food Safety Authority have decided that cloned livestock and their products are as healthy and nutritious as natural born animals.

How can they possibly know this? How can they know that there will not be unforeseen dangers? How do they know that one in ten consumers of cloned animal produce will not develop genetic abnormalities or cancer?

I don't know. And, with all due and relevant modesty, I would add that I am a qualified doctor and registered general practitioner whose warnings on health issues have repeatedly been proved accurate. I'm not entirely sure what qualifications the eurocrats have. As far as I can find out, no research has been done. The EU has admitted that 'the available data for risk assessment are limited', and that there are gaps in our knowledge about the welfare of the animals involved. The EU has also conceded that 'the health and welfare of a significant proportion of clones have been found to be adversely affected.'

The EU eurocrats in charge of forcing us to accept cloned animals concluded that: 'It is very unlikely that any difference exists in terms of food safety between food products originating from clones and their progeny compared with those derived from conventionally bred animals.'

How reassuring is that word 'unlikely'.

What I can tell you is that just at the time that the EU decided that cloned foods would be safe to eat in Europe, the Food and Drug Agency in the USA was about to decide whether or not cloned foods were safe for Americans to eat. The American Government was known to be keen to promote cloned animals in order to boost the income of American companies. And European farmers were worried that they would be uncompetitive if American farmers were allowed to use cloned animals and they weren't.

Several EU countries have refused to accept the EU's guidance and reassurance on genetically modified food and will almost certainly refuse to accept its guidance and reassurance on cloning. The British Government will, of course, accept the EU's decision even though this means rejecting advice from one of its own expert committees.

I do not, of course, suspect for a moment that the EU's decision had anything to do with commercial lobbying from European farmers.

4

Were We Taken Into The EU Illegally?

'We have before us an ordeal of the most grievous kind. You ask what is our policy? I will say: It is to wage war, by sea, land and air, with all our might and with all the strength that God can give us; to wage war against a monstrous tyranny, never surpassed in the dark, lamentable catalogue of human crime. That is our policy. You ask, What is our aim? I answer in one word: Victory. Victory at all costs, victory in spite of all terror, victory, however long and hard the road may be; for without victory, there is no survival. Let that be realised; no survival for the British Empire; no survival for all that the British Empire has stood for, no survival for the urge and impulses of the ages, that mankind will move forward towards its goal.'
WINSTON CHURCHILL, 1940

Many constitutional experts believe that Britain isn't actually a member of the European Union since our apparent entry was in violation of British law and was, therefore invalid.

In enacting the European Communities Bill through an ordinary vote in the House of Commons, Ted Heath's Government breached the constitutional convention which requires a prior consultation of the people (either by a general election or a referendum) on any measure involving constitutional change. The general election or referendum must take place before any related Parliamentary debate. (Britain has no straightforward written constitution. But, the signing of the Common Market entrance documents was, without a doubt, a breach of the spirit of our constitution.)

Just weeks before the 1970 general election which made him Prime Minister, Edward Heath declared that it would be wrong if any Government contemplating membership of the European Community were to take this step without 'the full-hearted consent of Parliament and people'.

However, when it came to it, Heath didn't have a referendum because opinion polls at the time (1972) showed that the British people were hugely opposed to our joining the Common Market. Instead, Heath merely signed the documents that took us into what became the European Union on the basis that Parliament alone had passed the European Communities Bill of 1972.

Some MPs have subsequently claimed that 'Parliament can do whatever it likes'. But that isn't true, of course. Parliament consists of a number of individual MPs who have been elected by their constituents to represent them. Political parties are not recognised in our system of government, and Parliament does not have the right to change the whole nature of Britain's constitution. We have (or are supposed to have) an elective democracy not an elective dictatorship. Parliament may, in law and in day-to-day issues, be the sovereign power in the state, but the electors are (in the words of Dicey's Introduction for the Study of the Law of the Constitution, published in 1885) 'the body in which sovereign power is vested'. Dicey goes on to point out that 'in a political sense the electors are the most important part of, we may even say are actually, the sovereign power, since their will is under the present constitution sure to obtain ultimate obedience.' Bagehot, author of *The English Constitution, 1867*, describes the nation, through Parliament, as 'the present sovereign'.

In 1972, when Heath decided to take Britain into the Common Market, he used Parliament's legal sovereignty to deny and permanently limit the political sovereignty of the electorate. Heath and Parliament changed the basic rules, and they did not have the right (legal or moral) to do that. The 1972 European Communities Bill wasn't just another Act of Parliament. Heath's Bill used Parliament's legal sovereignty, and status as representative of the electorate, to deny the fundamental rights of the electorate.

Precedents show that the British constitution, which may not be written and formalised in the same way that the American constitution is presented, but which is, nevertheless, enshrined and codified in the *Magna Carta* (1215), the Petition of Right (1628), the Bill of Rights (1689) and the Act of Settlement (1701), requires Parliament to consult the electorate directly where constitutional change which would affect their political sovereignty is in prospect. The 1689 Bill of Rights contains the following oath: 'I do declare that no foreign prince, person, prelate, state or potentate hath or ought to have jurisdiction, power, superiority, pre-eminence or authority within this Realm.' Since this Bill has not been repealed it is clear that every treaty Britain has signed with the EU has been illegal.

In 1975, when the Government changed, Harold Wilson sought to put right the clear constitutional error by organising a retrospective referendum (something quite unprecedented in British history) designed to obtain the permission of the British people for Britain to join something it had already 'joined'.

But, almost inevitably, the question asked in the referendum was also illegal since voters were asked: 'Do you think that the United Kingdom should stay in the European Community (the Common Market)?'

The problem was that since Heath had ignored the constitutional duties and requirements of Parliament, and had signed the entrance documents illegally, the words 'stay in' were deceptive. We couldn't stay in the EEC because, constitutionally, we had never entered. We couldn't enter the Common Market because Parliament did not have the right to sign away our sovereignty.

The referendum Wilson organised to remedy Heath's constitutional breach misled the electorate on a simple constitutional issue and was, therefore, itself illegal. (Wilson's referendum was passed after a good deal of very one-sided propaganda was used to influence public opinion. If the nation had voted against our 'continued' membership of the EEC, the political embarrassment for all politicians would have been unbearable.)

Attempts through the courts to annul our membership of the European Union on the basis that Parliament acted improperly have failed because Parliament, through its legal sovereignty, is the source of the law in Britain and the courts are, therefore, unable to challenge any Parliamentary Act.

Only Parliament can reclaim the legislative powers that Heath and subsequent Prime Ministers have handed to the European Union.

And so, only when Parliament is filled with honest politicians (not inevitably an oxymoron) who are not controlled by the private party system, will the mistake be rectified and our membership annulled.

Britain's entry into the Common Market (later to be transformed into the EU) was also illegal for another reason. The Prime Minister who signed the entry documents, Edward Heath, later confirmed that he had lied to the British people about the implications of the Treaty.

Heath told the electorate that signing the Treaty of Rome would lead to no essential loss of National Sovereignty but later admitted that this was a lie. Astonishingly, Heath said he lied because he knew that the British would not approve of him signing the Treaty if they knew the truth. Heath told voters that the EEC was merely a free trade association. But he was lying through his teeth. He knew that the original members of the EEC had a long-standing commitment to political union and the step-by-step creation of a European superstate.

Edward Heath received a substantial financial bribe for taking Britain into the EU when he was Prime Minister. (Heath was no stranger to bribery. One of his aides gave a senior Labour Party official £25,000 for details of Harold Wilson's election tactics.) The reward of £35,000, was handed over to Heath (in the guise of The Charlemagne Prize) for signing the Treaty of Rome.

Because of Heath's dishonesty, and fraudulent behaviour, we never actually joined the Common Market. And so all the subsequent treaties that were signed were illegal.

★★★

Britain's Treason Act (1351) is (at the time of writing) still in place. It states that: 'Treason is committed when a man be adherent to the King's enemies in his realm, giving them aid and comfort in the realm'.

And under the Treason Felony Act (1848) it is treason if 'any person whatsoever shall, within the United Kingdom or without, devise or intend to deprive our most gracious Lady the Queen (Elizabeth) from the style, honour or Royal Name of the Imperial crown of the United Kingdom.'

Our membership of the European Union will mean the end of the United Kingdom. So, since our membership of the European Union will doubtless 'deprive our most gracious Lady the Queen from the style, honour or Royal Name of the Imperial crown of the United Kingdom' Britain's entry into the Common Market, under Edward Heath's signature, was null and void for this reason too.

★★★

Heath committed an act of treason. He betrayed the Queen and he deliberately misled the British people.

Does any of this really matter to politicians?

Is there any hope that Parliament will repeal the 1972 European Communities Act and restore sovereignty to the people?

Not in the immediate future.

But the errors made by Heath and Wilson mean that when we want to leave the EU it will be very easy.

Because, officially, we never joined.

An independent British Parliament would simply have to pass one short Act of Parliament and give notice to the EU. We would then be out of this accursed club.

5

The EU and Our Money

'There is no art which one government sooner learns from another than that of draining money from the pockets of the people.'
ADAM SMITH

Britain is (or soon will be) the biggest net contributor to the European Union. According to the European Union, the total contribution of the United Kingdom to the EU budget will be 14,270,042,046 euros for the 2008 budget year. (In real money that's around £10 billion for the year.)

What does the EU do with all our money? (And the money it receives from other contributor countries.)

Well, it's difficult to tell because the accounts haven't been accepted by the official auditors for years, and it seems that no one really knows where the money goes.

Some ends up in private bank accounts, some is spent on administration, and some goes on huge salaries and massive expense accounts for commissioners, MEPs and bureaucrats. (There are in excess of 39,000 people on the direct EU payroll. Many more are making fortunes out of it.)

Some of it is stolen and some is spent promoting the EU, telling everyone what a wonderful organisation it is, designing flags and logos and indoctrinating school-children so that they grow up thinking that whatever the EU may be it is a good thing. (As well as having its own Official National Anthem – based on Beethoven's

'Ode to Joy' – the EU also has its own flag of course.)

That's the sort of accounting we're likely to get from the EU. The EU is an unending story of fraud and waste.

The few quid that is left when the EU bureaucrats have filled their purses and wallets and safe deposit boxes is distributed to the poorer parts of the EU. There is an EU rule that regional aid goes to areas of the EU where the income per head is less than two thirds of the EU average. In the past, some of this money has even found its way to the poorer parts of Britain. For example, Scotland, Wales and bits of Cornwall used to get a few quid tossed their way. (Naturally, every pound that comes from the EU comes with a good deal of EU flag waving.) The EU uses money as a carrot, to attract poorer countries into the EU. The EU redistributes money to remove the differences between various parts of the EU Superstate; dragging everyone down to the lowest common denominator.

New countries which join the EU have immediate access to all the goodies. And the best goody of all is the Common Agricultural Policy (CAP) which ensures that farmers get direct aid. It is through the CAP that the EU buys up all the excess milk, butter and cereals grown within the EU. The excesses are gathered together as milk lakes and butter mountains and then, sometimes, dumped in other parts of the world.

It is this dumping of cheap food which wrecks the farming economies of developing African countries and, in the long run, leads to starvation. The EU is one of the main causes of African poverty and the EU contributes hugely to starvation in the Third World. The world's poorest countries have to pay huge taxes and tariffs to trade with the European Union. Make no mistake about it, the EU's trade policies are largely responsible for the appalling poverty of the Third World. Pop singers who wanted to help stamp out starvation in Africa would do much more good if, instead of raising small amounts of money to donate as charity, they campaigned against the wicked greed and hypocrisy of the European Union.

★★★

It was French writer Voltaire who, in the 18th century, pointed out that: 'In general, the art of Government consists in taking as much money as possible from one group of citizens to give it to another.'

Voltaire realised that if you take money from Peter and give it to Pierre then it's a pretty fair guess that Pierre will like you quite a lot. If you do this repeatedly then Pierre is likely to expect the generosity to continue. Peter, however, is likely to become rather resentful.

The result of the fact that poor countries are entering the EU will be that those parts of the UK which have in the past received money from the EU (and which have, as a result, been enthusiastic supporters of the EU) are going to have to face a rather bleaker future.

Scotland, Wales, Cornwall and Merseyside have in the past received money from the EU. And the people in those areas have, not surprisingly, been firm supporters of the EU.

Oh dear.

Guess what.

Now that the EU has just had an influx of poor countries, the average EU income has dropped.

Just about every region of the new member states will now benefit for aid.

Scotland and Wales and Merseyside can go whistle. Their days of EU money will soon be gone. Cornwall will probably be the only part of the UK which will still receive a little EU money.

Maybe the Scots and the Welsh will now change their views about the EU.

Vernon Coleman

6

Fraud in the EU

'For the past eight years the Court (the European Court of Auditors) has had to refuse to issue the required 'Statement of Assurance' that money has been properly spent.'
THE TIMES, 17TH MARCH 2004

The EU has, virtually since its inception, been a playground for criminals – some of them working for the organisation and some of them simply taking advantage of the stupidity, incompetence or dishonesty of those working for it. In the days when the EU was still known as the EEC, a number of entrepreneurs got rich by taking advantage of the EEC's confusion of import-export subsidies and the EEC's Common Agricultural Policy which provides farmers and traders throughout Europe with protected prices and subsidies which guarantee them profits. It is these subsidies and guarantees which have led to the creation of the EEC's most famous creations: butter mountains and wine lakes.

The first rogues to take advantage of this scheme bought a trainload of butter which they then sent on a Grand European Tour, visiting only countries which were members of the EEC. Every time the train passed over a frontier the tricksters would claim a massive subsidy from the EEC, simply filling in a few forms to confirm that they intended to convert the butter into another product. At the end of the train's Grand Tour, after pocketing ten million deutschmarks in subsidies, they stopped the train and sold the butter for what they had paid for it.

Once this scheme became known, other adventurers decided to take advantage of it and soon the railways and roads of Europe were congested with trains and lorries packed with travelling produce. The cost to European taxpayers was phenomenal. Before long the tricksters realised that actually buying the damned butter and paying for it to be carried around Europe was an unnecessary expense. All they had to do was claim that they had bought the butter (or whatever). The transactions existed only on paper. When it had become clear that it was possible to fool the EEC simply by filling in forms, a whole new generation of fraudsters decided to join in. Another popular scheme involved claiming value added tax rebates on goods which were alleged to be travelling between one EEC country and another.

The bureaucrats in Brussels, who were either embarrassed by all this or angry because they weren't being given big enough bribes, constantly changed the regulations in order to try to stop these activities. But their attempts were futile. Every time they sealed up one loophole another one appeared.

The fraudsters who helped themselves to millions in this way were, of course, never prosecuted. Even when they were identified there was no effective means of starting a prosecution. In which country had the fraud taken place? In what country had the criminal law been broken? Where should the prosecution be initiated? The problem was that no criminal law had been broken. The EEC wasn't a country. There was no one able to prosecute. And so the fraudsters went free and tottered off to Switzerland with their millions. (Of course, it is doubtful if the EEC would have wanted to prosecute even if they had been able. Prosecuting would have merely drawn attention to the problem and made the EEC look even more foolish and pointless in the public's eyes.)

★★★

No one illustrates the link between the Labour Party and the EU better than the Kinnocks.

Kinnock was a European Commissioner while his wife sat as an MEP. According to one estimate, the pair of them were raking in £500,000 a year from various wages and benefits paid out by the EU.

Kinnock was European Commissioner in charge of anti-corruption in the EU. (No giggling. This is serious.) Sadly, he wasn't enormously successful in dealing with the problem. Indeed, the national audit office reported that the amount of 'waste' doubled in the year after he took over and 10,000 individual cases of corruption were uncovered. (Naturally, no one knows how many remained uncovered.)

When a brave woman who was the European Commission's chief accountant spoke out about 'dangerous failings' in the EU's £673 billion annual budget she, like a long line of other whistle blowers, discovered that telling the truth about EC crookedness is not a wise career move.

She was sacked and sent home without any tea.

Kinnock was not sacked and did not resign.

Now that he has retired from the EU, Kinnock will get a pension of £63,900 a year from a pension pot worth more than £2 million. (Curiously, that is £500,000 more than Englishmen and women who save towards their own pensions will be allowed to accumulate under new Government legislation).

Kinnock, who once described the House of Lords as nothing more than descendants of brigands, muggers, bribers and gangsters, has also entered the House of Lords.

I hope he feels at home there, surrounded, as he will be, by so many of Tony's other cronies.

★★★

'Opportunities for fraud are open and they are taken advantage of. The most elementary precautions are neither taken nor even contemplated.'
MARTA ANDREASEN, THE EU'S FORMER CHIEF ACCOUNTANT WHO WAS SACKED BY FORMER EU COMMISSIONER NEIL KINNOCK AFTER REVEALING THAT THE EU'S ACCOUNTING SYSTEMS WERE OPEN TO FRAUD.

★★★

The EU's internal fraud busters reckon that proven scams (the ones it knows about) cost the EU around £590 million a year. Other observers put the figure much, much higher.

Finally, in early 2008, European Union finance ministers started discussing proposals designed to clamp down on valued added tax fraud which, the *Financial Times* reported, cost the EU's member states tens of billions of euros every year. That's a lot of taxpayers' money.

The VAT fraud they were talking about stopping has been going on for just about as long as the EU has been in existence. Swindlers buy goods VAT free from one member state, sell them on with tax added in another state and fail to pass the tax on to the authorities. It's a breathtakingly simple fraud. And breathtakingly profitable. It's been going on for decades. According to the *Financial Times* the size of the fraud has actually grown sharply in recent years.

How much has this fraud cost taxpayers across Europe? It's difficult to say. But since the fraud has been going on for decades and has been costing tens of billions a year, the total cost must run into hundreds of billions. A lot of people have become very rich from this fraud. It's not surprising that so many people are keen on the EU.

★★★

There was widespread laughter around Europe, particularly among those who know how the EU works, when the EU was said to have reservations about Bulgaria becoming a member of the EU because of internal corruption. The words pot, kettle and black were widely translated.

★★★

One EU official was found to have created false travel documents and to have claimed £465,000 for meetings which were never held.

That's just one EU official.

There are thousands and thousands of them.

How many of them are 'on the fiddle'?

Your guess is as good as mine.

★★★

In 2007, the Metropolitan Police was asked to investigate Gordon Brown MP (then Chancellor of the Exchequer) for: 'misfeasance in unlawful disbursements of many billions of pounds Sterling since he became Chancellor in 1997 to a body (the European Union) whose accounts have not been signed off as correct for twelve successive years and where fraud and corruption is endemic, thereby occasioning actual loss and waste of public funds, contrary to the Government Resources Act, 2000.'

★★★

The European Court of Auditors, described as the 'financial conscience' of the EU, has rejected the European Union's accounts for more than a decade.

One MEP has admitted that the EU's constant inability to satisfy the auditors is unacceptable and that the failure to satisfy its own auditors means that the European Union has 'begun to look like a banana republic'. (If it were a banana republic the EU would, of course, be too bent to satisfy its own requirement that bananas be straight). Auditors routinely complain that the EU's budget is full of errors and that the failure to follow the correct procedures means that the accounts mess is impossible to untangle. Fraud, corruption and theft are endemic. Inevitably, there are rumours and suspicions that money from the EU finds its way into the pockets and campaign funds of politicians who suddenly (and often inexplicably) become forgetful about where their money and campaign money has come from.

According to a report prepared by independent forensic accountants, and commissioned by Ashley Mote MEP, the UK Government's own Resources Act 2000 calls for public accounts to 'present a true and fair view'.

But, it seems, the British Government ignores its own legislation on matters relating to the EU.

The same Act of Parliament demands that the Government checks that money provided by Parliament is expended for the purposes intended by Parliament.

Since the EU cannot provide any real assurance that this has happened, the Government is ignoring its own legislation in relation to the EU.

The accountants' report states that the EU's treasury function has never been audited independently – although a major public company would be audited independently on a regular basis. The report points out that payments worth 27 billion euros were 'simply not registered in the European Commission accounts'.

'The EU has 'lost' some 600 billion euros over the years,' claims Mr Mote MEP, who points out that there is nothing in British law to prevent the Government halting all British contributions to EU funds and putting the money into an escrow account pending the introduction and enforcement of proper auditing.

★★★

Back in 1967, work was started on a new building for the EU. The European Commission immediately leased the building from the Belgium Government. After EU staff moved into the building in 1991 it was discovered that the whole erection was stuffed with asbestos. The staff evacuated themselves.

In 1995, the bureaucrats finally got round to organising the removal of the asbestos from the now empty building. This took another four years.

Naturally, we paid for the whole of this disaster.

We spent £370 million buying the offices in the centre of Brussels. And we forked out another £338 million of our money to renovate the building. (And we paid out £96 million in rent so that the bureaucrats would have somewhere else to put their filing cabinets while the improvements took place.)

Much of the cost of repairing and renovating this wretched building has been the result of bureaucrats behaving like bureaucrats. For example, they spent 12 weeks trying to decide on the type of light bulbs to put in the building.

The project manager, responsible for at least some of this wonderful work, was a certain Mr Neil Kinnock.

The construction of the Scottish Parliament building (Scotland's Regional Assembly of the EU) also went way over budget. Hundreds of millions of pounds were wasted.

Economist Milton Friedman was right when he observed that the best purchases are made by people spending their own money.

★★★

If awards are given out for cheek, the European Commission would have a shelf full of them.

The European Commission and European Parliament want to put pressure on individual states to force them to provide proof that the money they've received from the European Union has been well spent.

The auditors of the EU accounts found huge errors in £72 billion of the £80 billion spending money that the EU had given to national governments in 2006.

The EU's complaint was that governments were unable to show that they sent the money to the right recipients. They were supposed to have used the EU money on infrastructure, training, job creation and so on but there was a rather comprehensive lack of evidence to prove that they'd spent it on bridges and ditch digging rather than investing it in fast cars, expensive champagne and fun nights out with partners other than their legal spouses.

The EU's anti-fraud commissioner complained (and you're going to admire this) that such lax financial controls gave Europe (by which he presumably meant the EU) a bad name.

For years the EU has had two main headquarters, one in Brussels in Belgium and one in Strasbourg in France. Once a month a convoy of lorries moves documents from Brussels to Strasbourg (and then back again). This entirely pointless exercise costs the best part of £100 million a year.

★★★

The EU has for some time been planning to augment its enormous income from the individual member states (soon to be broken up into regions, of course) with its own schedule of taxes.

A document released by the European Commission entitled Tax Based EU Own Resources: An Assessment showed that the EU has, since 2004, been looking at nine new types of special EU taxes. The areas where the EU has shown particular interest are:

1. An EU personal income tax, which would probably be in the form of a levy added onto national income tax.
2. An EU company tax. The snag with this is that it would undoubtedly lead many companies to set up headquarters outside the EU.
3. An EU tax on road travel.

4. An extension of VAT which would almost certainly result in the end of the UK's zero rating on essentials such as food in shops, children's clothing and shoes, books and public transport fares.
5. A special EU tax on financial transactions
6. An EU tax on energy use
7. An EU tax on air travel
8. An EU tax on communications – including phone lines and broadcasting.
9. Special, additional EU taxes on alcohol and tobacco.

But these are merely additional, temporary taxes intended to provide a short-term boost to the EU's vast multi billion pound budget. In the medium term there is no doubt at all that the EU intends to control all taxes throughout the EU region. The EU has already said that the 'unequal tax treatment of equivalent EU taxpayers would probably be considered as discriminatory and against the ideals of European construction'. So, clearly, taxes will be the same in all EU countries.

★★★

Recent EU legislation enabled tax authorities in EU member states to share information. Moreover, an international task force (known as the Joint International Tax Shelter Information Centre) has been established to enable tax authorities in different countries to coordinate their findings about taxpayers. The Inland Revenue is now authorised by EU legislation to send the information it acquires about British taxpayers spontaneously to tax collectors everywhere. Similarly, tax collectors in other countries now send information about British citizens with accounts or homes abroad to the Inland Revenue.

Moreover, a meeting of EU finance ministers in September 2004 agreed to set up a working group to work out how best to achieve direct-tax harmonisation between EU member countries.

This is likely to lead to the EU replacing individual, national tax systems and replacing them with a single EU wide system. The EU will simply encourage individual nations to 'adjust' their tax rates to match general EU rates.

The British Government has, of course, stated that it is firmly opposed to harmonisation of tax rates within the EU.

However, as long as Britain remains a member of the EU, the Government will have no authority to approve or oppose these changes.

7

The Euro – An EU Disaster

As I have constantly predicted since its inception and introduction, the euro has proved to be a disaster.

The original plan – indeed, the assumption, was that all national members of the EU would abandon their national currencies and adopt the euro. But first Denmark and then Sweden voted to reject membership of the single currency. Both proved that it was possible to survive happily without the euro.

In the summer of 2005, dissatisfaction with the euro reached a high and it began to look as though the euro had only a very limited life expectancy. If the euro had relatives they would, in June 2005, have already been gathered by the bedside awaiting the worst.

By the time that France and Holland rejected the EU constitution (the one that has now been snuck back into existence as the Lisbon Treaty) it was clear that the days of the euro were already numbered. In June 2005, one leading Italian politician called for his country to hold a referendum on whether or not Italy should abandon the euro and bring back the lira. The Italians were blaming the euro for rocketing prices. Italian experts claimed that their country's economy had been crippled because the interest rates set by the European Central Bank were too high for their country. By early 2008, Italian euro bonds were selling at a significantly lower price than German euro bonds even though the euro is supposed to be a single currency.

In France and Germany (where unemployment levels have been between 10% and 15% since the introduction of the new currency) the euro is widely blamed for the economic problems with which the two countries are struggling. The Dutch claim that the value of the euro makes them feel poor.

Early in the summer of 2005, the Germans were talking about quitting the euro and going back to their beloved mark. German officials were secretly discussing the possibility that the euro might collapse. Leading French politicians talked about changing the rules which govern economies within the eurozone and dumping the so-called stability pact set up to force countries to abide by strict rules on allowable budget deficits.

There is little doubt that if referendums on the euro were held throughout Europe, the result would be an overwhelming vote of no confidence in the single currency.

Throughout all this, the British Labour Government has maintained its enthusiasm for the euro and its determination to abandon the pound sterling and take England into the euro as and when they think the time is right (for which read, when they thought they could trick the public into accepting the decision). Can there have ever been a more bizarre example of rats actually wanting to board a sinking ship?

(Incidentally, it is now clear that our traditional currency (pounds, shillings and pence) was got rid of in order to prepare us for entry into the euro.)

★★★

Currency unions have usually been the beginning of political union. It is what happened in Germany in the 1800's. Bismarck's task of unifying the German states was made much easier by monetary unification.

If Britain had joined the euro our economy would be in an even greater mess than it is today. During Gordon Brown's tenure of incompetence, Britain's housing market boomed to absurd levels and personal indebtedness rose dramatically. The egregiously incompetent Brown, the most imprudent Chancellor Britain has ever had, created one of the greatest artificial booms of all time. If Britain had been in the euro for the first seven years of the 21st century (where interest rates were two to three per cent) the nation's economic situation would have been even worse.

The euro's one-size-fits-all policy has already created chaos throughout the rest of Europe. There is a dangerous property boom in much of Europe (at its worst in Spain to Ireland) and personal debt has risen to crazy levels.

A recent survey of German women showed that 71% want the deutschmark restored.

France, Germany and Italy were, before the introduction of the euro, among the world's most prosperous and technologically advanced countries. These nations are now sinking fast. Their industries (and jobs) are under siege. The euro has destroyed living standards, is destroying culture and, by destroying economic strength, is destroying the influence of those countries which signed up for it.

★★★

Nations which have abandoned their currency and taken up with the euro (including France and Germany) now merrily ignore the EU's rules when it suits them.

Theoretically, all members of the EU are linked together and the member nations which share the common EU currency are tied to one another particularly tightly.

Normally, when an individual country runs into financial trouble its government can put up interest rates or devalue its currency. But in Europe this isn't possible. All member countries are tied together. Right at the beginning, before the euro was introduced, even the intellectually disadvantaged bureaucrats of the EU realised that this could cause problems and that the citizens of individual countries which were careful and responsible might end up supporting the citizens of countries with less responsible governments.

To try to prevent this happening, the EU drew up a 'stability and growth pact' requiring all countries sharing the euro to keep their budget deficits below 3% of GDP at all times.

When Portugal exceeded the 3% deficit, the Portuguese Government tried to do the right thing: they slashed public spending. This pushed up unemployment and made the local recession worse. The Portuguese paid heavily for their profligacy.

But France and Germany don't consider that they play by the same rules. When France and Germany broke the 3% rule they simply ignored the pact and told other countries that the rule didn't apply to them. The European Court of Justice insisted that France and Germany had to obey the rules like everyone else. France and Germany just ignored the Court. EU ministers in Brussels eventually agreed to drop any disciplinary action against them. 'These rules were not invented for us,' said the French and German Governments.

France and Germany violated the 3% limit on budget deficits for three years in a row and a whole filing cabinet full of exceptions has been devised and published to ensure that they can now easily evade sanctions in a way that would make veteran tax evaders grin with delight.

Greece breached the euro area's budget deficit ceiling of 3% of GDP every year between 1998 and 2003. The Greeks even breached the rules in the years when they supposedly met the Maastricht criteria for entering the euro. The Greeks went unpunished for their sins.

On the other hand, an English greengrocer who sold bananas by the pound was arrested.

Just a few years ago, anyone who opposed the euro was regarded as a financial Luddite.

The only good thing that has happened to Britain in the last decade has been that we did not join the euro.

But that was only because at the time the Labour Party wasn't arrogant enough to refuse to have a referendum they'd promised and which they were aware that they would lose.

When the British bank Northern Rock got into trouble it was British taxpayers who were told that they had to foot the bill – and effectively find £3,000 each to shore up the bank.

But what would have happened if Britain had exchanged sterling for the euro? Would the EU have supported Northern Rock? Good question. If a Spanish or Polish bank collapses will citizens throughout the rest of the EU be expected to put their hands in their pockets? Another good question.

In an attempt to avoid having to find out whether doughy German burghers would bail out flighty Italian bank depositors, the EU responded to the Northern Rock crisis by flooding Europe with euros, hoping that the waves of liquidity would prevent similar problems developing in the euro-zone part of the EU.

The Northern Rock fiasco has been handled with the Government's usual unwavering incompetence. The result is that Brown and his inept chums have made a disaster out of a crisis.

But at least it has been a British mess. British bankers created the mess. And British politicians made it worse.

Heaven knows how bad things would have been if the EU had been involved.

Vernon Coleman

8

The EU's Regionalisation Of Britain

'All men having power ought to be mistrusted.'
JAMES MADISON

'The issue today is the same as it has been throughout all history, whether man shall be allowed to govern himself or be ruled by a small elite.'
THOMAS JEFFERSON

'All the great things are simple, and many can be expressed in a single word: freedom, justice, honour, duty, mercy, hope.'
WINSTON CHURCHILL

In order to create a new United States of Europe the eurocrats realised that they needed to get rid of all existing nations and nationalities. They 'bought' Scotland and Wales by giving them what look like parliaments but which are, in reality, merely regional assemblies. Since both parts of the UK are relatively thinly populated (and are economically weak) the EU didn't feel the need to split them up any further. But breaking up England was essential. The Scottish and Welsh, easily bribed, felt happy about the EU. This effectively isolated England and enabled the EU to set out its plan to break up the United Kingdom.

★★★

Thanks to the EU, Scotland, Wales and Northern Ireland all have their own assemblies (as a treat they are allowed to call them parliaments for the time being). They all now have clear national identities.

Many nationalists in those countries believe that they have won a sort of independence and that their parliaments are the first step towards self-rule.

Oh dear.

They are so wrong.

Their assemblies/parliaments exist only because the EU wants them to exist.

In the United States of Europe, Scotland, Wales and Northern Ireland will all be regions with their own regional parliaments. (Northern Ireland will become a region of the EU, alongside Southern Ireland. The Irish question will, therefore, be solved by the EU. There will be nothing left for the Irish to fight about. The only thing British Prime Ministers have done towards creating peace in Ireland has been to continue to keep us in the EU. It's an expensive price to pay to stop the fighting in Northern Ireland.)

Scotland, Wales and Northern Ireland have parliaments but England doesn't. The reason for this is quite simple. If the EU gets its way there will be no England. There will, instead, be a series of nine English regions – each with its own regional assembly. How can I prove this? Easy. The nine regional assemblies already exist. One of them, the London Assembly is functioning. The other eight exist in secret – though they are being given increasing amounts of power by the Labour Government.

★★★

Regional Assemblies are, it is claimed, there to offer the English people more democracy. This is a lie. They are there because they will replace England when the EU becomes properly divided into regions.

The Regional Assemblies are already set up. They have buildings, staff, members, huge budgets and power. They operate in secrecy because the members are appointed not elected.

In an attempt to bring Regional Assemblies out into the open, and to make them acceptable to English voters, the Labour

Government decided to have a referendum in the North East; to ask the people there if they wanted to have a regional assembly. Labour chose the North East because they thought that was where they stood the best chance of winning the vote. They spent a lot of time and public money campaigning for a 'yes' vote. The Government never mentioned that the Regional Assembly was part of the EU plan for a United States of Europe. Nor, as far as I am aware, did any national newspaper, national TV or radio station make this clear.

When the people of the North East voted on whether or not they wanted a Regional Assembly, 197,310 voted 'for' and 696,519 voted 'against'. It was a humiliating defeat for the EU, for Labour and for flirtatious former croquet player 'Fat' John Prescott (who had 'masterminded' and spearheaded the 'yes' campaign).

How appropriate that the Government's humiliating defeat at the hands of voters in the North East should have taken place on November 5th 2004 – the night when the English celebrate Guy Fawkes's attempt to destroy Parliament.

The Fascist Labour Government naturally pretended that the unsuccessful attempt to force a Regional Assembly on the people of the North East was an act of political generosity on their part. Their line now is that the voters of the North East have stupidly turned down a great gift.

Politicians and national media all carefully avoided the truth; which is that the North Eastern Regional mini parliament already exists. As do other Regional mini parliaments around the country. They may be secret. The members may be unelected. But they already exist.

And both politicians and the national media also carefully avoided the fact that these new Regional Parliaments are nothing to do with providing an extra layer of political representation for English voters but are simply part of the EU's plan to get rid of England and the House of Commons and to replace the former with nine EU regions and the latter with nine regional EU parliaments.

The significance of the vote rejecting the North Eastern Regional Assembly cannot be over-estimated. This was one of the most important votes in England's history. (You wouldn't know this from the way our utterly dishonest media dealt with the election. Not one TV network ran a programme dealing with the election. Not one national newspaper put the vote result on its front page the next day.)

Europhiles were said to be devastated.

But they did not, of course, close down the regional parliaments they had already set up.

Including the one in the North East of England.

Despite the resounding 'no' vote, the North East of England has a Regional Assembly.

The Regional Assembly building was already fully-staffed and operational when the people of the North East were asked to decide whether or not they wanted one. And the 'parliament' was filled with appointees. None had been elected to represent the people in the Regional Assembly.

That's democracy EU and Labour style.

★★★

The Regional Assemblies were established under the Regional Development Agencies Act 1998 which itself came as a result of the 1992 Maastricht Treaty which adopted the EU Regionalisation Plan. The Plan will abolish England's 48 counties and replace them with nine European regions.

The regional assemblies 'carry out a wide range of advocacy and consultancy roles with national government bodies and the European Union' but their public profile is very low. Each acts as a Regional Planning Body with a duty to formulate a Regional Spatial Strategy, replacing the planning function of county councils. They will, in due course, report directly to Brussels.

The members of eight of the nine English regional assemblies are not elected. They are 'appointed'.

The single exception is the London Assembly, which has 25 directly elected members. It was created under the Great London Authority Act 1999 but is, effectively, the ninth of the regional assemblies set up to 'manage' the nine regions which England will become when it is officially destroyed by the EU.

There is, curiously, some inconsistency in the naming of the nine assemblies. They are:

- London Assembly
- East of England Regional Assembly
- East Midlands Regional Assembly
- North East Assembly
- North West Regional Assembly
- South East England Regional Assembly
- South West Regional Assembly
- West Midlands Regional Assembly
- Yorkshire and Humber Assembly

The 2004 vote was an attempt by the Government to formalise the existence of these already existing assemblies. When the voters of the North East of England rejected their assembly, the Government quietly abandoned its plans to make the assemblies elected. But the eight unelected regional assemblies (including the one in the North East) remain in place and, despite the referendum defeat, the Government has no plans to disband them.

At no point has the Government ever admitted the truth: that the nine assemblies are, in reality, merely physical manifestations of regions devised by the EU to replace England. (It is incidentally, to fit in with these EU regions that the police in England are being reorganised into 'regions' which don't seem to make much historical sense but which make a great deal of sense as far as the EU is concerned.)

The physical addresses and telephone numbers of the eight unelected regional assemblies are not advertised widely. But key the names of the assemblies into an Internet search engine and you'll find them easily enough.

The post democratic society we have been promised is, it seems, already with us.

★★★

'England is divided into eight geographic regions, often referred to as the standard regions of England...'
ENCYCLOPEDIA BRITANNICA

★★★

The Labour Government likes to take the credit for the elected assemblies for Scotland, Wales and Northern Ireland. And they like to take credit for giving London a new Mayor and new independence.

But, in reality, these changes are all part of the regionalisation process and the instructions came, as usual, from Brussels. The Government was merely complying with instructions from the EU to split the UK into 12 regional governments.

The plan is that the EU will deal directly with these regional governments – completely by-passing Westminster and making the Houses of Parliament redundant.

New Labour has taken great advantage of the bizarre interregnum through which we are passing. After the formation of the Scottish Parliament, the Labour Party still allowed Scottish MPs sitting in the House of Commons to vote on issues which only affected English citizens. This wicked abuse of Parliament enabled Labour to push through Bills which were deeply unpopular with English voters and their parliamentary representatives. The Scottish MPs who helped push through the legislation knew that they had nothing to lose because their constituents would not be affected.

This was as daft and as dishonest as allowing Argentinian MPs to vote in the Scottish Parliament.

★★★

The Labour Government has given the unelected Regional Assemblies complete authority over housing and planning strategies. For example, the East of England Regional Assembly has decided to build 478,000 homes in Essex, near to 600,000 which have been built since 2001. Numerous people and local bodies objected to this plan but the decision made by the Regional Assembly cannot be opposed or overturned.

Regional Assemblies are not elected bodies, they are appointed EU quangos, made up of people who have been selected and appointed by Labour.

★★★

EU bureaucrats are working on a scheme to erase all national borders within Europe. In addition to the smaller regions which have been prepared for years (Scotland, Wales and the nine regions which England is to become), they have created a number of new European super regions. There is, for example, a new region called the Arc Manche which consists of northern France, western Belgium and southern England (including London). The first meeting of the Arc Manche transnational region took place in Sussex in October 2006 and was chaired by a Frenchman who is the 'president' of the region. Western Britain will be grouped with parts of France, Spain and Portugal to form the Atlantic region. Eastern Britain will combine with parts of Sweden, Denmark, Germany, Belgium, the Netherlands and Norway to form the North Sea region. (It doesn't seem to matter to EU bureaucrats that Norway isn't a member of the European Union.) There is another region consisting of Ireland and Wales while most of Scotland will combine with parts of Norway, Greenland, Iceland, Sweden and Finland to become the Northern Periphery. (The EU obviously doesn't care that Greenland and Iceland aren't members of the EU either.) The EU has demanded that maps and data within member states be brought into line with the EU's specifications.

The end of the EU will probably come when the French eventually realise exactly what the EU plans to do to their country. The English may take these things lying down (in the mistaken belief that none of it really matters). The French, who are never shy about making their views known, will riot when they realise precisely what the EU has planned for France.

9

Has The EU Prevented
The Third World War?
(As Europhiles Claim It Has)

The EU claims to have been the reason why there has been no war in Europe since the Second World War. This, of course, is nonsense. The EU has done nothing whatsoever to prevent wars developing in Europe. Europeans fought for reconciliation long before the EU existed and rather than encouraging peace it was, remember, the EU which supported the NATO led bombing of Yugoslavia. And the EU is creating its own army. EU forces are not designed for self-defence but for military operations anywhere in the world. The EU says that its army will be used for the 'export of stability'. (The phrase 'export of stability' goes in the book of military euphemisms together with such other gems as 'victims of friendly fire'.)

Famous old English army regiments are disappearing because they have to make way for the European Army or 'rapid reaction force' (which was formed as a result of the Amsterdam Treaty in 1999). The distribution of the EU's regional defence forces will fit in nicely with the unelected regional parliaments which we already have.

Europhiles claim that the EU has helped create peace and prosperity and freedom. This, of course, is a neat piece of mythology created to provide a raison d'être for an organisation which has cost its members billions of pounds in membership fees and provided nothing but an endless stream of red tape and unwanted legislation in return.

There is no evidence that the EU has created peace in Europe, and it is patent nonsense to claim that without the bureaucrats in Brussels, the French and the Germans would, by now, have been fighting World War III. Any peace and prosperity which have been enjoyed have been a result of the same global factors which have led to rising productivity and increased trade in Asia and the USA.

★★★

'It's an age-old mantra that there have been no wars in Europe since 1945 thanks to the Treaty of Rome and the EU. We have not had any wars with Japan either since that year – and we are not bound to them nor have their laws imposed on us.'
DEREK BENNETT, ANTI-EU CAMPAIGNER, UKIP CANDIDATE AND PUBLISHER OF EUROREALIST NEWSLETTER.

★★★

Far from helping to create peace, prosperity and freedom the only available evidence suggests that the EU is likely to damage all these.

Britain's independence and democracy is clearly threatened by the thousands of new laws coming from institutions in Brussels over which British electors have absolutely no control. Divisions between member states over the rights and wrongs of supporting American imperialism have created tensions between member nations of the EU which probably would not have existed if the members were stand-alone countries. The dispute over the invasion of Iraq revealed that the EU is split into two quite separate factions. The one most closely identified with the French wants the EU to become an independent player on the world stage and to become a counterbalance to the power of the USA. The other, obviously identified with the British, wants to see the old Western alliance, forged during the Cold War, respected, maintained and strengthened. The europhiles in the French Government fear the United States of America and believe that a united Europe may help hold back the more dangerous Americans. The Labour Party believe that trying to create a counterweight to balance the power of the USA is both misguided and dangerous. The split in the EU which resulted from the differing attitudes of the two factions was as much about a struggle for the control of the EU as it was a struggle for the oil in Iraq. The Spanish Government's decision to align itself with the USA and Britain (despite some 96% of Spanish electors opposing such a viewpoint) took place because the Spanish Government feared that it had for too long been dominated by the all-powerful Franco-German axis in European politics.

Vernon Coleman

10

The Party System Has
Betrayed Us

*'Socialism is usually defined as 'common ownership of the means of
production'. Crudely: the State, representing the whole nation, owns
everything, and everyone is a State employee.'*
GEORGE ORWELL

*'You are not here to enjoy the trappings of power, but to do a job and uphold
the highest standards in public life.'*
TONY BLAIR, ADDRESSING LABOUR MPS IN MAY 1997.

'We will clean up politics...'
NEW LABOUR PARTY MANIFESTO 1997

If we are going to save our country from the grasping hands of
the European bureaucrats, one thing is certain: none of the three
leading political parties will take the action we need. None of
them will loosen the ties holding us to Europe.

New Labour, the Conservative Party and the Liberal Democrats
all seem convinced that Britain cannot exist without being a
member of the European Union. For all practical purposes, Britain
has become a one-party state.

England needs to get rid of its existing three-party political
system and start again – from scratch.

The first thing we all have to accept and understand is that the

85

big three parties don't exist to protect Britain or, indeed, to defend or protect the voters. The three political parties in Britain exist to defend themselves. And the politicians who are members of those parties are in Parliament to promote themselves and their own interests. The party system has given us unending government by liars, cheats, hypocrites, incompetents and self-serving buffoons.

The tragedy today, and the reason for many of our problems, is that the great majority of politicians have never done anything else for a living – and cannot and could not do anything. They are, almost by definition, vain and ambitious and their reliance on politics as a means of earning a living means that they will do anything – including lie and deceive – to hang onto office. Only when the lies run out do they resign. Honour is, to them, an unaffordable luxury. They never stand up for unpopular causes – even if they believe in them. Their policies are ruled by political correctness rather than passion. Every penny they've ever earned has come from taxpayers via the Government. They are 21st century Puritans, oppressing those who pay their fat salaries out of a mixture of necessity and an entirely misplaced sense of moral and intellectual superiority. Modern governments are comprised of crooks and morons. But crooks and morons (and many are both) who look good and smile well.

Successful politicians are also actors (think of Clinton and Blair). They can smile and look sincere and convincing even when they are lying (and even when the majority of people they are addressing know that they are lying). Successful politicians are unhindered by conscience. They don't give a damn about people or their responsibilities. They care only about their own careers. A set of good teeth and a full head of hair are far more important to them than principles; principles are an unaffordable luxury, a burden too heavy to be carried in the modern world of politics.

'Above all, the European Economic Community takes away Britain's freedom to follow the sort of economic policies we need.'
Former UK Prime Minister, Tony Blair, writing in his personal manifesto when standing for Parliament in Beaconsfield in 1982

'We'll negotiate a withdrawal from the EEC which has drained our natural resources and destroyed jobs.'
FORMER UK PRIME MINISTER, TONY BLAIR, PLEDGING HIS OPPOSITION TO THE EEC WHEN STANDING FOR PARLIAMENT IN SEDGEFIELD IN 1983

'On the day we remember the legend that St George slayed a dragon to protect England, some would argue that there is another dragon to be slayed: Europe.'
FORMER UK PRIME MINISTER TONY BLAIR, IN PATRIOTIC AND VOTE WINNING MOOD ON ST GEORGE'S DAY 1997 IN AN INTERVIEW WITH *THE SUN* NEWSPAPER

'I am a passionate pro-European. I always have been.'
FORMER UK PRIME MINISTER TONY BLAIR, SPEAKING TO THE EU PARLIAMENT IN 2005 AND THINKING, PERHAPS, ABOUT THE POSSIBILITY OF BEING OFFERED THE JOB OF THE FIRST PRESIDENT OF THE EUROPEAN UNION.

★★★

The Labour Party, which one might have imagined to have been populated by more caring and honourable individuals, has turned out to be packed with MPs exhibiting just as many prejudices, just as many examples of selfishness, just as much enthusiasm for privilege and just as much blindness to injustice as the Tories in the dull, dark days of John Major.

The constant stream of stories exposing MPs (and Government Ministers) as greedy and grasping doesn't seem to shock us any more. It should. There are just 646 MPs at the moment and yet a huge proportion of them are palpably dishonest. The Global Corruption Barometer survey conducted by Transparency International (a not-for-profit organisation) showed that, when asked to rate people for corruption, the British responded by putting politicians right at the top of the list – above all other groups (but only slightly above the British legislature, whose representatives are also widely regarded as corrupt).

Politicians are the people whom we pay to run the country on our behalf! If the proportion of dishonest doctors (or even lawyers) was as high as the proportion of dishonest MPs there would, quite rightly, be an outcry.

But these days we seem to accept that our political representatives will be crooked.

How things have changed.

Up until 1911, MPs were paid nothing. Serving as an MP was seen as a privilege and a duty. MPs often had other jobs (running farms and businesses or working as barristers, doctors, journalists or union officials) and sat in the House of Commons as true representatives of the people they knew and worked alongside. Gladstone, Disraeli, Churchill and company had no need of expenses or research assistants.

Today, most MPs have never done any other work and know nothing of the real world outside the three political parties. Many are given their seats as a reward for sucking up to a sitting, powerful politician. The routes to power include simply sharing a flat with a future politician. These ladder-climbing nonentities do what they are told. If they are told to vote for war, they will vote for war. If they are told to hand over our country to the European Union they will do that too.

In return for their obedience they are paid fat salaries. And expenses. Lots and lots of expenses.

Half a century ago MPs took no expenses at all except a pittance for the cost of postage. But in 1957, MPs voted to allow themselves a parliamentary allowance of £750 to cover basic costs. That was the opening of the flood gates. Today, MPs receive a vast variety of expenses. And under the Labour Government the expenses MPs have claimed have risen dramatically. In 2001, MPs claimed a total of £20 million in expenses. In 2004, they claimed a total of £78 million for doing the same work. On average each MP claims £120,000 in expenses. In early 2008, it was revealed that one Conservative MP, Derek Conway, had paid his younger son £45,000 for being a research assistant even though the son was then a student at Newcastle. Then it emerged that he had paid a similar sum to his elder son when he had been at Cambridge. A son, who supposedly helped Mr Conway's secretary admitted that he had never met the secretary and didn't seem able to recollect precisely why his father had given him £10,000 bonuses. The money had, of course, been provided by taxpayers. In the end, Conway, who had paid nearly £400,000 of taxpayers' money to his wife and two sons had to pay a penalty of £13,161 and was suspended from the House of Commons for ten whole days. ('Hasn't he suffered enough?' asked the Speaker of the House, Michael Martin.)

When all this had been revealed it suddenly became clear that huge numbers of other MPs were behaving similarly. MPs from all three major parties could be heard justifying the fact that they too employed their relatives at taxpayers' expense. Other members turned out to be claiming rent for houses they owned outright. And husband-and-wife MPs turned out to be charging twice for the same home. The Commons Clerk employed to oversee MPs' expenses turned out to have enjoyed a £39,000 kitchen refit at taxpayers' expense.

The MP whose generosity had triggered the case had the party whip withdrawn (which meant that he could stay in Parliament but not under Conservative Party discipline) and other MPs seemed to think that he had been treated severely. (Non-MPs wondered why Conway hadn't had his collar felt by the constabulary. Is it not fair to suspect that if one of Mr Conway's constituents had been guilty of benefit fraud or tax evasion on such a scale he would have been facing a hefty fine and a term of imprisonment?)

After the revelations about Mr Conway, the Speaker of the House of Commons organised an inquiry. He put the inquiry into the hands of a committee of six. Five of the six members have themselves been criticised over their own financial dealings. One, for example, claimed £3,300 on his House of Commons expenses to buy a quad bike, although as far as I know he was not seen riding it around the Palace of Westminster.

Once the floodgates were opened, the stream of revelations seemed unstoppable. The ex-Work and Pensions Secretary Peter Hain (who had resigned after a little 'misunderstanding' and incompetence involving £100,000 in donations) disclosed that he paid his 80-year-old mother £5,400 a year of taxpayers' money for 'secretarial assistance'. It turned out that nearly a quarter of MPs employed at least one family member at the taxpayers' expense – often registering family members under different names to avoid detection.

And, sadly, it turned out that even the Speaker himself wasn't entirely above suspicion.

Mr Michael Martin, the Speaker, receives the same salary as a Cabinet minister (£137,579) and has a huge pension and palatial apartments overlooking the Thames. He admitted that he used air miles, accumulated when he flew at taxpayers' expenses, to fly seven members of his family on business-class trips from Glasgow to London for a New Year break. I will avoid commenting on the fact that internal flights are usually frowned upon as contributing unnecessarily to global warming. In the past five years Mr Martin has, it is said, claimed more than £75,000 for overnight stays away from London and more than £20,000 for lawyers to defend him against newspaper attacks. His wife (his wife, note) has allegedly spent more than £28,000 of taxpayers' money on air fares and taxis.

Here are some of the allowances to which MPs are currently entitled:

1. A massively over-generous travel allowance. Free rail travel. A per mile car allowance that is far better than any business would offer. The MP puts in an invoice and gets 40 pence a mile for using his car. Oh, and three free trips a year to European cities of the MP's choice.

2. An Additional Costs Allowance for accommodation away from a first home. This one allows MPs to keep a second home at taxpayers' expense. MPs claim huge sums of £20,000 to £40,000 for running their often modest-sized second homes. How they justify the costs they claim I cannot imagine. Does it cost you £40,000 to run your home? The money is often used to pay the mortgage interest on a second home (thereby enabling the MP to buy another house at the taxpayers' expense).

3. Up to £43,000 a year in petty cash expenses. Until recently MPs could claim this allowance without having to produce a receipt for any expense smaller than £250. (Try making a claim to the taxman for something costing 10p without having a receipt.) MPs can also claim £400 worth of shopping each month without having to bother keeping receipts.

4. Staffing allowances which enable MPs to hire husbands, wives, lovers, mistresses and children as secretaries, researchers and personal assistants.

5. Computer equipment, provided free on loan. The equipment includes a personal digital assistant. (In 2008, MPs demanded that they also be given BlackBerry devices.)
6. Massive pensions. MPs have awarded themselves the best pension scheme in Britain – and quite possibly the world. The annual bill to the taxpayer for funding MP's pension scheme is more than £20 million.
7. Free car parking in Westminster worth £26 a day.

These, remember, are the people whom we hire to manage the country for us. There are far more crooks in the House of Commons than there are in the average prison (where cells are often filled with old aged pensioners who couldn't afford to pay their rates, and demonstrators complaining about Government policy.) Our lives are controlled by a parliamentary conspiracy of crooks, liars and traitors.

To all this must be added the jobs 'on the side' or 'after resignation'. Time and time again, disgraced Ministers who have had to resign because of incompetence or dishonesty grab jobs with huge salaries – often either working for the EU or for the private companies they were responsible for regulating just months earlier.

After his decade as Prime Minister and war criminal, Tony Blair retired with a pension (paid by taxpayers) of over £1,000 a week, which he proceeded to enhance with a series of extraordinarily well-paid jobs. There was, allegedly, a ridiculously overpriced offer of £4.6 million for his memoirs. (It is difficult to see how the publishers can ever possibly make a profit from this. If the book he eventually writes sells for £20 in hardback the publishers would need to sell between 2,000,000 and 2,500,000 copies to cover the cost of the advance. I find it difficult to believe that so many people in Britain would pay out good money for Blair's memoirs. I hope no one will feel that I'm being cynical about this but it seems to me that large international publishing conglomerates don't always aim to make a profit when they make an offer for a book by a politician. Could the payments be a reward for favours provided in the past or favours to be requested in the future?) And an estimated £1,000,000 a year for insipid, meaningless speeches at dull, pointless gatherings. And then there were the 'jobs'. Most notable of these, perhaps, was the appointment with J. P. Morgan, the banking company which had been asked to run a bank in Iraq after Bush and Blair invaded it. How much was he being paid? One BBC 'expert' suggested it had to be more than $5 million a year. And what would Blair be expected to do for that? Blair has no relevant banking experience, and *Moneyweek* magazine guessed that Blair's role would be 'to help his employers cut corners, get around rules, subvert regulations...Otherwise why has he been hired?' There is something distinctly distasteful about a former Prime Minister selling his contacts and influence in this way – especially since those contacts and influence were acquired at the taxpayers' expense. Indeed, it doesn't take a good deal of cynicism to arrive at the feeling that Blair bought his well-paid jobs by sacrificing British soldiers and the security of the British electorate to buy popularity in the United States of America. In several books written long before he retired, I forecast that as soon as he left office Blair would take on jobs with rich American corporations. Nothing about Blair is much of a surprise to anyone.

★★★

'The ideal government of all reflective men, from Aristotle onward, is one which lets the individual alone; one which barely escapes being no government at all.'
H. L. MENCKEN

★★★

Why do the three main parties in Britain all support the EU? Why, when it is clear that a majority of the British people do not trust the EU and would, if given a chance, vote to leave it, do the three main parties, Labour, Conservative and Liberal Democrats, all support the EU?

It makes no political sense. Not since 1983 has a major political party in the UK talked openly about leaving the UK. Today, I believe that if one of the three main parties were to adopt a clear anti-EU stance that party would win any general election with ease. But none will. They all give the appearance that they know better than the people who put them into power what is good for the country.

I am always unwilling to accept conspiracy theories. But, as Sherlock Holmes pointed out, when you have excluded all other possibilities then whatever you have left, however seemingly impossible it may be, must be the only realistic solution. The only possible explanation is that the three main political parties in Britain are controlled by, and in thrall to, the European Union.

How could that be?

As I have pointed out elsewhere in this book, Edward Heath received a substantial financial reward for taking Britain into the EU when he was Prime Minister. The reward of £35,000, paid personally to Heath, in the guise of The Charlemagne Prize, was handed over to him after he had signed the Treaty of Rome.

Was Heath any worse than any other MP of modern times? I don't think so.

How much bribery currently goes on within the EU? That, of course, is impossible to say with precision. Bribery is, by its very nature, a secretive business. Neither those doing the bribing nor those being bribed are likely to talk much about what they are doing.

Questions relating to slush funds have been asked in the European Parliament. But so far there have been no replies.

According to the International Currency Review, the EU operates a secret bank account which it uses to distribute money to many of those involved in treaty signings. The International Currency Review has reported that in 2004 a total of $5 billion was allocated from secret slush funds to 'procure' the European Constitution Treaty. Of this sum $2.5 billion was allegedly allocated and paid out after the inter-governmental conference in the summer of 2004. Sums of $100 million were, it is claimed, allocated for each of the 25 EU member states with the bribery funds being remitted to various officials in each country. It is alleged that another $2.5 billion was due to be paid out on final ratification.

Search the World Wide Web and you will find plenty of reports alleging the existence of European Union slush funds. These allegations are substantiated by the knowledge that the EU is riddled with crooks and fraudsters. The mainstream media, ever obedient to the EU, has not, of course, reported or investigated these allegations.

Of one thing I am sure: those who support and protect the EU are well-rewarded. Conversely, those who oppose and criticise the EU are not.

★★★

The mass of people in England just want to get on with their lives. They want to live in a safe, secure environment with a decent infrastructure run efficiently and economically by the people who are paid to do just that. They want to be treated with respect, and possibly even with compassion, by the people they hire to look after them. And they want to be left alone as much as possible, free of unnecessary interference from the state. In addition, most people are prepared to believe that complex geo-political issues are probably best left to the experts.

But just look at the calibre of people who are running things.

The politicians running our Government are not experts in anything except lying, deceiving, spinning, self-aggrandisement and survival. Not one of these buffoons could run a corner shop successfully. They are driven not by a great desire to defend and protect Britain and its inhabitants but by a burning desire to better themselves. (It's worth remembering that most Labour Ministers are Scottish, and an unhealthily high percentage of Scots hate the English and believe that they have a duty and a responsibility to avenge imagined past injustices.)

Today the country is run by, and for, professional politicians; an unpleasant breed of thick-skinned, vain, insensitive men and women who are in politics because they weren't good enough to succeed in proper jobs. They know that general impressions are more convincing and more important than details. They know that facts can be dismissed, brushed aside, and swamped with empty promises, lies and carefully controlled news management. They know that in the end well-told lies can be more convincing than the truth. They know that if they are cornered they will probably be able to survive simply by repeatedly denying the truth.

People always find it hard to see through lies which they want to believe are the truth. It is the good-natured honesty of ordinary people which politicians use to enable them to lie, lie and lie again.

And from small lies leaders can go on to bigger ones with great ease. The politician feeds the voters with what they want to hear. The politician, like the drug pusher, gives his constituents what they want and what they demand.

The very size of the big lies they tell confuses us. Most of us never tell really big lies. We may tell small ones. But we don't tell huge fundamental lies which contradict the facts. We don't for two reasons: we suspect we will be found out and we don't feel comfortable with it. It's wrong.

So we believe what the politician says. What he is saying is so important that he couldn't be lying. Could he? And, besides, we elected him in the first place. We wouldn't elect such a bad person would we? That is an intolerable thought.

Politicians know that most people believe big lies more readily than they believe small ones. They know that to question a big lie is to question the liar. And they know that once you do that you have to question all the other stuff. And they know that means admitting that you were wrong when you trusted him or her in the first place.

Most people don't want to do that. Most people carry on believing and trusting because that's the easy way out.

★★★

'It is dangerous to be right when the government is wrong.'
VOLTAIRE

★★★

Never, in our history, has the country been run by people with such little knowledge, such little inspiration and such little genuine passion. We are being managed by men and women who would be stretched to serve as local councillors; men and women who would have risen far above their potential and capability if they had been pressed into running the village fete.

For the past two decades Europe has, in the words of Business Week magazine, 'lived through a series of economic lies'.

There were the false promises that the single market would boost economic activity, that the euro would turbocharge growth and that the expansion of the Economic Union to the East would make Europe strong again. The truth is that despite all these changes (or, rather, because of them) the EU has become an also-ran economy.

Today, the EU is synonymous with high unemployment, slow growth, protection of industries which ought to be allowed to die quietly and the suppression of new, growing industries. And, of course, a constant bias towards France and Germany.

And yet Britain remains a full and committed member of the EU, paying huge amounts of money for membership of the club.

What do we get in return?

Er, nothing.

Why are we members?

Good question. No possible answer.

What was ever in it for Britain?

Er, nothing.

Why are our politicians so desperate for us to become ever more closely aligned to Europe?

Because they want to climb aboard the EU gravy train for politicians.

Is being a member of the EU making our lives better or worse?

Worse.

Even members of the media seem noticeably reluctant to question the value of the EU. Could this be because the EU often sponsors and subsidises parts of the media?

Why does the European Union really exist? What is it for? Who really benefits?

These are questions which no one ever asks.

The truth is that Britain gets nothing out of the EU. It costs us money to be members of a club which is strangling all our industries with red tape, adding thousands of pointless new laws and regulations to our own over-extensive legislature and taking away our sovereignty and independence.

France, on the other hand, gets a good deal out of the EU. A very good deal. Thanks to the Common Agricultural Policy (which France devised and has carefully protected for decades) small French farmers receive steady, substantial subsidies from British taxpayers.

So, why do all three political parties support our membership of a corrupt and failing organisation which is charging us huge fees for the doubtful privilege of losing our sovereignty and our freedom?

In theory, it doesn't make much sense.

Opposition to the EU is so widespread that there is no doubt that if one of the big three parties announced that it was campaigning for us to leave the EU it would win the next election at a canter. Actually, even promising to offer a referendum on whether or not we should leave would probably be enough to win a sizeable majority (even though Gordon Brown dramatically devalued the manifesto promise).

Could all these politicians be either so stupid or so ill-informed that they cannot see the EU for the grasping, pointless and dangerous organisation it has become?

No, of course not.

The only alternative explanation is that they are bent.

Eliminate the impossible and you are left with the unpleasant truth that the vast majority of our leading politicians have been bought.

(The politicians have presumably not noticed that the EU will abolish the Labour, Conservative and Liberal Democrat parties. Only pan-European parties will be allowed. But maybe they have noticed that parties which criticise the EU will not be allowed at all.)

I believe that the politicians who support or promote the EU do so largely for personal gain. Thanks to the EU gravy train, numerous political no-hopers have become wealthy. Greedy politicians desperate for wealth (and a chance to have their egos massaged) have sold their country and betrayed their heritage. There is no excuse and there can be no forgiveness. Theirs are heinous crimes.

The party system which we now accept as a fundamental part of what we perceive to be 'parliamentary democracy' is not a fundamental part of public life in Britain. The political parties in Britain are merely private organisations which have no constitutional rights or privileges. They are run to implement the policies of their leaders rather than that of their members. The three main parties in Britain have no constitutional status, and the leaders of those parties have no rights other than as elected representatives sent to Parliament to 'manage' the country on our behalf.

★★★

'It would be nice to have a world devoid of psychopathic leaders. For two reasons this is unlikely ever to come about. First, throughout history the possession of psychopathic traits has proved a useful passport to high office. Men or women who are unfettered by moral scruples, who are prepared to lie or cheat their way to the top, who will make promises they know they cannot keep and may, in extreme cases, think nothing of assassinating their rivals, have a huge advantage over those held back by notions of fair play…the possession of psychopathic traits is advantageous to a leader. They give him more degrees of freedom in his control and manipulation of those under him and most particularly in his dealings with potential enemies.'
NORMAN F.DIXON

★★★

How do these corrupt, dishonest and self-serving people get into power?

Everyone I ever speak to claims never to have voted for Labour. So, how did they ever win?

I think the answer is simple.

I think that the people who voted for New Labour did so for purely personal, selfish reasons. They didn't do it because they thought that New Labour would make the nation a better, fairer country. They didn't believe that New Labour would look after the sick, the frail and the disadvantaged more wisely and more compassionately than any other party. They didn't believe that New Labour would provide a better infrastructure or defend them with more vigour, more determination and more loyalty. They voted for New Labour because they believed that in doing so they would best preserve their benefits. (Remember: one in five children in the UK lives in a household dependent on benefits.)

The politicians who run the country are self-serving, and the people who put them in power are self-serving too.

Has the time come to reconsider the validity and fairness of the sacred principle of 'one man one vote'?

The original concept of giving every man and woman a vote

was based on the unarguably fair notion that everyone who contributes to society should have a say in how it is run.

But things have changed.

Today, it is perfectly possible for a government to get into power – and to stay there indefinitely – simply through winning the votes of people who make no contribution to society.

So many millions now receive state benefits, and are wholly dependent upon the government for their income, that a political party which is prepared to pander to them, in order to win their votes, while at the same time ignoring the needs and rights of those who work and pay tax, could stay in power for years.

I believe that the Labour Party is in power because it gets votes this way. Those who voted for Labour in the last election could only have done so for entirely selfish and personal reasons. The Labour Government has been so discredited that it is impossible to believe that anyone could have voted for them for any other reason.

And it is because they know that this is where their votes come from that the Labour Party has done nothing to stop the epidemic of benefit fraud which is destroying the welfare state. The Labour Party doesn't care too hoots that those who are genuinely in need are being pushed aside and abandoned. All the Labour Party cares about is staying in power and enjoying the perks and the money that come with the power. If this means pandering to those who prefer not to work then this is what they will do.

It is part of our electoral tradition that prisoners do not receive a vote. Why, after all, should people who do not make a positive contribution to society have a say in how society is run?

It would make just as much sense to withdraw the right to vote from those who are long-term benefit claimants.

Our present system is ludicrous and quite unfair. It's like allowing those who receive donations from a charity to decide how the charitable contributions should be distributed and how much those who contribute to the charity should give.

★★★

'What matters is not who votes but who counts the votes.'
STALIN

★★★

It is a myth that we have a three-party system. We don't even have a two-party system. The political parties we have are all parts of the same party; they all share the same basic beliefs.

Politics today is primarily about politicians rather than voters. The only people who get anything out of elections are the politicians, and people don't vote because the politicians aren't worth voting for.

After another low turnout at the last general election, one Labour Minister stated that people didn't bother to vote because they were content. The truth, of course, is very different. People don't bother to vote because they know that their vote is worthless. Politicians ignore the people. And an increasing number of people now recognise that the vast majority of the laws and policies which control us and shape the way we live are sent to us from Brussels. Voting for MPs and MEPs makes no difference to the laws sent to us by the unelected eurocrats.

Very few sensitive, thoughtful, caring individuals go into politics these days. Decent people don't become politicians because they just don't want to expose themselves and their families to public ridicule and humiliation. Today, the only people who go into politics are the pompous, thick-skinned, greedy, self-centred people who see politics as a way to improve their status and their wealth. In the end, the people who run the country are the very people who should not be leading the country. We need leaders who care but instead we end up with people whose primary concern is not the good of the nation, or the welfare of the people, but simple self-preservation and self-aggrandisement. It is hardly surprising that there is plenty of fraud in modern politics but very little genuine passion. Those politicians who are led by an ideology (and there are few enough of those) use their ideology as an excuse to further their control, rather than to improve the state of the world they are supposed to be managing.

★★★

Elections are a sham. There are no real choices. It is always the government who wins, and never the people. All our major political parties are fundamentally fascist; they want to tyrannise us and impose their beliefs on us. Instead of wanting to create a free and liberated society, so that we can all get on with our lives, they want to expand their control over our lives and they want to interfere in every aspect of everything we do. All today's political parties want to violate our individual rights and to increase the rights of government. Those views are fundamentally fascist.

The three parties control what happens, and yet the three-party system is a confidence trick. There are no real differences between the parties. All three parties want Britain to be part of Europe. MPs who are members of these three parties represent (and vote for the interests of) their parties rather than the electors or the country.

English politicians are interchangeable. (Actually, to be accurate, most of them aren't English.)

Think of any leading politician. Now imagine him transplanted into another political party. It isn't difficult is it?

There is nothing much to help us distinguish between the three main parties; they have much the same policies and the same arrogance, they display the same indifference to the voters and they make the same mistakes. They share the same taste for power (for its own sake rather than for what it can be used to achieve) and the same denial of reality.

★★★

'The ideal government of all reflective men, from Aristotle onward, is one which lets the individual alone; one which barely escapes being no government at all.'
H.L. MENCKEN

★★★

We must take back the political power which is rightfully ours. We have to take back power from the crooks and the crooked institutions which now rule our lives. We have to take back power from the weak, spineless and unthinking politicians who serve those institutions with such uncritical faithfulness.

The people are now the only force of opposition; the only voice for freedom and justice is the voice on the streets.

What Britain really needs is a House of Commons made up of independent men and women who would keep their promises, who would stick to their manifestos and who would vote honestly and decently according to their consciences.

The biggest problem we have at the moment is that our destiny, our welfare and our history are all in the hands of political parties which have their own vested interests to pursue. Political parties need to grow and thrive in order to survive.

★★★

All organisations (and this seems particularly true of political organisations) develop their own (well-hidden) agenda: their own reason for being.

For the first time in history we have succeeded in creating a world, a society, which now exists solely to defend, protect and develop itself. We have created a society whose institutions have acquired power of their own. These institutions – governments, multinational corporations, multinational bureaucracies and so on – now exist solely to maintain, improve and strengthen themselves. These institutions have their own hidden agendas, and the human beings who work for them may think that they are in control – but they aren't.

The people who seem to be in charge of our institutions aren't in charge at all. There is no one actually running the EU – just as there is no one running the NHS. Both organisations are now out of our control. The EU, in particular, satisfies all the requirements for a truly fascist society. When the needs and rights of the individual take second place to the needs and demands of the State (or, in the case of the EU, the superstate) the State has become unarguably fascist. The bureaucrats working for the EU exist only to create rules. It is what they do. They have no experience of the real world and no understanding of how their new rules affect people's lives. And they don't care. In fact they love chaos and confusion – because chaos and confusion give them an excuse to create new laws. They love making new laws because when they make more laws they give themselves more power. And the more complicated the rules become the easier it is for them to argue that they need more staff and bigger offices. And if they have more staff (and more authority) they deserve to receive more pay. The EU bureaucrats are the perfect example of modern administrators gathering authority without responsibility. Those working for the EU have enormous amounts of authority but no responsibility at all. Every minor bureaucrat is a state-sponsored despot; this is fascism (or communism) at its very worst.

It may be a little difficult to accept the concept of institutions having agendas of their own but the reality is that this is exactly what has happened.

The people who appear to run large institutions, and who themselves undoubtedly believe that they are in charge, are simply institutional servants.

Consider, for example, the chairman and directors of a large multinational pharmaceutical company. These well-paid men and women will regard themselves as being responsible for the tactics and strategy followed by the company for which they work. But in reality it is the company itself – an institution which only really exists on paper – which is in real control.

Every multinational company has a constant thirst for cash. In order to satisfy bankers, brokers and shareholders, companies need to produce quarterly figures which show a nice big, fat profit on the bottom line.

The people who work for our imaginary drug company may think that they are in control but in reality they aren't. The directors have to do what is in their company's best interests. If they don't then their company will falter and that can't be allowed to happen. The company, the unimaginably powerful corporate demon, must come first.

So, for example, if the directors find that one of their products causes lethal side effects they may, as human beings, feel ashamed about this. Individually, the directors may want to withdraw the drug immediately and to apologise to the people who have been injured by their product. But this course of action would not be in the company's best short-term interests. Withdrawing the drug would doubtless cost the company money. Research and development costs would have to be written off. And apologising would expose the company to lawsuits. So the directors, acting in the company's best interests, must keep the drug on the market and deny that there are any problems. In these circumstances, the company (a non-human entity which only exists on paper) is in control. The decisions are made not in the interests of people (whether they be customers or directors) but in the interests of the corporate 'being'.

The problem is compounded by the fact that, big as they are, multinational companies have no souls and no sense of responsibility. Nearly forty years ago I wrote an essay which attracted a good deal of mail from readers because it clearly hit a nerve; the essence of the piece was my view that one of the major problems of our society is that responsibility has been separated from authority. I wrote the piece when I was still practising as a doctor, and I couldn't help but illustrate my essay by pointing out that the young hospital doctor has a great deal of responsibility but virtually no authority, whereas the hospital administrator has an enormous amount of authority but virtually no responsibility. I warned that this constant separation of these two would lead to great problems.

Responsibility has been totally separated from authority. No one in authority seems to be held responsible for their incompetence. A list of all the failures, stupidities and waste of the last decade would fill twelve volumes. The pointless, cruel wars which have been started without public support. The Child Support Agency which collapsed, causing social mayhem and financial bedlam. Billions have been wasted on consultancy fees without any possible advantage to the voter. The intrusive NHS computer scheme is, as I write, two years behind schedule and its costs have tripled to £20 billion. Think of the absurdities of the Dome, the worries created when the Inland Revenue lost the confidential records of over 20 million citizens, and the constant rise in costs of the Olympics. The list goes on and on. In contrast, I find it impossible to think of any way in which our society has been improved in recent years. Everything is getting worse and it is the politicians who are to blame. Politicians lie with impunity; they hardly ever resign (and never through embarrassment, shame or on a matter of principle). Bureaucrats, civil servants, soldiers (killing colleagues in friendly fire incidents) and the police are just a few of the many who have vast amounts of authority but who carry no sense of responsibility.

And, of course, corporations and political parties have no responsibility whatsoever – but they have great authority over us and our lives. Moreover, corporations (represented by their slaves – the people who think they are running them) never think beyond the next set of profit figures; they are ultimately ruthless and (since they are inanimate and bloodless) utterly 'cold blooded'. They are also ultimately short-sighted. Big institutions, like computers, are inherently, irretrievably, stupid. They do not realise that their behaviour will, in the long run, lead to their total destruction – partly because it will annoy and alienate their customers and partly because it will eventually result in the deaths of many of their customers.

By and large, the men and women who run large drug companies, arms companies, food companies and genetic engineering companies don't really want to destroy the world in which we all live. They know that their families have to breathe the same air as you and I. They know that they too need good food, clean drinking water and a healthy environment.

However, despite the evidence being to the contrary, the people who run these companies probably think that they are doing good and useful work. They have denied the truth to themselves in order to avoid coming face to face with a reality which would probably drive them insane if they accepted it. It is only through denial and self-deceit that most of the men and women who work for tobacco companies can continue to sell a product which causes so much misery and so much death. Adolf Hitler killed fewer people than the big tobacco companies have killed. But I doubt if many of the people running big tobacco companies think of themselves as evil.

I have met men and women who run large organisations (such as drug companies). Some recognise that what they are doing is immoral, and they excuse themselves with such trite and shallow phrases as 'If I didn't do it someone else would' and 'I've got to pay the mortgage'. These are, of course, variations on the same excuses favoured by the men and women who operated the gas chambers during the Second World War. The brighter and more sensitive individuals usually see through these excuses in the end; they often become depressed.

But many men and women who work for large organisations quite honestly and sincerely believe that they are doing useful and indeed valuable work. They have become so deeply institutionalised, and are driven so completely by the needs of the corporate beast, that they genuinely feel no shame about what they do. They have rationalised their actions and denied to themselves the truths which are apparent to outside observers.

Occasionally, this constant denial and self-deceit breaks down and absurdities appear. For example, British Members of Parliament have, as members of an institution, consistently voted to allow multinational corporations to pollute our drinking water and to tamper with and pollute our food. And yet MPs themselves, as individuals, are so conscious of the value of the pure food and clean drinking water that in the House of Commons they have arranged to be given spring water to drink and to be fed on organic food which has not been genetically modified. The men and women who vote to allow our water to be polluted and our food to be genetically modified are voting as representatives of institutions rather than as representatives of people. They know that they are creating a world in which the food is unfit to eat and the water unfit to drink. But they can't stop it happening because they are operating for the benefit of institutions rather than people. The huge organisations which now run the world have developed identities, strengths, purposes and needs of their own. And in order to continue to grow in size and in strength those organisations need to ignore or suppress as much of the truth as they can – and to ignore the truths which they cannot suppress. Obviously, the people who work for those institutions must also ignore and suppress the unpalatable truths (and they must find ways to hide from the reality of what they are doing).

How else can anyone explain the fact that the American Government has decided to continue to damage the environment – despite knowing the consequences? How else can anyone explain the fact that because antibiotics are being consistently and deliberately and knowingly used irresponsibly, infectious diseases are once again a major cause of death? How else can anyone explain the fact that genetic engineers are creating foods which may or may not be safe to eat? How else can anyone explain the fact that drug companies keep on producing – and selling – products which do more harm than good?

The industrialists, the politicians and the administrators who allow these things to happen are just as vulnerable to the consequences of their actions as you and I. They – and their families – cannot buy immunity to the problems which they are creating.

The need to produce short-term profits means that commercial organisations must follow policies which lead to short-term advantages – even if those policies are disadvantageous for customers, employees and shareholders. The long-term interests of these three groups are pushed aside in favour of the needs of the corporation. Naturally, the rewards paid to the select few individuals who serve the corporations needs most assiduously become obscenely over generous. It is, after all, in the institution's interests to ensure that the directors who defend the institution should be well-rewarded. Short-termism has always been a problem in central and local government, where the overriding aim of politicians is usually to get re-elected (it is alleged that this was Blair's first aim when moving into Number 10, Downing Street) but it has increasingly become a serious problem in industry where companies now desperately need to produce a constant stream of quarterly profits. Large corporations are like huge rudderless tankers; they plough on regardless, unstoppable and unsteerable; the captain and crew reduced, in practice, to the status of mere passengers.

The selfish, self-centred amoral materialism which has characterised political life for the last few decades, and which has simultaneously accompanied a downfall in morality, can no longer be seen as just another unfortunate blip in human development. The horrors of today will not be easily conquered, and will not be conquered at all unless we acknowledge the breadth and depth of the exceptional problem we now face.

Some years ago, Dr Albert Schweizer saw the first signs of what has happened. 'Another hindrance to civilisation today,' he wrote, 'is the over-organisation of our public life. While it is certain that a properly ordered environment is the condition and, at the same time, the result of civilisation, it is also undeniable that, after a certain point has been reached, external organisation is developed at the expense of spiritual life. Personality and ideas are often subordinated to institutions, when it is really these which ought to influence the latter and keep them inwardly alive.'

Today, the over-organisation of public life has a momentum of its own; public individuals and public bodies are pushed this way and that by corporate lobbyists. The direction they finally take depends on who pushes hardest.

No one has control of anything any more.

Campaigning charities exist not to fight for the cause which led to their foundation but to provide salaries, perks and pensions for their employees. If you doubt this just look at the accounts for any successful, professional charity. The chances are that between 50% and 75% of the gross income goes towards paying the organisation's costs; in other words the organisation exists largely to sustain itself.

And political parties are much the same; they exist to provide comfortable employment for the paid employees, social support groups for voluntary workers (who usually spend most of their time concerned with constitutional minutiae and fighting one another for power within the organisation) and power, money and status for the party's political representatives: the MPs and the councillors. Political parties exist to win seats and to win elections. That is all they exist for.

The interests of the modern political party no longer match the original aims of the founders; they are far removed from the original concerns and passions which led to their foundation.

The Labour party doesn't really care about the English people or about England. The Labour Party doesn't care whether England exists or disappears; it doesn't care about Scotland, Wales or Northern Ireland; it doesn't care about the NHS, the railways or the security of old people in Birmingham, Manchester or Leeds.

The Labour party is an organisation and organisations don't have feelings, passions or purposes. Organisations exist only to exist. And as with so many organisations the Labour Party is run for the benefit of the people who run it: the managers, the office staff and the other employees whose salaries and pensions are paid by it.

The same thing is true of the Conservative Party. And the Liberal Democrat Party. And in the end it will be the same of any large, successful political party.

★★★

Our first step to freedom must be to free ourselves of the 'party system' and return to the days when our Parliament consisted of honest, caring individuals whose only concern was the future safety and welfare of the people they represented – and the country of which they were citizens.

And that would be a real revolution.

It is not the duty of a government to micro-manage people's lives. It is the duty of a government to provide a safe, effective, unobtrusive infrastructure which allows citizens the freedom to do their own thing. Ayn Rand, the author of *Atlas Shrugged* and founder of the philosophy of objectivism, declared that the only true purpose of politics is to protect individual rights. And she was right.

It will take some time to get rid of the party system. But once there are a few genuinely independent MPs in Parliament, the present dishonest system will start to crumble. How will the party whips respond when a growing number of MPs cannot be bullied or bribed into acting in a particular way? As the number of independent MPs grows so the power of the parties will collapse. Eventually, the independent MPs in the House of Commons will have the majority. They will be able to form a Government themselves. And the parties will be finished. We will have a House of Commons populated by rational, individual MPs who are not driven by absurdities such as political correctness and multiculturalism.

The party system has betrayed us and it's time we changed it. The Government should be the servant of the Commons and the Commons should be the servant of the people. That's not the way it is as the moment. If anything the system works totally the other way around.

★★★

'Those who are unafraid to say they do not know become wise. Those who insist they know never learn. Those who pay attention to their weaknesses gain strength. Wisdom and strength come from the courage to see things as they are.'
Taoist philosophy

Sadly, I believe that the United Kingdom is finished.

The Scottish Parliament, and the Scottish nationalists, have seen to that.

The Scottish and Welsh nationalists think that their countries are heading towards independence. They don't realise that they are heading not towards independence but towards European regionalisation. The Scottish Parliament is, in reality, merely a Regional Parliament of the EU. The same is true of the Welsh Parliament. But the Scots and the Welsh don't realise this. They enthusiastically support membership of the European Union because they foolishly and naively believe that staying in the EU will enable them to reach full independence.

Scotland and Wales will survive only as regions of the EU. But that is more than will happen to England. When the European plan reaches its final stages, England will become nine anonymous regions. English history and culture will be forgotten.

★★★

'What was it that at every decisive moment made every British statesman do the wrong thing with so unerring an instinct?'
GEORGE ORWELL

★★★

In many British elections there is a less than 50% turnout.

In 1997, Labour got a massive landslide victory with less than 50% of the popular vote. Since only about two thirds of the electorate bothered to vote, Blair received the support of around one third of the electors. That was enough to give him a 'landslide'. So, in the year when Tony Blair got an overwhelming, unprecedented majority in the House of Commons, two thirds of the British people either didn't vote for him or didn't want him as Prime Minister.

Millions have given up voting in political elections because they don't think their vote is going to make any difference. There are, they believe, three reasons for this.

First, modern politicians lie. They regard campaign promises and manifesto pledges as gimmicks to win elections.

Second, there is no significant difference between the main parties.

Third, once they get into power politicians don't take any notice of the wishes of the people. They turn into dictators.

The turnout at all forthcoming elections will, I suspect, be an all-time low. How can citizens be expected to have respect for a Government which starts illegal wars? What is the point in voting when the Government starts a war against the wishes of the people?

People don't vote in political elections because they don't think there is any point. They don't like politicians.

The problem is that politics has become a career. Politics has become something people no longer choose to do because it is a way to improve society, or a way to correct injustices, but because it offers a good way to earn a living and get on in the world. Just a few generations ago most of the people who went into politics did so because they wanted to put something back. They had either been born to wealth and position or they had earned wealth and position through their own talents and hard work. Most were gentlemen and were not easy to bribe (because they were already rich and they already had all the status and social position they needed). Alec Douglas-Home (coincidentally the only Prime Minister ever to play first class cricket) was probably the last British Prime Minister who could be described as a 'gentleman' without risking a lawsuit under the Trades Description Act. Today's politicians are an entirely different breed to yesterday's men. Which one of today's raggle-taggle bunch could possibly be described as a 'Statesman' in the mould of Disraeli or Churchill? Today's average MP has no skills, and no job experience. This is particularly true of Labour MPs, though it applies to MPs on both sides of the House; if they lose their jobs their future will be bleak. It is, therefore, perhaps not surprising that most MPs think solely of their careers and allow themselves to be treated as voting lobby fodder.

Our world is run by people who may be formally educated but who have never learned to question what they have been told and have no valid life experience with which to create judgements. The average citizen has less respect for politicians than any other group except lawyers. (Is it merely a coincidence that most politicians were trained as lawyers?)

★★★

Our 'leaders' are, almost to a man and woman, professional politicians who have risen, by default, far beyond their meagre potential. They are in power because no one else wanted what they wanted quite as much; no one else was prepared to sacrifice their integrity on the altar of their ambition. New Labour politicians don't understand the world or the needs of ordinary people. They live a life divorced from the real world. (Frighteningly, a remarkable number have children following in their footsteps. These nonentities are creating new political dynasties.)

Today's British politicians are in Parliament because they want power. They call it patriotism, service and leadership. But it's really the power they want. And why do they want the power? Simple. They want the power because it is the best (and for them probably the only) way they know to get rich.

Today's politicians are in it for the money and the glory rather than because they want to serve the people. Blair, for example, was probably only Prime Minister because he couldn't make it as a rock star. Does anyone in Britain still believe that Blair (the man who did the impossible and made Thatcher look caring) led New Labour because he believed in a fairer, better society?

★★★

The main political parties are clearly determined to throw out our heritage. The Labour storm-troopers seem to believe in all things modern, in progress for its own sake, regardless of whether it is what people want or whether or not it works. Traditions are neither respected nor preserved.

Among today's 'professional' politicians money always buys a hearing for its point of view. (There are many ways for a 'backer' who wants a particular policy pushing through to 'support' a politician. Numerous politicians have been paid huge fees for unsaleably dull autobiographies and there are many politicians around the world benefiting from absurdly inflated speaking fees and interest free loans.)

Yesterday's MPs, often exceedingly wealthy in their own right, could afford to be independent and, on occasion gloriously bloody-minded. It is hardly surprising that when things go wrong, today's MPs and Ministers lie, and look for someone else to blame, rather than resign. Today's politicians have no experience and no achievements of their own. They are professional politicians; following a career because it satisfies their vanity, their ego and their yearning for wealth and power. They have little or no interest in serving the public or in improving the nature of the world in which we live. They are in politics for what they can get out of it, rather than what they can put in. They have no passion for improving the world and they have no experience of competence. Never having run anything (a business or a professional practice) why should they suddenly be capable of running huge departments? Besides they have no real control over day-to-day issues. The big decisions are made by civil servants in Brussels. The end of the 'gentleman amateur' in politics meant the end of honour and justice in Parliament.

Their immorality (and lack of scruples) has, through spin and deceit, led all our institutions down a dangerous spiral into a world where the only thing that seems to matter is who wins. Politicians no longer lead the electorate. Instead of 'leading' they merely try to please enough electors to stay in power. Labour politicians realised some time ago that they could win an election (and subsequently stay in power) simply by appealing to people who don't pay tax. At the last general election, New Labour was voted into office by people who have a strong, personal vested interest in our current illogical and unfair benefits system.

Because they are always looking for money (either for themselves or for their next political election campaign) politicians are easily 'bought' by lobbyists. There are numerous examples of politicians taking advantage of their public position to obtain better holidays. Two recent former British Prime Ministers gained enormously from having been popular in America, and there has been an almost endless trail of politicians moving from public life into corporate boardrooms. There is little doubt that many politicians regard political life as some sort of apprenticeship which, when served, entitles them to cash in and earn huge amounts of money in the city of London. Professional, career politicians are prepared to lie and to cheat and to deceive if that is what it takes to be successful. And because so many of them do lie and cheat and deceive then that is now what it does take to be successful.

Politicians make promises they know the electors want to hear, even though they have no intention of ever honouring those promises. Modern politicians don't resign if they are caught out. They just lie and cheat some more in the hope that they can get away with whatever it is that they have done. And then, at worst, they just lie low for a couple of years before they make a comeback. Dishonesty is now so rife among politicians that it has become almost impossible for an honest, decent politician to succeed at all. Indeed, politics is now such a discredited part of public life that very few honest, decent people want to have anything to do with it. For the time being at least, the crooks have taken over.

All things considered, it is hardly surprising that millions of people don't bother voting. Why should anyone vote?

'Politicians are all crooked,' wrote one reader to me. 'Why should I bother voting for any of them?'

Conservative party sleaze usually involved sexual indiscretions. Labour party sleaze usually involves greed, dishonesty and money. The sexual indiscretions may well have a devastating effect on the candidate's family but they don't affect the voters very much. The greed and dishonesty do. Within weeks of taking power, the Labour Government was embroiled in a financial scandal when it was revealed that Government policy on tobacco advertising had been changed (coincidentally, of course) at just the same time that the Party had accepted a seven figure donation from an individual who stood to gain a great deal from the change. Since then, everything has been downhill and Labour politicians have proved themselves to be as every bit as greedy as their Conservative predecessors. The only reason Labour politicians don't receive their money in brown envelopes is that the sums involved are too great to fit into envelopes.

★★★

'Make yourself sheep and the wolves will eat you.'
BENJAMIN FRANKLIN

★★★

But although people don't bother to vote in political elections, they still love voting when they think it is worthwhile and when they think their vote will make a difference. They do it all the time. They vote in their millions to subject minor celebrities to great indignities in the television programme *I'm a Celebrity – Get Me Out Of Here*. They vote for their favourites in *Pop Idol*. They vote to have obnoxious players thrown out of the *Big Brother* house. In these 'elections' people actually pay to cast their vote. In many areas of the country, more English people voted for candidates in the *Big Brother* house than voted in the last Parliamentary elections.

★★★

We have to break the three-in-one party system which has for so long held a stranglehold over British politics. We must fill Parliament with people who care about nothing but the voters and the country; parliamentary representatives who will think only about the needs and wishes of the voters and the good of the country when they are voting in the House of Commons. We have to vote for representatives who know that if they fail to represent the wishes of the voters, or at least satisfy the voters that they have voted honestly and honourably, then they won't be elected at the next election. Vote not for the party but for the individual. Whenever possible always vote for the independent candidate. If there isn't an independent candidate, vote for the candidate representing the smallest party. Do not, under any circumstances, vote for a candidate representing one of the main three parties.

Even if your independent candidate turns out to be an incompetent crook we will all be better off. One incompetent and crooked MP can do far less damage than an incompetent and crooked political party.

Is it possible for us to regain power over our representatives this way?

Yes.

Is there a choice?

Well, there is always a choice.

If you want things to continue to get worse you can carry on voting for the present corrupt and incompetent system.

Or if you want a better life and a better world then you can vote for genuine change.

Most of the members of parliament we have now will not rescue us from the EU.

Theoretically and historically, MPs are there to represent and protect the interests of their constituents. But today their main function is to act as lobby fodder for the party leadership, to be fed into the lobbies and counted.

If an MP's party is not in Government, he or she has no power. If his or her party is in Government, the amount of power he or she has depends on his or her influence with the leader (i.e., were they at school with him, have they ever shared a flat with him and so on).

In practise, the average MP who sits for one of the big three parties is representing not his constituents, the people who voted for him, but the party machine which selected him to represent the party at an election.

Most MPs are merely bit part actors, fit to open fetes, kiss babies and write patronising, self-glorifying rubbish for the local newspaper.

I believe that we can change the way our nation is governed by voting not for candidates who represent the three big parties but by voting for candidates who represent smaller parties or (better still) stand as true independents.

Independent MPs have an enormous amount of power in the House of Commons. They can do a great deal of good for their local constituents. The vote of an independent MP cannot be relied upon by a big party machine. An independent MP cannot be told to vote one way or the other. He cannot be threatened with expulsion from the party or bribed with a promise of minor office or a peerage. The independent MP must truly represent the interests of the people who sent him to Parliament. If he doesn't they won't vote for him again. The independent MP can demand things for his constituency and have a reasonable hope that his demands will be met. He will, at the very least, have a much greater hope of success than the MP who represents a party – whether that party be in or out of power.

At each and every forthcoming election vote for anyone whom you think might possibly be able to defeat the Labour, Conservative and Liberal candidates.

That's real tactical voting. And it will give us back our Parliament and our country.

Vernon Coleman

11

The EU, the Law and Your Disappearing Freedom

'The officers of the new EU police force, Europol, are immune from criminal prosecution should they break the law while carrying out their activities.'
ARTICLE 5, PARAGRAPH 2 OF THE EU COUNCIL ACT (1998)

Our Parliament at Westminster is subordinate to the European Commission in Brussels from whence comes a constant torrent of new regulations.

They are called 'regulations' and 'directives' but, make no mistake about it, they are 'laws'. Regulations from the EU come with the strength of law. They are undeniable and unalterable. They have to be passed by our own Parliament at Westminster. MPs don't have a choice. Like MEPs in Brussels, MPs sitting in London are just a huge and very expensive rubber stamping machine.

Politicians at Westminster take responsibility for the new laws from the EU (even though they may not agree with them) because they know that they have no choice. And if they are seen to question the laws which emanate from Brussels they will expose the whole sham that is now the British Parliament. British civil servants now exist not to oversee new laws devised by British politicians but to oversee new laws passed by EU civil servants.

The constant flow of new laws is designed to help increase the speed of integration, to cement the power of the European Commission and to keep us occupied with minutiae so that we

117

do not have time to realise what is happening. We are kept so busy worrying about the size of our ducks' eggs and the shape of our bananas that we have no time left to reflect on the loss of our freedom, our independence and our sovereignty.

Ignorance of the law is no excuse for breaking the law. But how can anyone possibly know all of the 100,000 laws which we have been given by the EU? How can anyone possibly be familiar with the endless rulings, technicalities and amendments? We've come a long way from the Ten Commandments.

There are now so many EU laws that it is virtually impossible for anyone to get through a day without breaking several. When there are so many laws that no one knows what they are, and everyone regularly breaks them without thought, knowledge or regret, then respect for the law disappears. But it is not just respect for the small laws which disappears: respect for the big laws goes too. The EU has devalued the law and our attitude towards it.

The EU bureaucrats are demanding an 'evaluation of the quality of justice' in the EU. They want a 'European judicial culture'.

And they are getting it.

In order to allay our fears, the bureaucrats say that they will 'respect legal traditions' in individual countries.

But their idea of 'respect' is clearly not the same as mine. The EU has already failed to respect English legal traditions with the introduction of its pan-European 'arrest warrant' whereby suspects can be arrested without the need for anything as inconvenient as 'evidence'.

The EU bureaucrats (perhaps we should call them 'masters' because that is a better description of their role in our lives) want 'common standards of procedure in criminal proceedings'. And so the EU will in future be responsible for defining both criminal offences and penalties. The aim is to 'increase the efficiency of prosecutions' and to secure more convictions.

It is undoubtedly for this reason that the Labour Government has been busy attempting to get rid of such inconvenient legal nonsenses as trial by jury. It is far easier to get convictions when the decision about whether or not a defendant should be found guilty can be left in the hands of politicians, lawyers and bureaucrats.

★★★

Englishmen and women were given their freedom hundreds of years ago under the *Magna Carta*. Those rights have now gone.

So, for example, in contrast to other European countries, England has always had the right to habeas corpus. The principle of habeas corpus was already common law by the time the *Magna Carta* was signed in 1215. The principle of habeas corpus was enshrined in law when the Habeas Corpus Act was passed in 1679. The Latin means 'you should have the body' and it means that under this Act a judge can order the Government to bring anybody in its custody to a specified court for a trial to ensure that he is tried according to the due process of law. The purpose of the Act was to stop the Government imprisoning people without good reason. We are losing our habeas corpus protection from the Government and for this we can thank the EU.

We can also thank the EU for the fact that the Government is replacing coroners with its own political appointees. It is, of course, much easier to avoid legal embarrassments if your own appointee is making the decisions.

★★★

'No free man shall be taken or imprisoned or dispossessed, or outlawed or exiled, or in any way destroyed, not will we go upon him, nor will we send against him except by the lawful judgement of his peers or by the law of the land.'
CLAUSE 39, THE *MAGNA CARTA*

★★★

The *Magna Carta*, provided the foundation for parliamentary government around the world. Parliamentary democracy originated in England. The *Magna Carta* and the Bill of Rights gave every English citizen fundamental rights. We allow MPs to act on our behalf but as citizens we retain the power. According to Lord Chief Justice Coke, writing in the 'Origin of the Common Law of England' our common law comes from King Brutus (who landed in Totnes in 1104) and cannot be altered or revoked by any Act of the crown. In other words, the common law rights of British citizens cannot be given away by the British parliament and they cannot be revoked by the EU. If we accept the *Magna Carta* as the basis of British law, and the fundamental statement of our rights, every British Prime Minister who has signed a document handing over our rights to the European Union has been wasting ink. None of the documents they have signed has been valid in law. Neither Parliament nor the Sovereign has the power to sign away our rights or to allow a foreign power to govern us.

The new legal system which the EU (and Labour) is imposing on England will mean the end of habeas corpus and the end of the *Magna Carta*. There will be no juries, the authorities will be able to lock you up without trial and if, when you do come to trial you are found not guilty the state will be able to keep re-trying you until they get the 'right' verdict.

★★★

'To no man will we sell, or deny, or delay, right or Justice.'
CLAUSE 40, THE *MAGNA CARTA*

★★★

The EU's corpus juris now controls our whole legal system. Under corpus juris the Government (and its agents) are above the law and cannot be prosecuted. In 2004, a total of 45,000 policemen were let off for speeding (even though they had been caught by speed cameras and had killed 44 innocent people). Under EU law, the police are exempt from prosecution. Under new legislation we can all be arrested and held in prison for breaking any one of the EU's 100,000 laws. How many of them do you know? How many of them do you break each day, without knowing? The EU laws on arrest now allow the police to arrest any one of us without charge and to hold us indefinitely, without the right to see a solicitor, make a telephone call or have a trial. Under the Serious Organised Crime And Police Act of 2005, we can be arrested and held in the cells by any police officer for anything. You can be locked up for dropping litter or putting your litter in the wrong sort of rubbish receptacle. In addition, the authorities now have the power to confiscate anything you might possess, including your home. And the authorities have the right to move you around. If a Minister says 'This is a national emergency' he can close down a town to block access to it. (I have experienced this at first hand when I was due to speak at a peaceful anti-vivisection rally in Oxford. When I got close to my destination I found that the roads were blocked. A police sergeant allowed other travellers to pass but stopped me because I was attending the rally.) The EU has more power over our lives than Hitler had over the Germans in the 1930s. Under EU law the shoot to kill policy adopted by the police did not require any democratic authorisation. When an innocent Brazilian was shot dead in Stockwell underground station he was being held down by two police officers at the time. He was shot with dum-dum bullets which are outlawed under the Geneva Convention. The police cannot be prosecuted for killing innocent people any more than they can be prosecuted for speeding. Since 1992, 30 people have been shot by the police. No policeman has been convicted of any crime even though some of these people were no threat to anyone.

★★★

As a British citizen and a citizen of the EU, you are obliged not only to be aware of, and to obey, all British laws and all EU laws (there are well over 100,000 of those in existence already) but also to be aware of and obey all laws in all other EU member countries.

Any EU citizen can now be extradited to any European country which is also a member of the EU. There is no right to trial by jury. The protection of habeas corpus (traditionally provided by English law) has gone.

One problem with this new EU law is that there are still many different laws in existing European countries. Activities which might be illegal in Greece or Romania might not be illegal in Britain. The extradition process was introduced to help integrate former European nations into the United States of Europe. But it was introduced before the various countries had managed to integrate their legal systems. All Englishmen and women are now subject to all English laws, all EU laws and all the laws which may exist in other EU nations.

If you accidentally break a law when you are on holiday in Spain, the Spanish can demand that you be extradited and taken for trial in Spain. If you are at home in England, doing something on the Internet and you break a law in Germany then you can be extradited to Germany for trial, sentence and punishment. (Anyone living in the EU who uses the Internet today should make sure that they are familiar with all the laws currently existing in their own country, with all the laws existing within the EU as a whole and all the laws existing in individual EU nations.)

The only people exempt from the extradition law are German citizens.

Englishmen and women can be extradited to Germany.

But German men and women cannot be extradited to England.

(Oh, and if you are British you should remember that you are also subject to American law. Britons can now be extradited to the USA for trial if they are deemed to have broken American laws. Naturally, this law operates one-way only.)

A European evidence warrant allows judges in EU countries to order the seizure of evidence abroad. It is believed that Austrian judges probably used the EU warrant in 2006 to require British police to confiscate and hand over private documents owned by David Irving, the British historian and author, when he stood trial for Holocaust denial in Vienna, even though Holocaust denial is not a crime in Britain.

The EU arrest warrant gives foreign courts and police the right to arrest any British subject on British soil. The British citizen has no rights. All the traditional rules, providing protection for the citizen, have been abandoned. There are no extradition procedures. For example, consider what happened to a 19-year-old British man who was arrested and accused of counterfeiting four euro notes while in the Canary Islands. He was arrested by the British police and handed over to Spanish police at Heathrow. He was taken to Madrid where he was denied bail. Since the Spanish judicial holidays were about to start he was held in a Spanish prison for two months. He was then told by his Spanish lawyer that if he continued to plead innocent he could spend another year in prison before facing trial but that if he pleaded guilty he would get a suspended sentence and a fine. Although he had not been found in possession of any counterfeit money he did what most people would do: he pleaded guilty and got a two year suspended sentence and a small fine. Guilty or innocent?

I have no idea.

But it doesn't sound much like justice.

Why did the British judge allow the Spanish police to take the Briton to Spain when he knew that the Spanish courts were about to start a two month holiday?

No one bothered to answer that.

The Government's official response?

'We have to have faith in our European partners.'

Thanks to the EU, if you do something which is a crime in another EU country while travelling or, more likely, while using the Internet, you are likely to find yourself extradited, imprisoned and tried in a foreign country for an offence you didn't even know was an offence.

★★★

'The power of the executive to cast a man into prison without formulating any charge known to the law, and particularly to deny him the judgement of his peers, is in the highest degree odious and the foundation of all totalitarian government whether Nazi or Communist.'
WINSTON CHURCHILL

★★★

The fundamental difference between English justice and French justice is that we were given our basic rights (in the *Magna Carta*) whereas the French took theirs (as a result of the French Revolution). The EU is now imposing the French legal traditions on England. The result is that we are acquiring a legal system which we don't understand and don't know how to use and don't feel comfortable with.

The bottom line is that the European Court of Justice, which follows the concept of corpus juris (an idea which is quite alien to English Common Law) has now successfully supplanted the traditional English legal system. The ECJ in Strasbourg is a higher court than anything in Britain. It exists, at least in part, to ensure the integration of separate EU countries into the new state of Europe. It can and does make new, irrevocable laws to govern the citizens of the individual countries which are now part of the new Europe.

The freedom of British citizens was built upon English Common Law (one of England's greatest gifts to the world). It was English Common Law, with the principles of trial by jury and habeas corpus, which guaranteed our liberty.

No more.

The European Commission, run by unelected bureaucrats, has pushed aside centuries of English law and replaced it with European law. The European Court of Justice exists not to guarantee the freedom and liberty of individual citizens but to protect the corrupt and dishonest bureaucrats who now rule our lives.

It is worth remembering that although the British Government has always obeyed the European Court of Justice, other governments are not so obedient. After British beef exports had been banned as a result of the Mad Cow crisis, the ECJ eventually ruled that imports could be allowed again. The French Government merrily ignored the ECJ ruling and continued to refuse to accept British beef. Naturally, the French were allowed to get away with this.

Thanks to the EU, we now have to obey their laws.

But they don't.

12

The EU Is Destroying Business (Particularly Small Businesses)

'Prosperity is not a gift from the government or anyone else. Free enterprise, not government, is the source from which our blessings flow.'
RONALD REAGAN

Like businesses throughout the EU region, English businesses are being buried under new legislation. Nine out of ten British companies sell nothing to other countries in the EU. And yet all British companies are subjected to damaging and restricting EU regulations.

Since the EU compliant Labour Party took over, there have been 66 tax rises in England. Even more significantly, however, has been the increase in the number of new regulations. Labour claims to be 'friendly' towards business. This is number 384,376,363 in an endless series of Labour lies. Every single day since Labour came to power they have introduced an average of 15 new regulations, and as a result it is clearly impossible for anyone running a small company to remain aware of what is, and is not, the law. And yet the penalties for ignoring these new rules are often serious.

The result is that small companies are doomed. I suspect that the EU doesn't like small businesses because they are difficult to control and are considered impractical and unsuitable for existence within a large, fascist superstate.

★★★

EU rules have already resulted in massive unemployment in Europe. In many other European countries (including the large ones – France and Germany) the official level of unemployment is now running at between 10% and 15%. In Britain, the figure has been kept lower than this but only because the Labour Party has proved more adept at massaging the figures than have other European governments. Only people who are receiving the 'jobseeker's' allowance are included in Britain's official figures. There are, in fact, another eight million people of working age who are not working and who are not looking for employment and who are (to use the official phrase) 'economically inactive'. The Government encourages this and provides financial incentives for the long-term unemployed to claim incapacity benefit rather than unemployment benefit. (Those who claim to be too stressed to work can receive a third more than those looking for work.)

★★★

The Labour Government has successfully kept unemployment figures low in five main ways.

First, although they pledged to cut welfare spending before they were first elected back in 1997, (Tony Blair made cutting the welfare burden a central part of his pre-election strategy telling voters: 'Judge me upon it – the buck stops with me') Labour has deliberately encouraged widespread fraud and has dramatically increased the number of people receiving incapacity or sickness benefit. Many of the 2.7 million allegedly 'on the sick' are suffering from common and often trivial health problems which don't necessarily stop more honest people from working. The vast majority of this 2.7 million claim that they have been too ill to work for over a year. Minor aches and pains (particularly backache) used to be favourite excuses but today the most common complaints for those claiming incapacity benefit are ill-defined, difficult-to-prove mental disorders such as 'stress', 'anxiety' and 'depression'. Payments which were originally designed to support those who had been injured in industrial accidents, or literally worn out by years of hard labour, are now handed out to those whose work experience is modest or non-existent. There are 500,000 under 35-year-olds claiming sick benefit. Those claiming sick pay receive a third more per week than those who are honestly trying to find work. Unemployment costs the nation around £4 billion a year. Alleged incapacity costs the nation in excess of £16 billion a year. Many who are claiming benefits have no idea what work entails and, after years of sitting at home watching television, need training in the art of getting up in the morning and doing what the boss wants without giving him a mouthful of abuse. EU regulations have encouraged a destructive and unhealthy way of life.

Officially, doctors believe that a quarter of sick note requests are dubious and a fifth are just plain bogus. Unofficially, they believe that the figures should be reversed – with no more than a fifth of claims being honest. Once someone starts receiving sick pay they have a one in five chance of returning to work within five years. Once they have been off work for a year the average duration of their sick pay will be eight years. (For many, the years of sick pay will segue neatly into years of pension.) Every year taxpayers hand over £2.4 billion in incapacity benefit to people who have nothing physically wrong with them but who claim that they are too 'stressed' to work. There are, according to the Government's own figures now over a million people in England who receive long-term incapacity benefit for stress and similar conditions. One claimant, receiving a total of £37,400 a year in State handouts, said that he had been too depressed to work for seven years after the death of his father. In 2004, a Bank of England study estimated that 500,000 men had deliberately left their jobs to claim incapacity benefit because it was so generous. Many admitted that if they worked and paid tax they would take home less money than if they simply claimed benefits.

Even Labour Ministers themselves have had to admit that many of those claiming incapacity benefit are fit enough to work. According to a Minister for Work, speaking in December 2004, a third of 2.7 million claimants could start work immediately and another third could return to work in 'the longer term'.

The Minister admitted that the Government had, for years, done 'almost nothing' to encourage people to come off incapacity benefit and confessed that only 3% of those living on incapacity benefit were actively trying to get employment. The Government won't do anything about this massive fraud (in which it is complicit) because if it did then the unemployment figures would rocket. And politically that just isn't acceptable.

In February 2008, an adviser hired by the Government, claimed that up to two thirds of the people claiming incapacity benefit are not really entitled to the State handout. David Freud, an investment banker hired by James Purnell, the Work and Pensions Secretary, said the disability tests used to award state aid were ludicrous and could be costing billions of pounds.

We have, it seems, created a system which encourages laziness and reliability on the State. The very basis of freedom is taking responsibility for oneself. But Britain's Government has encouraged people to hand over all responsibility for themselves to the State. That is, bluntly, a waste of a life. It certainly isn't 'living'.

The Government's second method of keeping the unemployment figures artificially low has been to increase the number of people on its own payroll. Since Labour took over the ruining of the country in 1997, Gordon Brown, (whom history will show was probably one of the worst chancellors the country has ever had) hired new Government employees at an average rate of well over 500 a day. The result is that in a period when English manufacturing industry lost a million jobs, the Government's payroll increased by almost exactly the same number. A million productive workers have been replaced by a million parasitical bureaucrats who have a negative effect on the nation's productivity. (As a measure of the destruction of the British manufacturing industry it is worth noting that the value of all the engineering companies quoted on the London stock exchange is less than a third of the value of just one German engineering business – Siemens. British industry has been destroyed by the EU because, unlike other governments in Europe, the British Government has, as I will show in my chapter in this book on gold-plating, insisted that its corporate citizens follow every new piece of legislation to the letter.)

And the Government pays its staff well with taxpayers' money. In 2005, the average hourly wage for Government employees was £11.32. That was £1.50 an hour more than the average wage in the private sector. And remember that Government employees work short hours, have excellent sick pay cover, suffer far less stress than employees in industry and can look forward to excellent index-linked pensions. It is hardly surprising that Government jobs are so popular. The British economy may seem to be doing well but it has been artificially sustained by Government spending sustained by Government borrowing. For Gordon Brown to describe himself as having been a prudent Chancellor is as honest as it would have been for Tony Blair to describe himself as having been a peace loving Prime Minister.

It is hardly surprising that the rate of unemployment has remained artificially low. One in five employed people in Britain now work for the Government. (In some parts of the country the figure is much higher than that.) The vast majority of the new jobs have been for bureaucrats doing worthless and entirely unnecessary jobs. (Indeed, most of the jobs are worse than useless in that they involve creating new paperwork and enforcing pointless new EU regulations which slow down the work of those who are trying to do real jobs). Government ministers repeatedly promise to cull civil service jobs but instead of cutting the number of public service employees, the Government has consistently increased the taxpayers' burden.

(The added advantage, to the Government, of all these Government employees is, of course, that they will vote Labour in order to keep their jobs. The Government is using taxpayers' money to ensure that it remains in power.)

The third way the Government artificially keeps the unemployment figures low is by providing a variety of schemes allegedly designed to 'train' and 'prepare' the unemployed for work. Everyone involved (employees and 'employees') knows that these schemes are fraudulent and that their sole purpose is to help the Government massage the official figures.

Fourth, the most cynical scheme of all is, perhaps, the policy of encouraging teenagers to carry on with full-time education for as long as possible. Since students now have to pay for their fees, this scheme doesn't cost the Government a great deal but it does keep vast numbers of young people off the unemployment register. The colleges and universities which have been set up to provide courses for this vast army of students have been encouraged to offer courses which are not intellectually demanding and which offer attractive-sounding subjects for study. It is cheaper to teach cake decorating and nail filing than it is to teach dentistry or plumbing. And cake decorating and nail filing are doubtless easier to learn too. So, as a result, a nation which is desperately short of dentists and plumbers, is now awash with hairdressers, brewers and nail technicians while countless thousands are graduating with utterly worthless or impractical diplomas in media studies, film-making and tourism.

Finally, the Government has one other way of 'reducing' the unemployment figures. It is called the 'head-in-the-sand' technique. There are more than one million people in England who are under the age of 25 and who are neither working nor studying. None of these people (and there are, remember, a million of them) counts towards the official unemployment figures because they are not actively seeking work.

★★★

'The difference between a welfare state and a totalitarian state is a matter of time.'
AYN RAND

★★★

As Britain adopts more EU regulations, so her attractiveness to employers falls. During the 1980s and 1990s, Britain was a popular and competitive destination for big companies who wanted a toe in Europe but who didn't want to be suffocated by the EU's red tape. No more.

EU laws mean that any employer who employs a woman of child-bearing age (or, indeed employs any man with a wife or partner of child-bearing age) must be stark raving bonkers.

Thanks to EU legislation, employers have to allow female members of staff to take up to twelve months off if they have a baby. And new fathers can have time off too. The new parents will, of course, receive money as a reward for their fecundity. Some of the money will come from their proud employer and some from long-suffering taxpayers, and it will be paid for the whole of their post-natal rest period. The employer has to keep the job open while the new parent is learning to change nappies and burp the baby.

Thanks to the EU, under European law it is now also compulsory for employers to allow employees with disabled relatives time off work whenever they feel it necessary. It is, indeed, compulsory for an employer to allow any employee as much time off as they need in order to care for any relative or friend who needs attention. In practice, this means that an employee who wants time off work to accompany a disabled relative or neighbour to the hospital or the dentist must be allowed to take time off. Employers who try to fight this will be in breach of the law (and will, of course, be branded uncaring and cruel by people who know nothing of the responsibilities and obligations endured by those struggling to run a business in the 21st century, while hemmed in by rules and regulations designed by people for whom work is an occasional, moderately entertaining interlude). Since the definition of a carer is now extremely wide, and many people who aren't really ill are officially designated as disabled, there are at least six million people in the UK who are officially classified as carers.

Oh, and if an employee becomes blind or deaf while they are employed, it is illegal to sack them. 'Quite right, too,' you might think. But should it really be the responsibility of an employer to continue to care for an employee who has lost a vital sense? Shouldn't the State take on that sort of responsibility? If you run a small business with, say, three employees and one of them becomes blind or deaf how do you cope? You should, according to the people who make the rules, adapt your business for the blind or deaf individual. Effectively, this means that running a small business is now a complete lottery. If an employee becomes unable to work (and in many businesses blindness or deafness would effectively mean 'unable to work') then the business will go bust.

There is now even a rule (and even I find this one difficult to believe) which says that if an employee wants to write a book they should be allowed to take the time off to do it. Great. Just what I needed. Eight million British civil servants all writing books. And there is, so I have been authoritatively advised, another law which says that if an employer who is planning to expand decides, after studying all the regulations and laws, 'Oh, to hell with it, I can't put up with this any more, I'm not bothering to hire anyone' then he is breaking the law by not hiring anyone having said that he was going to.

If, despite all this, you are brave enough to want a new member of staff, you must take great care. Mention that you are looking for a man or a woman, or a young person or an older person, and you will get into serious trouble. One employer got into trouble for inserting an advertisement announcing that he was looking for a 'hard worker'. This, he was told, was illegal because it discriminated against people who weren't hard workers.

It is the disruption all this causes, rather than simply the financial cost, which is so destructive to small businesses.

The EU bureaucrats and lawyers who think up this nonsense, work in an environment where money is no object and where employees can disappear for years at a time without anyone noticing. Neither politicians nor bureaucrats understand that it is not appropriate for businesses to be compelled to provide what is, in effect, charity, to people who take on work which they are either unwilling to do or incapable of completing. Business owners also have responsibilities to customers, other employees, shareholders and, indeed, themselves.

A small businessman who employed a husband and wife team to run his shop would be ruined by such legislation. How can a small employer possibly manage a business when his staff regularly fail to turn up for work because they're attending to private, personal matters?

No wonder that more and more small employers now prefer to hire older staff who are less likely to have relatives who need care.

I can't help wondering how long it will be before the EU insists that conception leave should be made available for couples who want to start a family.

Maybe I shouldn't give them ideas.

Actually, to be perfectly honest, I wouldn't be surprised if they hadn't already passed a law about it.

After all, EU policy now entitles employees to work at home and to choose when and how much they work. The bureaucrats who think up this largesse know damned well that their office can survive perfectly well if the entire staff takes a year off. But they have no experience of the real world and have no conception of the disruption this legislation can cause. Employees working for the EU and for government departments enjoy all these perks and more. Is it any surprise that three quarters of young people say that they want to be public employees. That is their ambition. Could this possibly be related to the fact that public employees enjoy flexitime, shorter hours, massive, guaranteed pensions and far greater job security?

★★★

The EU's Working Time Directive obliges employers to spend vast amounts of money monitoring their staff and keeping detailed records to make sure that no one works any more hours than the EU allows. The cost to industry, and to taxpayers, is phenomenal. The NHS, for example, spends over £250,000,000 a year satisfying the administrative needs of the Working Time Directive. No one knows just what the overall cost to the nation may be. (And, remember, we pay many billions of pounds a year for membership of the EU.)

★★★

Thanks to the EU, companies must ensure that at least 85% of their staff are able to cope with the demands of their jobs. Repetitive and boring jobs must be eliminated as far as possible. At least 85% of employees must have a say about the way they do their work – including some control over the pace at which they work and the timing of their breaks.

And employees must be consulted on all changes, must be offered reasons and must be provided with a timetable.

It isn't difficult to tell that these regulations were thought up by bureaucrats who have never ever run a proper business – or even worked for one – but who work in a protected and cocooned environment where money is never a problem and work, which is something fitted in between breaks, consists of thinking up new rules which make their own lives better and better, without regard for others or for the community which pays them.

★★★

Employers are expected to collect taxes of various kinds and to redistribute this money as credits. The average company payroll has become incredibly complicated; cluttered with credits and deductions.

Much of this new legislation is produced without any warning or consultation. It suddenly appears on the statute book and becomes law, sometimes with a few days' notice, sometimes overnight. It is not unknown for new legislation to be introduced retrospectively. Naturally, this means that it is now possible to break a law which doesn't exist at the time you break it but does exist at the time you broke it by the time someone totters round to arrest you.

As a publisher I have, several times, discovered the existence of new legislation completely by accident.

On one occasion when I heard of a piece of new legislation which affected publishers I telephoned a specialist lawyer for advice. He hadn't heard of the new legislation at all and was unable to help me. He rang me back later to confirm that the legislation existed. It had crept into being with virtually no one being aware of it.

Every businessman can tell his or her own horror story of working within the EU and struggling to cope with the incomprehensible demands of an increasingly bizarre bureaucracy seemingly determined to suffocate everyone under a blanket of Kafkaesque red tape.

The single market (which was the original purpose and promise of the EU) is further away than ever. What we have now is more legislation and more red tape, layer after layer of it added on top of national layers and making the whole thing incomprehensible even to lawyers. The red tape and the extra laws make life ever more complicated for individuals as well as for companies and businesses.

★★★

The new EU constitution gives workers extensive rights over employers.

For example, it gives members of the armed forces the right to be members of trade unions and to go on strike. The bureaucrats have not yet worked out what will happen if the crew of a battleship decide to go on strike during an engagement with another vessel. Nor, I suspect, have any of the pen pushers worked out what will happen to the old charge of mutiny.

New laws now mean that women who want flexible working no longer have to show that their employer could let them work part-time or flexi-time without detriment (as they had to under the old law) but only that the existing corporate policy has a disproportionate effect on women as primary child carers.

Bonkers?

You decide.

One employment tribunal has already decided that a woman in the Royal Navy suffered sex discrimination because her bosses refused to let her cut her working week down to three days after the birth of her second child. The woman brought the action because she said that she found it difficult to combine her family duties with the 120 mile round trip to the base where she was working.

(There might be those, probably not sitting on tribunals, who would consider that the navy could not be held responsible for her choosing to work 120 miles from her home. And there might be others, again probably not the sort of people destined for places on tribunals, who might wonder how the armed forces can possibly be expected both to operate a fighting unit and to provide part-time work for their employees.)

★★★

The EU bureaucrats may have meant their legislation to improve the security of employees. In practice the EU legislation has dramatically reduced the security of employees and has made millions virtually unemployable in private industry. Vast numbers of employers now prefer to take on part-time employees for the simple reason that by doing this they can avoid some of the EU legislation governing the way employees are treated. (Many employees like part-time work because it means they can also claim benefits.)

The EU has also made it enormously difficult for entrepreneurs to start businesses. And EU legislation has made it nigh on impossible to 'grow' a business once it has started.

'Running organisations that employ lots of people is increasingly difficult,' wrote a successful entrepreneur in the *Financial Times*. 'No wonder the Rich List is full of more property entrepreneurs than any other kind. Inanimate objects like buildings can't sue for unfair dismissal for discrimination over age, race, faith, gender, or sexual orientation – or demand flexible working or maternity rights...Legislators who have never met a payroll refuse to understand that when they gold-plate employment rights, they ultimately destroy jobs and prosperity.'

★★★

Today, as Labour brings more and more EU legislation into the country, foreign investment is falling dramatically. For example, foreign investment in England fell from £15.6 billion in 2002 to £8.1 billion in 2003. Professional advisers are now telling multinational companies not to come to England.

Labour's high tax policies haven't helped, of course, but it is the EU regulations which are scaring away multinationals and threatening England's future financial stability.

To regain our national strength we need to leave the EU and get rid of all the daft laws and regulations with which we have been saddled.

As fewer and fewer companies open factories and offices in Britain, and the ones which are here decide to leave, so the tax burden on the companies remaining will grow. And as hard-working citizens give up and emigrate, so taxes on individuals will have to soar.

★★★

The unelected, overpaid bureaucrats who run the EU (and, therefore, our lives) don't like people who are independent. People who are independent ask too many questions and have a tendency to be difficult. The bureaucrats don't like the self-employed either. People who work for themselves (rather than for a large business) are too difficult to control and to keep tabs on. Large corporations are usually keen to cooperate with the bureaucrats. They can (and do) negotiate profitable quid pro quos. People who are independent and self-employed threaten the system, are often annoyingly independent and invariably have little interest in cooperating with the bureaucrats.

It is hardly surprising, therefore, that the EU and the Government are doing their best to get rid of small businesses and the people who run them.

And they're doing well.

Three out of five new businesses now fail within their first three years. Most of the people whose businesses fail blame the same factor: increasing interference and red tape. Some of the interference and the red tape obviously comes from the EU. The rest may appear to come from the Government but most of it comes from the EU.

The Government and the EU are working hard to improve the level of failure. Their immediate aim is clearly to see four out of every five small businesses fail. Ultimately, their aim, if things go according to plan, must surely be to see five out of five new businesses fail.

★★★

We have come a long way from the days of the Luddites and the Tolpuddle Martyrs. Today it is entrepreneurs who need protecting from the bureaucrats, rather than workers who need protecting from exploitative employers.

Two thirds of the registered businesses in Britain have only one employee – the owner. As in all countries it is these small businesses which keep the economy moving and which create new ideas. Not one distinctively new electric home appliance has ever been created by one of the big corporations. The first washing machine, electric cooker, dryer, iron, electric lamp, refrigerator, radio, toaster, fan, razor, lawn mower, freezer, air conditioner, vacuum cleaner and dishwasher were all created by small inventors working alone or with a very small group of people.

It is a short-term tragedy and a long-term economic disaster that both the British Government and the European Union seem determined to destroy entrepreneurs by suffocating them with red tape.

No sane person who knew what they were getting into would start a business in Britain today. Two thirds of small businesses in Britain claim it has become more difficult to run their businesses in the years since 1997.

★★★

All this red tape is helping to ensure that our world is changing faster than most of us realise. Companies are being driven abroad because of the extra costs of the red tape showered upon them by New Labour and the EU. The result is that both service and manufacturing jobs will in the future be done in the Far East rather than in Britain.

Employees there are also cheaper, better and more reliable (there are 1.5 billion people in Asia keen and eager to work for $1 an hour) but it is the absence of red tape and crazy regulations which really make it so attractive for employers to take work there.

There are, for example, no daft rules such as those allowing new parents to take a year off work every time they choose to have another baby.

Of course, it isn't just the red tape which employers want to avoid. Big manufacturers are also transferring their factories to China and Indonesia because it is easier to find loyal, hard-working employees there. The trend to litigation has not yet surfaced in Asia. One manufacturer reported that he could get parts made in China for $100 (including the cost of employing two agents and paying for air freight) whereas in the UK the same parts cost $1,000 to make. 'And the parts made in China are better,' admitted the manufacturer. 'Their quality control is much better than ours.' Europe and America have to get used to the idea that the 21st century will belong to Asia.

For several years, Europe has (like the USA) faced brutal competition from car manufacturers in Japan and Korea.

But instead of attempting to deal with the problem by looking for ways to improve productivity and efficiency, the EU has destroyed Europe.

European firms are now uncompetitive because of the ruinous blizzard of regulations with which they have been showered by EU bureaucrats, themselves protected from the real world by their own secure contracts, their absurdly generous sickness schemes and their vastly over-generous pension programmes.

Bizarre working practices, over-protected workers, a 35 hour week, corporate pension schemes – all these things have helped to make Europe uncompetitive compared with Asia, and helped to destroy European businesses.

And things are going to get worse. Much, much worse.

The European clothing industry has been moving manufacturing to China just as quickly as bosses can close down factories in

Europe, and the EU has already been reduced to begging China to 'voluntarily' restrain its textile imports, claiming, rather pathetically, that if China doesn't stop exporting textile products to Europe there will be massive job losses in EU countries.

Not surprisingly, the Chinese Foreign Minister rejected this pathetic whinge as 'over-protectionist, irrational and unreasonable'. (If a bookseller complained to the boss of Tesco that the supermarket's ability to bulk buy gave them an unfair advantage, and they were selling books too cheaply and damaging the bookseller's business, do you think the Tesco man would apologise and put up his prices?)

The EU's request was particularly pointless for, even if the Chinese had agreed to accommodate the European plea, the manufacturing would have gone to Thailand or Vietnam.

The truth is that China, an emerging power with very low labour costs, is now doing to Europe and America what Japan did a generation ago and what America did to Europe a century ago. (The Chinese are also stealing product designs in exactly the same way that Japan did a generation ago and America did over a century ago. However, the Chinese are not following the American example and patenting natural plants so that they can charge indigenous peoples hefty fees to use the naturally occurring products which they have been using for centuries.)

European manufacturers are at a disadvantage because of high wages, low working hours and low productivity and the influence of unions on working practices.

Having been mollycoddled by the workplace protection provided by the EU, many Britons now seem to find it difficult to offer much in the way of service. Telephone receptionists are frequently churlish and often downright rude. So, hardly surprisingly, call centre work is going to India (where workers speak English and do not mind being kind and courteous to strangers). Administrative work is going abroad too. The big banks are already starting to move thousands of jobs to India, and eventually all will have to send work there in order to compete. Time after time employers have admitted that staff in India are paid less but they are better educated and provide a better service. The advantages are so great that no company can resist and survive.

It is only a matter of time before middle level management jobs are moved abroad too. This will lead to the de-industrialisation of Britain and the Western world. Countries such as Britain will be left with an ageing infrastructure built for the industrial revolution. Cities built for their water access (for example, Liverpool) will cease to have a purpose and millions of people who cannot adapt will never work again. The only real growth industry will be in the demand for hands-on service work (such as plumbing) which cannot be done from abroad. That is where the future lies. And yet the Government continues to push thousands of students into college to study subjects (such as computer studies and media studies) for which there will never be a great enough demand.

The other change forced upon Britain by home-grown and imported red tape is the fact that many companies now use short-term contracts for staff in order to avoid employment laws, and to make themselves more flexible. This is a wise move for companies but can be unnerving and unsettling for individuals who have to cope with uncertainty and insecurity.

Forty years ago I wrote a science fiction story describing a world in which people worked for just one day in their lives. In my story, work was something people looked forward to. Their day of work was their big moment. In Britain today, the idea no longer seems quite so absurd.

★★★

The EU has had a devastating and destructive effect on business. It has, single handed, been responsible for destroying most of what was left of British industry.

I have for many years argued that companies are amoral and have agenda and requirements of their own.

My argument, as explained earlier in this book, is that the directors and executives of big companies have no control over the companies for which they work because it is the company's needs which must always come first. The company needs to make quarterly profits to satisfy corporate analysts. The company needs to produce rising dividends in order to satisfy shareholders. The employees, however elevated and well-rewarded they may be, are there simply to ensure that the company's needs are met. The modern company is a bit like the man-eating plant in the spoof version of The Little Shop of Horrors. It is never satisfied, can never be satisfied, and is unconcerned with the well-being of the humans who work for it or tend to its needs.

In an utterly misguided attempt to deal with this problem, the rather simple-minded bureaucrats who run the European Union (and, therefore, our lives) have spent several decades attempting to control modern companies and turn them into socially responsible entities.

In this fruitless and destructive endeavour, they have been supported by eurocrats who have spotted the financial advantages of heaping many of the State's responsibilities onto corporate structures.

Because very few (if any) bureaucrats or politicians have any real commercial experience (or, indeed, any experience of what life is like in the real world) they have done some pretty staggering (and probably irreversible) damage to the competitiveness of European companies.

Today, in rather pathetic attempts to keep the EU happy, even modestly sized companies employ Corporate Social Responsibility (CSR) Officers, maintain CSR Departments, promote their CSR initiatives and spend fortunes on hiring CSR consultants.

Vast amounts of time, energy and money are wasted on pointless exercises in corporate political correctness.

In England, the Government forces companies to use their payrolls to perform at least 23 jobs which should be done by the Government. (When Labour came to power in 1997, the figure was 15). These delegated jobs include doling out maternity pay and tax credits and collecting fines and student loan repayments.

It is hardly surprising that the incidence of bankruptcy among small businesses (particularly those which are labour intensive) has reached record levels. The EU increasingly forces employees to take on responsibilities which have nothing to do with employment – responsibilities which belong either to the individual employee or to the State. No caring employer is going to refuse time off when an employee has a genuine emergency. But the problem is that the EU now forces employers to allow their staff to take time off to deal with ordinary routine, run of the mill day-to-day problems. It is now employers – particularly those struggling to run small businesses – who need rights. The pendulum has swung too far. The EU has actually created an impossible situation in which sensible employers who care about their responsibilities to their other staff and their customers have no choice but to do their best to avoid employing staff who have children, who could get pregnant or who care for disabled relatives. (To get round this the EU has made it illegal for employers to ask questions such as 'How old are you?' of future employees. It is indeed almost impossible for prospective employers to ask any questions. An employer has to accept what information he or she is given – and hope for the best. This is in a world where we are all constantly encouraged to be on the lookout for terrorists, money launderers and people who don't sort their rubbish properly.)

The small tragedy is that by forcing companies to take on inappropriate and pointless responsibilities the EU bureaucrats have simply provided the slaves of the corporation (from the directors and the executives downwards) with a neat cop-out.

If corporations pay lip service to the bureaucratic requirements of the EU then the EU will leave them alone.

The big tragedy is that by forcing corporations to take on responsibilities for which they are not designed or well-suited, the EU bureaucrats have done lasting and severe damage to the efficiency and effectiveness of European companies, and to the employment prospects of millions of European workers who must rely for their livelihoods on corporate employment.

It is largely thanks to the EU that many European companies are now closing local plants, sacking their workers and moving their production, or their services, to another continent. China and India are gobbling up the work.

And it is largely thanks to the EU, a series of incompetent governments and the witless greed of Labour in stealing £5 billion a year from British pension funds, that many large companies are now so burdened by their pension responsibilities that they can no longer function as companies operating in their area of expertise but are effectively no more than investment funds managing the company pension scheme.

The truth which EU bureaucrats have failed to spot (because of their ignorance of the way things move in the real world) is that corporations have no social responsibility other than making the maximum possible profits for their shareholders. That is why companies exist. It is all they exist for.

It was Adam Smith, the author of *The Wealth of Nations*, who first pointed out that: 'It is not from the benevolence of the butcher, the brewer, or the baker, that we expect our dinner but from their regard to their own interest.'

(I doubt if Smith was the first to realise this truth, but he was the first to express it so neatly, and so he is entitled to the credit for it.)

Self-interest is the reason why capitalism works.

Investors put their money into companies not out of a sense of public service but so that they will receive a return. Employees go to work not through altruism but so that they will be able to feed, clothe, house and entertain themselves and their families. Self-interest is the very basis of our society.

And what is true for bakers and shoemakers is equally true for companies making bread and companies making shoes.

The company which makes a profit will serve its shareholders and its employees well.

It is the role of Government to prevent corporate excess and corporate crime. It is the role of Government to introduce legislation which will effectively control companies and make sure that they earn their money without damaging individuals or society. And it is the role of Government to introduce penalties and sanctions which ensure that just laws are obeyed and, most important of all, that it is in the interests of the company that the laws are obeyed.

The politicians of Labour and the bureaucrats of Brussels simply don't understand this.

★★★

If you live within the EU, have a pension and don't work for the EU or a Government department, you are probably going to be much poorer in your old age, or have to work longer than you had expected, thanks to the EU.

In 2007, the EU brought in a new directive on the activities of institutions for occupational retirement pensions. Article 17 (para 2) specifies the assets direct benefit schemes must have in order to absorb discrepancies between anticipated and actual expenses and profits (bear with me because this is important stuff) and refers back to a previous life assurance directive which was due to be repealed by a new solvency directive (believe me I'm making this as simple as I can though I confess I'm not entirely sure I understand it either).

To cut a long story short (and I can hear the sighs of relief at the back of the class) what all this eurocrat blather means is that pension funds are probably going to have to reduce their equity exposure and increase the number of bonds they hold (EU and Government bonds will do nicely, thank you).

So what, you may well ask.

Well, the 'what' is that over long periods (and pension funds usually operate over long periods) equities invariably do much better than bonds.

So, if the EU forces pension funds to hold less of their assets in equities and more in bonds, the result will be that when pensioners want to take their pensions, there will be less money available.

Ah, but the EU has an answer to this little problem.

And its answer is that schemes will simply have to increase their assets.

By a lot.

Or pay less in pensions.

So, all of this means that, thanks to the EU, your pension probably just became either worth a lot less or likely to cost you a lot more.

Unless you work for the EU, of course.

If you work for the EU you will get a very fat pension which will be paid for by taxpayers and so you don't have any worries at all.

★★★

Most companies (and nearly all small ones) loathe the European Union. But a few multinational corporations (particularly American ones) are EU supporters and have a really loving relationship with the eurocrats.

Now, why on earth would that be?

The answer is simple.

Large companies are not as right wing as their critics often suggest. Large companies don't believe in free thinking, in free enterprise or, indeed, in free anything. But they do believe in dictatorship, a single world government and state socialism.

The thing is that at the two extremes of the political spectrum, political beliefs merge into one; there is no difference between the far left and the far right.

It was, you may remember, the same few powerful companies and organisations which financed both Hitler and Stalin. (How many remnants of those same greedy vultures now control the EU I wonder?)

Statism (an updated version of communism) and state control suits the needs and interests of big corporations much better than the 'small is beautiful' philosophy.

Left wing politicians (such as some members of the Labour party) have a great deal in common with those who represent multinational corporations. Try defining the philosophical difference between China and your average multinational and you'll see what I mean. (It is, perhaps, not quite so surprising that the representatives of large nations and large companies enjoy each other's company in organisations such as the Bilderbergers.)

It is the dislike of the 'small is beautiful' philosophy, and an affection for large, bureaucratic organisations which can be controlled more effectively, which has made the EU and the Labour Government conspire to banish almost everything small and independent from our lives.

Small hospitals, small medical centres with just two or three doctors working there, small post offices – all these are being banned as a result of instructions from the EU. The EU and the Government want only large hospitals and super surgeries with ten doctors and a team of full time administrators. These can be controlled far more efficiently, and can be fitted much more comfortably into the statist world of the all-conquering European Union.

★★★

The EU has established a European Corporate Governance Forum to coordinate the corporate governance regimes of member states and to create new regulations. And the EU has already got three new directives on company law planned and designed to stamp the EU's authority on corporate governance.

145

There will soon be yet more laws and yet more regulations controlling British companies. It will mean that legal, accounting and auditing costs will rocket, that bosses will have to spend more time dealing with paperwork and less time running their businesses, that companies which are on the edge will fail and that thousands of people will lose their jobs.

Experts are agreed that one thing a mass of new corporate governance regulations, guidelines, laws and rules will not do is prevent another corporate scandal. Fraudsters who want to lie and cheat and steal will simply ignore the new rules in the same way that they ignored the old ones.

(The EU, like most fascist dictatorships, hasn't really caught on to the fact that you can have as many laws as you like and terrorists, money launderers and fraudsters will ignore them all. Laws only restrict the activities of people who try not to break them. Laws do nothing to restrict the activities of people who ignore them.)

These new rules and regulations will, of course, affect and afflict companies in other EU countries.

But English companies will suffer more than other companies in Europe for two reasons.

First, the British Government gold-plates EU legislation (see my essay on this in this book). And, second, British companies are often listed on the American stock exchange. This means that they are also susceptible to onerous American regulations.

The EU is controlled by people who have never done a proper day's work. They have pushed the power pendulum too far towards the employed rather than the employer. Means testing, political correctness and multiculturalism are weapons which they are using to destroy small businesses and to promote the EU State and the multinational corporations who work within the EU State.

The supporters of the EU know that they must destroy small businesses because the people who run small businesses are true capitalists and the true epitome of freedom.

Destroying small businesses, and promoting and protecting large ones, are essential principles upon which the EU State is built.

13

The EU Has Produced Over 100,000 New Laws – And They're Still Coming!

'Once a country applies to join the EU, it becomes our slave.'
EU OFFICIAL IN BRUSSELS

'Freedom does not die in one blow, it dies by inches in public legislation.'
LORD STRATHCLYDE

Most British people have grave doubts about the value of EU membership but no leading politicians seem to take this anxiety seriously. All major British political parties support the EU. Anyone even suggesting that Britain might contemplate rejecting closer ties to the EU (let alone leaving the EU) is regarded as a maverick and something of a closet racist.

And yet, being a member of the EU costs Britain a great deal of money. We pay heavily for our membership. But what do we get in return?

Well, we get miles (or perhaps that should be kilometres) of red tape (which make our lives miserable and stifles British business), and we get thousands of new laws and regulations thought up by unelected bureaucrats in Brussels.

According to the Government's own figures, the extra red tape added since 1997 costs taxpayers £12 billion a year.

The EU has so far given us over 100,000 new laws. Some of them may be called 'directives' or 'regulations' but when you can go to prison if you don't do what the State tells you to do I think the word 'law' is more appropriate.

These new laws now govern our lives and many have superseded long-established British laws.

Supporters of the EU frequently claim that critics have exaggerated the absurd nature of many EU directives.

They say, for example, that there are no directives insisting that bananas must be straight and that carrots must be of a certain size.

But there are. The EU is just as daft as it is often portrayed and its defenders are, quite simply, telling pork pies which may well satisfy EU requirements but which don't satisfy mine or, indeed, those of any clear-thinking commentators.

So, for example, European Union Directive 2257/94 states that it is a 'criminal offence to sell bananas of abnormal curvature' and European Union Directive 1677/88 refers to the curvature of cucumbers.

In addition, there are directives ruling that peaches must not be less than 5.6 cm in diameter between July and October, that Class 1 Victoria plums must measure at least 3.5 cm across and that carrots that are less than 1.9 cm wide at the thick end are not allowed unless they are sold as a special variety of baby carrots.

There is no doubt that absurd EU directives, dreamt up by eurocrats with far too much time on their hands and far too little to do, result in vast quantities of perfectly edible food being thrown away. In a world where millions of people are starving to death, such bureaucratic nonsenses aren't remotely funny.

'Bureaucracy is the death of any achievement.'
ALBERT EINSTEIN

To ensure that we all toe the line, the European Commission has set up a series of European agencies. We now have a European Food Safety Authority and a European Railways Agency which have the authority to dictate to civil servants employed by British

Governments. We have not of course, laid off any British civil servants, so the British taxpayers are now in the position of paying civil servants in London to do what civil servants in Brussels tell them to do.

Anyone who is any doubt about the fact that the bureaucrats in Brussels are planning a European superstate need only look at the development of European 'agencies' to see that while they weren't looking the Government has already moved.

There are now a number of EU agencies covering many different aspects of our lives. There are EU agencies controlling food, aviation safety and human rights.

These pan-european agencies (which were described in a White Paper on EU Governance in 2001) were set up to help organise a supranational system of government throughout Europe. The aim, quite simply, was to give the European Commission and its bureaucrats control over national civil servants in areas of policy and law enforcement. (The basic rule within the EU is that power can only ever be transmitted towards the centre of the EU.)

In particular, the EU, having spent 50 years creating over 100,000 laws, wants to take control of law enforcement without having to put up with interference from democratically elected domestic politicians.

And so the EU has created a whole team of agencies designed to take power from national governments and their civil servants.

Local, national, civil servants (those working in London and Paris, for example) are now employed to ensure that the wishes of the EU's agencies are carried out.

The bill for creating and running all these agencies (which, naturally, runs into billions of pounds a year) will, until the EU has its own European tax collectors, be met by national taxpayers in each individual country. The agencies will be able to charge for their regulatory services. In other words, we in Britain are paying the EU to run agencies to charge a fee to tell the civil servants in London (whose salaries and costs we also pay) what to do.

Businesses whose work brings them into contact with these agencies will have Kafkaesque experiences. Small businesses in particular, which do not have their own specialist translators and EU rule book interpreters, will find themselves spending days ringing bureaucrats in foreign agencies as they attempt to find out what they have to do to stay in business and out of prison.

I was recently sent official documents in German which relate to my work as an author and publisher. Knowing that the British Government is always ready to spend its taxpayers' money on providing documents in whatever language is required I wrote and politely asked if I could have copies of the documents in English. I was told that I had to find a translator because the documents were only available in German. At least, I think that's what the reply said. It was in German.

★★★

Since they came to power in 1997, Labour has consistently promised to cut Government bureaucracy. Like all Labour promises this is, of course, just a lie.

Today, in Britain, the civil service, the health service, local councils, schools, colleagues and universities, quangos and so on employ eight million people. (By the time you read this the figure will doubtless be much higher.) These are, I stress, employed by the nation rather than working for it. There is a difference.

Since 1997, the Government has (despite promises to cut staff and costs) added more than a million people to public sector staff. And the hiring is increasing because it helps keep down unemployment figures and because most of those hired will vote for the Government which has given them a job.

Just as private companies have at last realised that management consultancy is something of a fraud, the British Government is following the EU's example by wasting an increasing amount of taxpayers' money on hiring management advisors.

Vast quantities of money are now being spent on creating EU-approved league tables and targets which are always met because the figures are spun (fiddled).

Management consultancy fees paid by the public sector almost doubled in 2003 and now top £1.3 billion a year. Most of the money comes from central government clients.

There have for years been far too many managers in English industry. Now there are far too many managers in public sector areas too. Too many chiefs and not enough Indians. Astonishingly, there are now less than three employees for every manager in Britain.

Britain desperately needs less people giving orders and more people doing things. This is particularly true of the public sector.

Local councils now spend £24 every time they buy a £10 book because of the bureaucracy involved. As a result of this, most libraries will be closed in 15 years.

I believe we can blame the tragedy and dilution of the quality of life in Britain squarely on the European Union. I have no doubt that most councils are managed badly but it is largely thanks to EU employment policies that libraries now spend 54% of their budgets on staff and just nine per cent on books.

The National Health Service, to give another example, is now awash with highly paid managers who probably don't know the difference between a triangular bandage and a bedpan. There are far more managers than nurses working for the NHS. Actually, there are more managers than beds.

Most of the people newly hired by Labour are paid to do what can best be described as non-jobs which contribute nothing to our society. Indeed, many have a powerful negative effect since they are employed to enact legislation produced by the EU. Local councils all over the country are now hiring 'five a day coordinators' to persuade people to eat more fruit and 'real nappy officers' to persuade mothers to use old-fashioned nappies (a laudable aim, perhaps, but why do local councils need to use ratepayers' money to hire people to encourage this?).

On one typical day, *The Guardian* (seemingly the Government's official job centre noticeboard) had 124 pages of advertisements for jobs paying up to £150,000 a year. As an example, one advertisement for a job in the public health sector, asked for someone to work as a 'smoking cessation adviser for adults and young people'. Applicants were assured that 'a lack of clinical knowledge will not be a disadvantage'. For this, applicants were offered up to £24,424 a year.

It is in the Government's interests to keep hiring staff.

But that isn't the primary reason why they do it.

The bottom line is that huge numbers of the people the

Government are hiring with our money are being hired to satisfy the requirements of the EU.

If we leave the EU, our expenditure on worthless additions to the nation's payroll will plummet and we will all be far, far richer in every conceivable way.

★★★

British politicians pretend to run the country but in reality they don't – and they haven't done so for a long time. The EU has, for years, been producing and enforcing thousands of new laws and regulations. Most people are unaware of this because the British Government, desperate to hide the fact that the power now lies in Brussels rather than London, usually takes the 'credit' for new legislation.

For example, although the British Government claimed that it was their idea, the new laws allowing transsexuals to change their birth certificates and to marry were adopted by Britain because the EU told the House of Commons that we had no option. Similarly, the new laws entitling homosexuals to marry came from Brussels.

The Data Protection Act came from the EU too. Its real name is European Community Directive 95/46. You probably innocently imagine that the Data Protection Act exists to protect your confidentiality and privacy. But think about it. The authorities who rule our lives have for years been working hard at removing your rights to confidentiality and privacy. So what is the Data Protection Act really for?

Well, here's a hint: the Data Protection Act protects public figures (such as politicians). They can, with the aid of this directive, prevent newspapers and others printing material about them by claiming that personal data has been used.

You didn't really think they cared about you, did you?

★★★

The Labour Government reversed the last Tory Government's opposition to the EU's Social Chapter. As a result, UK employment law is now largely shaped by bureaucrats in Brussels. The bureaucrats there concentrate on protecting jobs and the 'rights' of individual workers regardless of the consequences for the viability of companies.

Bureaucrats, never having had proper jobs, don't realise that there is a link between companies going bust and rising unemployment figures. In particular, they seem unaware of the threat companies are facing from India and China where companies are relatively unregulated.

Heavy-handed employment law tends to have the most harmful effect on small companies, rather than large ones. Bureaucrats seem to think this doesn't matter. They appear to be unaware that if you kill off small companies you dramatically reduce the number of small businesses available to grow into big ones.

Directives pour out of the European Commission where bureaucrats who have no experience of (and little understanding of) the demands of building and running a business in the real world churn out bizarre rulings about the shape of bananas and duck eggs which may sound silly but which have a very real impact on all our lives.

The EU seems incapable of keeping its fingers and feet out of ordinary aspects of our everyday life and whenever they see a problem (or even the spectre of a problem) their first thought is to introduce a new law.

For as long as locals can remember there have been ponies on beautiful Dartmoor and Exmoor in Devon. Soon the ponies will be gone. Why? Blame the European Union which demands that every pony in the country have an expensive health certificate from a vet.

Why on earth does the EU want wild ponies to have health checks?

The new law is being brought in because ponies are eaten on mainland Europe and must, therefore, be regulated, officially approved and stamped. It doesn't matter in the slightest to the Brussels bureaucrats that these ponies will never be eaten.

Who will benefit? Well, try the vets. They will charge £50 for each certificate.

In the long-term – no one will benefit; there will be no ponies on Dartmoor or Exmoor and most of us will be poorer. Another victory for the bureaucrats. Another loss for common sense.

★★★

When Dwight D Eisenhower was President of Columbia

University in New York, USA he received a deputation from the faculty asking him to stop students walking on the grass in the main quadrangle.

'Why do they walk on the grass?' Eisenhower asked.

'Because it is the quickest route from the main entrance to the central hall,' they told him.

'So build a path,' said Eisenhower, an American general and 34th American President, who realised that there are times when there are better solutions to problems than simply making more silly laws.

Bureaucrats in Brussels have not yet learned this.

And so the EU is now banning hairdressing salons from giving customers free cups of coffee. And they are stopping supermarkets from offering free buses to pick up shoppers.

This is being done to protect hairdressers who don't have coffee pots and supermarkets which don't have buses.

Have you noticed that an increasing number of shops now make their customers queue for service? Shops which always used to have enough till operators to cope with all but the severest rush now have ropes and barriers built so that a queue of customers can snake around the shop.

Blame the EU for this unpleasant development. Another example of how the EU is wrecking our lives.

Employment legislation means that employers now have to get by with minimum staffing levels. It is cheaper to make customers wait, rather than to provide enough staff. And don't expect the staff to be polite. The EU has made it almost impossible for anyone to be fired for anything less than killing the customers.

Next time you have a shopping experience that is less than joyful murmur a word or two of thanks in the direction of Brussels.

(Oh, and it is entirely because of regulations thought up by unelected bureaucrats in Brussels that so many shops, doctors' surgeries and other places now close at lunchtime (the very time when working people need to use them).

Another example of life getting worse for ordinary citizens because of the EU.

★★★

Some of the daftest (and cruellest) new European legislation concerns animals.

During the last foot and mouth epidemic in Britain, we were forced to move our pet sheep around in the dead of night in order to avoid the teams of Ministry vets and policemen touring the countryside intent on murdering perfectly healthy animals to appease bureaucrats sitting somewhere in Europe.

(Animal lovers will be delighted to hear that we succeeded in keeping the sheep alive (and healthy) and in staying one step ahead of the bureaucrats, though the exercise did become rather complicated at times.)

The rules that caused this mayhem came from Brussels, and the way the problem was handled was dictated by faceless, brainless bureaucrats from the EU.

Much of the legislation produced by the EU causes great merriment when announced – though it is, of course, nevertheless perfectly serious legislation and invariably carries horrendous penalties.

For example, pig owners who want to take their pig for a walk must now apply for a licence from the relevant Government Department. Every pig owner in the UK has been sent (or, should have been sent) a leaflet on 'New Pig Identification Rules' telling them how to comply with the new 'Pigs (Records, Identification and Movement) Order 2003'. Pig owners are told: 'If you take your pig for a walk, you must have a pig walking licence.' They are, in addition, warned that before each outing they must notify the Ministry so that an official vet can visit and inspect the proposed route. (If pig walking becomes a popular activity the Ministry will doubtless have to hire regiments of extra vets.)

This new legislation only applies to pigs. Sheep and cow owners who wish to take their animals for a walk can do so quite freely. As far as I am aware no bureaucrat or politician has yet attempted to provide any logical explanation for this new (and very serious) piece of legislation. One suggestion was that pigs could not be walked in such a way as to spread infection. But since pigs are not the only animals to spread or suffer from infection this explanation is not logical.

I promise you faithfully that I did not make this up. It is a real piece of EU legislation.

★★★

Before it was elected, in 1997, the Labour Party announced itself firmly against animal cruelty. Though this is now difficult to believe, it sold itself as the party for animal lovers. The oh-so-eager-to-be Prime Minister (who would have promised anything to get himself into Downing Street) announced, among other things, that he would call for a Royal Commission to investigate the scientific validity of vivisection.

Naturally, within weeks of being elected, the Labour Party had abandoned all this fluffy animal stuff. Scared of upsetting the international pharmaceutical industry, they announced that there would be no Royal Commission on animal experiments after all. That, it was clear, was simply a vote catching ploy. They couldn't possibly have a Royal Commission because they, the drug industry and everyone else, knew damned well that any independent enquiry would be bound to find that vivisection is not just worthless but that it actually endangers the lives of patients.

But, there was another problem the Labour Party might well not have been aware of until they took possession of the large offices and the chauffeur-driven limousines.

The EU is an enthusiastic supporter of experiments on animals.

Around 80,000 chemicals are currently in use by manufacturers. Chemicals are used in pesticides, solvents, packaging, cars, appliances, toys and foods (particularly meat). Only 10,000 of the 80,000 have ever been tested for human health effects. Of these, 52 are known to cause cancer in humans and 176 are suspected of being carcinogens.

We simply don't know about the rest. No one has ever checked. Occasionally, it becomes clear that such and such a chemical or food constituent causes cancer. There is then a panic and all foods containing that chemical are removed from the shelves.

So now the EU is testing all 80,000 chemicals on animals. (So too is the USA. The EU is doing one set of tests. America is doing another set of identical tests.)

This is a total, utter waste of time and money.

Countless millions of animals will die in vain.

Vivisection is a barbaric waste of time, easily proven to be of no value whatsoever to human beings.

Animal experiments are conducted only because they enable drug companies to launch new products on the market without proper clinical testing. The EU is testing 80,000 chemicals on animals because the chemical companies know they can't lose. If a test on an animal shows that a chemical causes cancer, the test will be ignored on the grounds that animals and people are different. If a test on an animal shows that a chemical doesn't cause cancer in that animal the test will be used as proof that the chemical is safe. The EU is doing these tests because the chemical companies want them to do them.

How can I prove this?

Simple.

This is exactly what the drug companies have been doing for decades.

The pointless tests on chemicals on animals are to be done as a result of the EU Chemical Directive. Every piece of scientific evidence shows that this is an entirely pointless gesture but there is nothing any EU citizen can do about it. Parliaments are not allowed a vote on EU directives. The EU simply ignores the critics (the taxpayers who will pay for the tests). I know of no scientist who thinks these tests are going to be of any value. (I recently gave evidence to a House of Lords Committee explaining why animal experiments are of no medical or scientific value and should be stopped.)

The British Government admits that the new testing requirements (which will do little or nothing for human safety) will cost consumers a massive £22,000,000,000 over the next decade.

★★★

A new law from Brussels forces home-owners to spend up to £1,000 preparing an information pack on their house if they want to put it up for sale.

These compulsory information packs mean more red tape,

more work, and more power for the bureaucrats, the regulators and the inspectors.

The packs won't help buyers or sellers but they will delay the whole process and make it even more complicated and stressful than it is at the moment.

Despite the forms, dishonest people will do what they've always done: they'll lie.

The new EU-approved and enforced home-owners' packs will have to be updated every month or so if they are to be of any use at all, and naturally every home will have to be repeatedly surveyed by a professional, qualified and certified surveyor. There aren't enough proper surveyors around so a new breed of bureaucrats is being trained to do the work.

The British Government claimed credit for this piece of lunacy but in truth it wasn't their idea. It came from Brussels.

★★★

In future both companies and company bosses could face criminal prosecution if someone they employ is involved in a road accident. The company can be subjected to an unlimited fine and the boss can be given both a fine and a jail term. To defend themselves companies and employers have to show that they have a proper risk assessment policy in place. They must also show that they had taken steps to ensure that their employee avoided having an accident.

Just how a company or employer can do this has not, of course, been explained.

★★★

'The ideal tyranny is that which is ignorantly self-administered by its victims. The most perfect slaves are, therefore, those which blissfully and unawaredly enslave themselves.'
DRESDEN JAMES

★★★

New laws are coming into force so quickly in 21st century Europe that it is impossible to keep up with them. In today's EU no one is innocent.

Here's another example of rank stupidity: the EU's Investment Services Directive is demanding that all stock brokers conduct suitability checks every time a private investor trades. The broker must make sure that the investor knows exactly what he is doing, can afford the risks and is aware of all the possible consequences.

This new compulsory check will take about 30 minutes. It will inevitably mean that buying and selling shares will cost a small fortune and will become unreasonably intrusive and unbearably cumbersome.

An investor with a million pound portfolio will have to go through the whole stupid 30 minute question and answer session every time he wants to buy or sell a share.

The people thinking these things up, clearly advocates of a nanny state to end all nanny states, simply do not live in the real world.

★★★

Thanks to the EU, employers are now legally required to consult employees about all decisions which may affect employment prospects.

This new EU law will have a devastating effect on businesses.

If the people running a company want to do something which might have an effect on employment prospects they have to ask the employees for their approval.

It is, of course, difficult to think of anything a company might do which would not affect employment prospects.

If employees complain that they have not been properly consulted the company can be fined up to £75,000 for each offence.

★★★

The EU seems surprisingly unaware of the way its suddenly introduced regulations can affect millions of people. For example, when the EU issued directives on the prices car manufacturers could charge they probably thought they were helping car owners.

What no one at the EU seems to have realised is that by introducing their new directives too quickly millions of individuals, and thousands of companies, suddenly found that the value of their existing car had dropped – literally overnight. Car owners couldn't afford the lower priced new car because their old car had dropped in value.

The EU has even interfered in the football transfer market, giving players dramatically increased bargaining power. Unless these changes are changed again many clubs will simply go bust as they struggle to cope with the absurdly high wages (now often around £100,000 a week) that the EU has authorised players to demand.

The EU has interfered in the aviation industry too. Here the result has been to help national airlines (which have historically been subsidised and protected from the real world) and to damage low cost airlines which provide travellers with cheap transport around Europe. By making it illegal for small airports to encourage small airlines the EU will push prices up, increase overcrowding at large international airports and make it nigh on impossible for people to get around Europe as easily as they had got used to doing. Many flights to small regional airports will stop altogether, thanks to the EU. Just how any of this improves European life is something only EU bureaucrats can explain. Naturally, since they are unelected and unaccountable they aren't talking.

It was the EU which brought in the laws which have made it an offence to put up Christmas cards which feature Nativity scenes. And a new EU law makes it possible for workers to object to Christmas decorations on the grounds that they are contrary to their religion and create an offensive environment.

This new law doesn't just apply to offices and factories – it could apply to your home too. If you have a cleaner or a home help he or she could object if you dared to put up a Christmas card he or she didn't like.

Guidelines, devised by the EU, are so vague that they are a troublemaker's charter.

Workers whose religion involves abstaining from alcohol, now have the right to complain (and, naturally, seek compensation) if a fellow worker comes back to work smelling of booze, or, within their sight, hands a bottle of whisky or wine to a colleague as a gift.

Muslims or Jews could object if someone sitting in the same office starts to eat a bacon sandwich or if the works canteen offers ham sandwiches for sale.

The EU has even made it possible to break the law by talking about a television programme or film you saw at home.

The same tranche of EU laws mean that employees have to be given time off for religious holidays, festivals and for prayers. (The legislation lists 81 specific religious festivals which are officially acknowledged by various religions.) Naturally, agnostic workers who aren't given the same time off could complain that they are being discriminated against. If an atheist is confronted by religious workers he could complain that he had been teased or provoked or simply upset. Employers who don't provide prayer rooms for different religions will be acting in a 'discriminatory' way and therefore breaking the law. The EU legislation designed to combat discrimination in our society is so complex, unworkable and confusing that it provides endless work for lawyers.

(Naturally, employers will suffer enormously and many more will move work to the Far East. The only people who will benefit from this new legislation will be companies in India and employment lawyers.)

I rather doubt if there is anyone in Britain who hasn't broken at least one EU law this week.

When we are all lawbreakers then the law has no value and no purpose.

★★★

Creating higher levels of unemployment will not be the only consequence of the new EU employment legislation which I've described above.

This new legislation has, allegedly, been introduced to encourage tolerance and reduce discrimination. I believe that these new regulations will breed intolerance rather than stop it. If, before this legislation had been introduced, a Muslim had seen a card which a Christian had put up he would have probably commented on it and asked about it. The Christian might have then explained why the card had been sent. Everyone would have felt closer and would have had a better understanding of one another's beliefs.

The new legislation will stop people getting to know more about one another's beliefs. It will create resentment and bitterness. Beliefs and feelings will be hidden away.

Incidentally, different legislation already allows Muslims and Jews to kill animals by slitting their throats; a form of execution which many Christians find deeply offensive. Complaints about these practices have been rejected as racist.

★★★

'People are deceived en masse but enlightened one at a time,'
RICHARD BODDIE

★★★

It is thanks to the European Commission that the traditional gold and silver hallmarking system which has guaranteed the quality of British jewellery for around 700 years has been banished.

In future, jewellers will be allowed to certify the quality of their own jewellery and stamp it with a European standard hallmark in order to harmonise standards across EU.

As long as every single jeweller in Europe is entirely honest this will be no problem.

But will this be just another version of the ubiquitous and much derided CE mark – a pointless gesture towards quality, which some believe offers nothing to protect consumers but simply tends a low bow towards EU authority?

★★★

No one seems to care much about patients these days. A four hour wait in casualty is officially considered acceptable. (Though I bet Gordon Brown wouldn't have to wait that long if Mrs Brown was feeling less than perky.) And whatever the fiddled Government figures might show, hospital waiting lists are getting longer and longer.

The service patients get from GPs has also fallen dramatically.

If you can still get a doctor to come and see you at home at night or at weekends then you are one of the lucky few. Make the most of it because finding a doctor out of hours (any doctor – not just a good one) will soon be as big a long shot as winning the lottery. It will even make finding an NHS dentist look easy.

When I last practised as a GP (in the early 1980s), night and weekend visits were a routine and essential part of general practice. I was a member of what now would be considered a fairly small practice, and our duty roster for out-of-hours calls meant that although our patients wouldn't necessarily see the doctor with whom they were registered they would at least see a local doctor, a doctor they knew, a doctor who knew how the local hospitals worked and who, if necessary, had access to the patient's medical history. Working nights and weekends and bank holidays wasn't fun but it was, it seemed to me, an essential and integral part of the job.

Today, most family doctors work office hours – which means that they are unavailable for 75% of the time. If you need your doctor outside office hours you will have to speak to an agency doctor who will probably be sitting in a call-centre some distance from your home, who will be on-call for a vast number of patients, who will know nothing about you, who will have no access to your medical notes and who will probably be reluctant to visit you at home.

Not by any stretch of the imagination can this be described as an improvement.

So, who is to blame for this dramatic reduction in the quality of medical care in Britain?

You've got one guess.

And if you guessed the EU you get full marks.

It was, of course, the EU which decided that working hours now have to be limited and that the hours a doctor is on-call have to be counted in with his working hours. EU regulations now limit the number of hours doctors can work and the British Government has given GPs the opportunity to opt out of emergency work.

Things aren't helped by the fact that thousands of GPs are retiring early – fed up of NHS red tape which makes their working lives miserable. And the problem has been exacerbated still further by the fact that the regulatory and taxation framework put in place by the EU and the Labour Government has encouraged many married women doctors to choose to work part-time. And that problem, in turn, has been made worse by the EU and the Government imposing a discriminatory quota system on universities, and forcing medical schools dramatically to increase the number of women being accepted for medical training (regardless of their suitability).

163

As I have shown on numerous occasions, whenever doctors go on strike the number of patient deaths falls noticeably.

And so, theoretically, a cut in the number of hours doctors are allowed to work should benefit patients.

With doctors sitting at home watching TV, patients should be safer.

But nurses are now being allowed to make decisions which used to be made by doctors. Nurses will deal with emergencies. Nurses will perform procedures formerly performed by doctors. And nurses will make decisions on drug therapy and on which patients live or die.

The result, I predict, will be a rapid rise in the incidence of iatrogenesis.

It is, of course, sensible that doctors' working hours should be limited. When I worked as a young hospital doctor I often worked over 100 hours a week. I once managed the maximum of 168 hours work in a single week. By the end of the work I was operating like a zombie.

But the EU should have given governments more time to reorganise the NHS and to employ the additional doctors who will be needed.

Patients will benefit if doctors are less tired.

But the way the EU has introduced these changes – and the way governments have responded to them – will result in even more patient deaths.

Once again the EU has screwed up.

This time their incompetence won't just cost us money.

Thousands of patients will die unnecessarily because of this cock-up: as nurses struggle to do work for which they have not been properly trained.

The only thing I can promise you is that if a Labour Minister (or his or her family) need medical care, teams of fully-qualified doctors will be on hand day and night.

The Minister's life won't depend upon the quality of a life-or-death decision being made by a harassed, partly trained nurse. On the other hand, your life might.

The EU has dramatically endangered hospital patients too. The EU has ruled that junior hospital doctors are, like other health workers, 'working' even if they are sleeping or resting while on call. (A doctor in Germany made a complaint to the EU when doctors were excluded from the rules. And so now all doctors are working when they are sleeping. In a way this is fair enough; firemen have been paid for sleeping for years.)

However, in bringing in the new rules very quickly, EU bureaucrats have shown once again that they have no understanding of the real world outside their red tape lined office block.

This particular new ruling means that all hospitals in Britain will be short of doctors. It is impossible suddenly to find ten thousand more doctors.

The British Government has solved this problem by announcing that in future hospital nurses will prescribe drugs, give anaesthetics and perform minor surgery.

Thanks to the unelected, unaccountable bureaucrats of the EU, hospital nurses will be taking life and death decisions for which they have not, of course, ever been properly trained. Nurses will have to take more decisions and will have to provide routine and emergency night cover for patients without medical cover. (As the number of available nurses falls, I wonder how long it will be before auxiliary staff are left in charge at night.)

Naturally, the ambulance service, which is already overstretched, will not be able to cope with the extra demands on it. Ambulance service chiefs have already decided that in future they will no longer respond to every 999 call.

★★★

The European Bank has given the British Government instructions that if Britain joins the euro, the NHS must either be closed down or broken up into a series of private hospitals and private clinics. In order to prepare for this, the Government is introducing 'foundation hospitals'. Foundation hospitals will add to the already absurd amount of inequality within the NHS. The inequality will not be between rich and poor but between people living in place A and place B. Before long I suspect that house prices will respond to hospital quality in the same way that house prices respond when there is a good school in the neighbourhood. Houses near to a good, well-equipped hospital will rocket in value.

Houses near to a second-rate hospital with Victorian facilities and hardly any staff will collapse in value.

Britain will have to change the NHS a great deal. It is because of the EU that the Government is already privatising both hospitals and general practitioner services. This is to ensure that our health care services fit more closely into those in the rest of Europe (where the mixture of private and Government provided care is more heavily tilted towards private care).

Thanks to EU legislation the chances of seeing your own GP when you really need him or her (during a medical emergency) are close to nil. Since both partners in this relationship are unhappy, the likely consequence will be the development of private GP practices. It isn't difficult to see how they could work. A GP (or perhaps two) could set up a small practice. They would charge patients, say, £500 for an annual subscription (no more than a gym membership in many areas). There might be an additional small charge for home visits and for prescriptions. The result would be that GPs would get much greater job satisfaction and patients would feel much safer. A GP working this way would be able to manage with no more than 500 to 1000 patients and would, therefore, be able to provide a much more personal service. Those who can't afford the new service will have to make do with a constantly deteriorating NHS service.

★★★

While English taxpayers die in their thousands because hospitals take too long to perform basic tests (such as simple X-rays and blood tests) and uncomplicated, life-saving surgery, the EU and the British Government conspire to waste yet more money on pointless meetings.

At an estimated cost of around £500,000, the Labour Government booked more than 100 rooms at a five star hotel so that EU officials and health ministers from other EU countries (and their accompanying officials) could spend a weekend together.

But what were they meeting about?

At that time, the EU had no influence whatsoever over health care in individual countries.

So, either the EU officials were meeting to discuss ways to

standardise health care throughout Europe. Or, they were just meeting (at the expense of English taxpayers) to have a jolly good time.

★★★

An absence of decent health care means a dramatic rise in the incidence of amateur health advisers. I have stood several times in chemists and health food stores and listened in horror as assistants (who obviously have no training or knowledge on medical matters) have gaily given out very specific but totally erroneous advice – usually designed to sell one of their shop's products.

★★★

Politicians in the UK pretend that they have power.

But they don't.

When the new look driving licence was introduced in the UK we were told that it was the Government's decision.

It wasn't.

Every detail (including the EU ring of stars logo) followed new rules which came from Brussels.

In the long-term, the EU is planning to abolish British driving licences. Britons who want to drive will have to take tests every ten years (naturally, there will be a large fee involved). Drivers with medical conditions (including diabetes and heart disease) will be forced to take medical examinations (probably another large fee). Anyone with a health problem will have to prove that they are fit to drive.

The nonsense we have to go through when trying to open a bank account is a result of an EU directive on money laundering

Changes to school examinations, announced by the Government as if they were a brilliant new idea, were designed to fit in with school diplomas elsewhere in the EU.

When the Government announced, with its usual great pomp, that it had ordered water companies to spend £8.5 billion cleaning up Britain's water, the truth was that the clean-up has been ordered by Brussels.

Britain is always eager to cooperate and obey all the new rules but other countries simply ignore the ones that don't suit them.

Most British politicians claims to admire the EU.

Why don't they tell us where all these new rules are coming from?

Why are they afraid to be honest?

Almost every important change in English law and culture for several decades has been a result of legislation demanded by unelected European bureaucrats. The EU now reaches, uninvited and unwanted, into every aspect of our lives.

For example, a trivial thing, but today, on my desk I have a note from the Driver and Vehicle Licensing Agency telling me that I am going to be given a new Vehicle Registration Certificate which 'has been developed to comply with a European Directive, which requires member states to introduce a common format for Registration Certificates'.

★★★

Owners of cars which were no longer good enough to drive used to be able to sell them to scrap dealers. They would usually receive a few pounds for the wreck.

Today, thanks to new EU rules which define the ways in which cars can be scrapped, owners have to pay £100 to have an old car taken away.

The result is that millions of old cars are now simply abandoned. The bill for removing all these unwanted vehicles will run into hundreds of millions and will be paid by local authorities (and, therefore, by honest local ratepayers and by taxpayers).

★★★

The EU intends to introduce a new law forcing motorists to leave their headlights on all day. Motorists who drive without their headlights on will be fined and may accumulate points which will lead to the loss of their driving licence. The European Commission claims that between 1,200 and 2,000 lives will be saved by forcing motorists to drive with headlights blazing when the light is good. As you will expect with the EU, there is no evidence to support this claim. Nor is there any reason to suspect that there might be any saving of lives. The figure might as well have been plucked out of a hat. Indeed, for all I know it may well have been. Opponents have pointed out that if motorists are forced to drive with their headlights on, motorcyclists will be endangered (because they, who already ride with their lights on, will be less conspicuous) and, because headlights are often badly adjusted, other drivers may well be dazzled (and have accidents). It has also been pointed out that the new EU legislation will increase fuel consumption by an average of 5 per cent, thereby increasing costs and fairly dramatically increasing the rate at which oil is used up. When the EU invited members of the public to respond to their proposal, a grand total of 117 people (out of a possible 495 million) heard about the invitation and responded. The respondents were overwhelmingly opposed to the change. So, here is another new EU law which no one wants (apart from the EU and, presumably, lobbyists from the headlight bulb industry) and which will almost certainly do far more harm than good. It is, in short, yet another example of democracy not in action. When the EU finally collapses and is disbanded, historians may well look back and note that it was the constant introduction of nonsensical legislation such as this which was the irritant which destroyed the project.

It was, of course, the EU which was responsible for the daft rules which result in perfectly good furniture being thrown away if it doesn't have an EU acceptable fire certificate. Theoretically, the legislation exists to save lives. In practice, the legislation simply results in a vast amount of wastage and hugely increased profits for the furniture-making industry. There are some who wonder why old furniture, which currently has to be dumped in landfill sites, cannot be made safe by spraying it with a fire retardant.

Thanks to the EU, Britain's drinking laws have been revised to fit in with drinking laws throughout Europe.

The changes are producing huge problems and there is much opposition to the introduction of 24 hour drinking, but the changes will continue so that there is continuity among EU regions. The result is that, thanks to the EU, street crime and drunkenness are rising dramatically and in many parts of Britain law-abiding citizens are now afraid to go out of their homes after dark.

The problems are developing because Britain's drinking hours have been restricted for years. Because of the restrictions, many drinkers have got into the habit of binge drinking – trying to drink as much alcohol as they can before the pub or club closes. Newspapers and magazines have made heroes and heroines out of heavy drinkers.

In France, where cafes have been able to serve alcohol around the clock for many years, there is no culture of binge drinking.

Attempting to impose French regulations on English drinking are proving (literally) fatal.

Given the opportunity to drink alcohol for 24 hours a day, English drinkers simply binge all day and night. The publicans (or, rather, the companies which employ them) make lots of money.

This is yet another example of the EU failing to understand the importance of national differences, and the impracticality and danger of imposing standard regulations on non-standard cultures.

★★★

We used to put our rubbish in large holes (old mines and quarries) or use it to reclaim land from the sea. But the EU has banned this sensible use of waste and now pretends to want us to recycle in order to protect the environment. In reality, what happens is that millions of tons of our rubbish collected for recycling are exported (at enormous expense and a great expenditure of energy) to China and other Asian countries where they are buried in order to fill in large holes or to reclaim land.

To add insult to considerable injury, the EU is also planning to fine Britain £200 million a year (or more) for being in breach of EU rules on the amount of our rubbish 'they' allow us to send to our landfill sites. The EU's regulations and directives have created utter chaos. First there were plans to introduce a 'pay-as-you-throw' tax on rubbish. Then, it was pointed out that if you put a tax on each bag of rubbish that is left out for collection, the least scrupulous householders will be in and out of their homes all night long moving bags from outside their homes and putting them outside their neighbours'. The loser in this game of musical rubbish bags will, of course, be the weak and elderly residents who are too frail to play the game with the necessary degree of enthusiasm. In an attempt to obey the EU, and to cut down the amount of rubbish they dispose of, councils are collecting rubbish once a fortnight and limiting householders to the amount they can cram into a small plastic container. Collecting rubbish once a fortnight is, of course, a serious health hazard. Rubbish stinks and attracts rats. To sell us this nonsense we are told that we must reduce the amount of rubbish we produce by recycling far more. (No one explains precisely how we reduce the amount of rubbish we produce when everything we buy is double or triple wrapped and councils and the Government continue to bombard us with unsolicited leaflets and other printed debris). But the recycling story is a confidence trick. As long as the rubbish is officially classified as having been recycled no one cares what happens to it. All that matters is that the bureaucrats in Brussels are happy that we are doing what we've been told to do.

The whole sorry saga began in 1987 when a European treaty allowed the EU to control the way we dispose of our waste. Denmark and Holland were both running out of space to bury their rubbish and so, to cater for their specific needs, the European Commission began a new rubbish policy for the whole of the EU. As always, the policy was a mixture of compromise and misunderstanding and it has created chaos, confusion, bewilderment and anger. It has turned binmen from friendly street collectors into some of the most hated figures in our communities. The Landfill Directive of 1999 was the result of the EU's deliberations. A group of faceless, nameless bureaucrats decided that since Holland and Denmark didn't have enough space in which to bury their rubbish we should all phase out burying rubbish in holes in the ground (regardless of whether or not we had enough suitable holes) and instead start incinerating rubbish or recycling it. The one country in the EU that was doomed by the new directive was Britain because we have always used more of our rubbish for landfill than any other country. We had used our rubbish well and we had done more sensible recycling than virtually any other country in Europe. Now, thanks to the EU our rubbish policy is in utter chaos. Every aspect of our rubbish has been affected.

It sometimes seems that the EU can never leave anything alone if it works. They have not, it seems, ever heard of the phrase 'if it isn't broke don't fix it'. Our method of dealing with old car batteries worked exceptionally well. The proportion of old batteries recycled was 97%. But under the EU's new scheme the number recycled has dropped to under 80%. The EU has actually reduced the amount of recycling that is done. And the EU's policies on the disposal of fridges, old cars and old paint tins has produced an explosion of fly-tipping which has turned our roadside verges into a series of rubbish dumps and has created a whole new black market industry designed to evade the rules. Just this morning I was awoken at 7.00 a.m. by a good deal of noise in the street outside our home. When I looked out of the window I saw that a removal van full of old and clearly unwanted furniture had been backed up to the back of a council refuse lorry. The council's refuse collectors had collected our black bags from the pavement and were busily feeding a vast pile of old mattresses, chairs and tables into the machinery which chews up rubbish.

Finally, to make matters even worse, the British Government has been putting more and more taxes on landfill. Councils and businesses simply cannot cope. So, what's the bottom line? We are paying more money to the EU, we are recycling less rubbish, our towns and cities stink and are unhealthy, our countryside is littered with abandoned television sets, computers, paint tins, fridges, old cars, batteries and heaven knows what other rubbish (EU-approved but dangerous light bulbs will soon be added to the list), our privacy is being threatened by spy-in-the-bin cameras, identity thieves are having a field day (because of the rubbish bags left abandoned on our streets) and our relationships with our binmen have been destroyed.

Thanks to EU directives on the disposal of rubbish, householders in Britain are now paying more and more for a constantly deteriorating service. When a householder telephoned his local council to point out that rubbish left uncollected for two weeks was smelling badly and attracting rats he was told that he should double wrap every item of rubbish in plastic and then place the doubled wrapped items in a double layer of black plastic sack. It did not seem to occur to the council official that this would dramatically increase the amount of waste. Nor did it seem to occur to him that double wrapping waste food will not deter rats – who can gnaw through steel and tarmacadam. There are currently said to be 80,000,000 rats in Britain. The number is increasing daily and the rats are getting larger. Rats spread a number of dangerous diseases including Weil's disease, foot and mouth disease, toxoplasmosis, salmonella, e.coli, cryptosporidium and tuberculosis.

Despite the EU regulations, millions of householders in France and Spain still have their rubbish collected daily. That is, 'daily' as in every day of the week including Sundays and bank holidays.

★★★

The Labour Government blames the shortage of affordable housing on housebuilders who should, say the Labour politicians, have built more houses and should have kept the prices down.

Not surprisingly, the housebuilders don't agree with this criticism.

And they have good reasons for their point of view.

There have, they point out, been lengthy delays in obtaining planning permissions. Many perfectly reasonable applications have been refused, and red tape means that it can take the best part of a year to get a planning inspector to make a site visit. There is also a serious shortage of craftsmen. Misguided policies mean that the nation is awash with hairdressers, nail varnishers and would-be television presenters but desperately short of bricklayers, carpenters, plasterers, electricians and plumbers.

But it is the new laws (most of which were thought-up in Brussels) which are really at the root of the problem.

The EU and Labour have introduced an interminable host of new restrictions and building regulations (most of which have done nothing to make houses safer or better). All these new regulations have added enormously to the cost of building new houses and, therefore, to the cost of housing.

One building company, Taylor Woodrow, has reported that in 2004 it cost 60% more to build a house than it cost in 1997. And, they say, nearly half of that increase comes from new regulations.

Another housebuilder claims that two fifths of the cost increase in house building since 1997 has come from additional building regulations and restrictions (many of them from the EU), very little of which adds to the value of homes or people's enjoyment of them. It is hardly surprising that whereas 425,000 houses were built in the UK in 1970, anywhere near half that number seems to be about the limit of our ambitions these days. We have more people and we're building fewer houses.

If there is anyone to blame for the shortage of affordable housing there are only two possible culprits: the EU and the Labour Government.

Since the Labour Government has, on the whole, done nothing more than introduce regulations sent over from Brussels, it is the EU which is largely responsible for the current housing problem the nation faces.

Naturally, Labour Ministers refuse to acknowledge this pretty obvious cause-blame link. They do not dare to criticise the glorious new federal State of Europe – the fountain of such wealth for its bureaucrats and politicians. Instead of cutting back on some of the more absurd regulations from Brussels, Labour is insisting that developers provide a number of affordable homes every time they apply for planning permission for a new housing estate. Naturally, this simply bumps up the cost of the rest of the development. It is a typically Statist solution.

★★★

Under EU rules, farmers in Britain are forbidden to produce as much milk as English citizens consume.

However, under more EU rules farmers in France, Germany and Ireland can all produce more milk than their citizens use.

The result of this is that English supermarkets are able to buy cheap milk from farmers in France, Germany and Ireland. The supermarkets are, of course, also able to offer English farmers a knock down price for their milk.

EU legislation has forced the consolidation of farming and has produced huge farming conglomerates. Four fifths of Britain's potato crop now comes from 250 growers, down from 5,000 growers in 2001, in part because the requirements for what constitutes an 'acceptable' potato keep tightening. The same is true for all vegetables. Tomatoes must be between 53 and 63 millimetres in diameter. Tomatoes which aren't the right size are thrown away. Is it any wonder our food prices are rocketing?

In Britain, largely thanks to the EU, a thousand farmers and farmworkers a week now leave the land and either look for other work or join the growing millions on benefits. Those remaining have been advised to join in 'Soviet-style collectives' of up to 20,000 acres in order to produce acceptably shaped and sized crops at prices acceptable to the supermarkets.

France, where the Common Agricultural Policy has long made the EU popular among farmers, has lost half its farmers in the last two decades. The same thing has happened throughout Europe. As Poland is absorbed into the EU, experts believe that 70% of Polish farms will disappear.

What the eurocrats don't realise, of course, is that smaller farms actually produce more food than big ones.

The EU's policies may result in tomatoes, apples and potatoes all being the 'right' size but big farms are nowhere near as productive as small ones.

Farmers who work on ten or twenty acres get to know their land. They learn to intercrop plants which have different requirements, they walk across their fields noticing what is happening, they take care of their land and make sure that crops are rotated properly so as to produce the best crops. They use their land and their water much more efficiently than do the big farms with their massive tractors and their hired technicians. As the oil disappears, and fertilisers become too expensive to use, those few small farmers who have the skills to know how to use animal manure to revitalise their land will become increasingly important. But, thanks to the EU, there will be very few of them. The EU's policies are ensuring that our bleak future, threatened by the coming Oil Apocalypse, will be much bleaker than it might have been.

★★★

The quality of education is falling dramatically throughout Europe as individual member countries of the EU struggle to cope with new regulations and the philosophy of political correctness espoused by the EU.

In France, when 15-year-olds were given a dictation test that had been passed by most pupils in 1988, they performed abysmally. More than half scored zero and 80% failed the test. After ten years of schooling more than half the pupils who leave school in France are still semi-literate and incapable of writing a letter or e-mail.

The same is true throughout the rest of the EU where cultural and intellectual values have been devastated in recent years.

In 2005, the head of Ofsted, the UK's schools watchdog, warned that the behavioural and verbal skills of children starting school were at an all time low and that some five-year-old children couldn't even speak properly. Standards of literacy have tumbled as school teachers have abandoned old-fashioned teaching methods which worked (but which were regarded as too tedious for teachers) in favour of new, politically correct systems which are useless.

Astonishingly, it isn't just in academic areas that school children have been proved to be developing poorly.

English school teachers have admitted that they often have to teach children how to use a knife and fork in the school canteen and a survey by a restaurant chain showed that one in five children under the age of 11 usually eat all their food with their fingers.

The EU Energy Commissioner has called for a 55 mph speed limit throughout Europe. The Commissioner seems to think that this will cut fuel consumption and save oil. Sadly, I fear he is mistaken. My car is fitted with a gauge which tells me how much fuel it is consuming and the gauge shows, quite clearly and consistently, that my car is more efficient at a higher speed and that, consequently, consumption is higher at 55 mph than it is at 70 mph. A 55 mph limit would, like so many other EU regulations, slow everyone down, waste time, damage the economy and cause boredom and accidents. It would also result in more fuel being used. The one reliable thing about the EU, and its many well-paid representatives, is that it and they invariably manage to display a staggering level of stupidity and incompetence. Any business organisation which was as badly led and as grossly incompetent as the EU would have gone bankrupt years ago. (And its directors would by now be in prison.)

The EU seems determined to legislate on everything, manufactured or natural, inanimate or alive. Very few aspects of our lives remain untouched by the heavy hands of the EU's interfering eurocrats. Under EU regulations it is now illegal for you to repair your own plumbing, electrics or motorcar. If you buy a boat which is over six feet long, built after the EU Recreational Craft Directive of 1999, and you don't pay the EU £4,000 to measure the boat you can (and probably will) be sent to prison for six months. The EU has decided that British pubs must throw out all pint glasses which are marked with the crown symbol and replace them with glasses which are marked with the European Union mark. Even barometers have been targeted. The EU wants to ban them because they contain a small amount of mercury. Barometers have been around for 350 years (at least) and to the best of my knowledge no one has ever been injured by one (certainly not by the mercury locked inside one). The EU wants all barometers to be broken up and destroyed. The eurocrats don't seem to have realised that by doing this they will release all the mercury into the environment. But then, this is the same EU which is insisting that in future we must all use light bulbs containing toxic mercury vapour.

★★★

The EU wants to force Britons to make wills which are EU friendly. The EU has prepared common principles for will makers and wants a 'European certificate of inheritance' to be introduced. The EU's plans will, naturally, mean that the British inheritance rules will have to be abandoned. The new EU rules will, almost certainly, mean that French rules must be accepted and Britons will be forced to spread their estate among close relatives – whether they like the idea or not. It is because of French inheritance law that French farmland has, over the years, been broken up into thousands of tiny pieces. The expensive and absurd Common Agricultural Policy was devised to suit the needs of all those farmers with tiny pieces of land. In practice, the Common Agricultural Policy has dramatically increased the price of food, has made life much more difficult for British farmers and has resulted in impoverishment and starvation in the Third World.

★★★

The EU wants to force all service providers to store customers' Internet and phone data for up to three years. The information stored will include not just what was said, but where you were when you said it, lists of all the websites you visited, details of all your text messages and e-mails and details of everyone with whom you communicated.

The very fact that bureaucrats should even ask for this type of information to be kept is an outrage. But our politicians are, as usual, rolling over.

Britain's Home Office (which supports this ultimate Big Brother intrusion) claims that: 'We are aware that organised crime and terrorist activity takes place across international boundaries and for that reason the Government is keen to see the harmonisation of data protection laws that prevent criminals finding a safe harbour within the EU.'

Only the fascist American Government (which is, incidentally, now planning to give itself access to hundreds of millions of international bank accounts around the world) could dream of anything this intrusive.

Intelligence experts agree that what they need is good information based on specific threats rather than mass surveillance which will merely produce far more data than anyone can ever usefully analyse.

But neither the EU nor the Labour Government really believes that collecting this sort of information will stop terrorists.

They want to snoop on honest citizens so that they can make sure we are obeying all their laws, paying all the fines and paying all the taxes they want from us.

Moreover, they will make a profit by selling the information to commercial companies wanting to build up even more complete pictures of the consumers they are targeting.

The end result, of course, will be less not more security – both for nations as well as individuals.

It goes without saying that other Government departments and agencies will enthusiastically help themselves to this information.

The proposed legislation is almost certain to go through because individual countries in the EU already have such legislation on their statute books and can argue that all they are doing now is 'harmonising'.

Companies already store much of the information which the EU now wants. They store it for billing purposes and to comply with data protection laws (which, of course, have nothing to do with protecting the public or protecting the data).

The costs of storing all this data will be the responsibility of individual companies (who will, presumably, be able to share in the profits from selling the information on to outside agencies.) Naturally, in the end the costs will be met by customers and shareholders.

We will be paying for the EU to spy on us.

★★★

Many of the new taxes introduced by the Labour Party are, in fact, taxes invented by the EU. Our politicians are merely doing what they have been told to do, and implementing EU law.

The EU has an unquenchable appetite for money (largely because it is now an irredeemably corrupt organisation) and it has, therefore, devised a great many new tax raising regulations. If we remain in the EU we will find ourselves paying many more new 'stealth' taxes.

One suggestion from the EU, is that there should be a tax on computer ownership and use.

★★★

EU legislation is invariably designed to reduce any conceivable risk. Once the eurocrats spot a potential hazard they introduce legislation designed to avoid risk, responsibility and blame. It is this culture which has produced an imperfect storm of legislation and has destroyed our everyday life in so many crucial ways. Much of the daft over-protective legislation which has been enacted in the last decade has emanated from Brussels, not London.

So, for example, new EU legislation will force musicians to limit the number of pieces of loud music they perform on a single night. Orchestras and choirs may, however, be allowed to choose to wear earplugs. The new rule is part of the Control of Noise at Work Regulations. Evening concerts will, in future, have to be balanced with quieter pieces of music being sandwiched between louder works. A Government spokesman has suggested that if musicians lower the volume during rehearsals they may be able to play at full volume during performances.

It is thanks to the EU that every aspect of British life is being ruined by petty bureaucrats finding new and dafter ways to implement health and safety legislation.

It is the EU we must thank for the fact that morons with chainsaws are cutting down horse chestnut trees so that children don't hurt their fingers playing conkers, and idiots from councils everywhere are covering dance floors with carpet so that dancers don't slip over while doing the foxtrot.

The EU makes daft rules like these because the EU is a fascist organisation and is, therefore, determined to control every aspect of our lives by making minute decisions about what is, and is not, good for us. When making these decisions for ourselves we simply have to decide whether the pleasure we get from the activity (playing conkers or ballroom dancing) is worth the risk. We weigh up the pros and cons and we make a decision accordingly. Most of us choose to take a number of risks in our daily lives because everything we do involves a risk and if we don't accept some risk then we won't ever do anything. But the fascist State (in this case the EU) looks at things rather differently. As far as the EU is concerned there is no advantage whatsoever to the State in us playing conkers or dancing the foxtrot. Activities such as these are not productive. And so the EU outlaws these activities (and thousands of others like them) because they add nothing to the State but may affect our productivity and, therefore, inconvenience the State.

It may sound silly to say that the people who stop children playing conkers are fascists but, in fact, that is exactly what they are. You don't have to wear shiny jackboots to be a fascist. All you have to do is constantly to put the needs of the State above the wishes of the individual.

★★★

The letters CE which now appear on just about everything you buy stand for Conformité Européenne and not Church of England. The mark indicates that the manufacturer has satisfied EU requirements for the product concerned. You will note that this book does not contain a CE mark. It contains too high a percentage of truth and far too low a bullshit content to satisfy EU requirements. As you might expect, the EU publishes a vast quantity of information about when the CE mark can, and cannot, appear, what it should look like and where it should be placed. Manufacturers who fail to adhere to the EU legislation must remove their product from the market. They may also be fined and sent to prison though the EU warns that in some circumstances penalties may be greater than 'a fine or imprisonment'. (Clearly, the EU must have quietly introduced some variety of corporal or capital punishment.)

★★★

The EU has given broadcasters permission to advertise their goods in films and television shows. Product placement has been popular in the USA for some time but the EU has now given the go ahead for 'selling by stealth' to be introduced by European broadcasters.

★★★

Thanks to the EU, Britain could well be in the dark soon.

Around a quarter of Britain's electricity comes from nuclear power stations – all but one of which are due to shut in the next two decades. They are old and need replacing. It takes at least a decade to set up a replacement nuclear power station.

So, it is clear that if nothing is done very quickly the lights will start going out in Britain within a few years.

The only sensible solution is to 'go nuclear'. Leading environmentalists and greens such as James Lovelock (the inventor of the Gaia hypothesis) reckon that we will never be able to obtain enough electricity from wind, wave and solar power and must start building more nuclear power stations.

But the Labour Government and the EU are worried about nuclear power. They think terrorists might hijack a power station and drive it to Brussels.

So we've still done nothing about our impending shortage of electricity.

And, thanks to the EU, there is another little problem which seems guaranteed to turn our coming emergency into a real crisis.

The EU has told Britain that two thirds of our coal-fired supply plants must shut down by 2011.

Since Britain gets 36% of her electricity from coal-fired supply plants, this crisis is now already active.

You will be relieved to hear that France does not face this problem since the French get 80% of their energy from nuclear power, and so the EU ruling does not affect them.

★★★

The EU and the USA Treasury have told European banks that they must pass details of international transfers to American justice authorities. So, if you are British and you have a holiday home in France and you send some money to a French bank so that you can pay your bills, the CIA and the FBI will be informed that you are moving money between countries and that you should be considered a possible terrorist or money launderer. Thanks to the EU, banking confidentiality is now just a memory.

★★★

The EU now allows the USA to retain information about passengers for up to 15 years and places no limits on what the Americans can do with the data. The European Union's top data protection official has warned that this will put at risk the privacy rights of air passengers. The deal made by the EU allows the Department of Homeland Security in the USA, as well as American Customs, to have access to private data about European citizens. The deal allows for names and addresses, phone numbers, credit card details, past flight details and dietary requirements to be handed over and retained (or mislaid) by the Americans.

★★★

The single market was launched in 1993 to establish the free movement of just about everything within the member states of the EU. The idea was companies can sell their products anywhere within the EU, and that individual professional qualifications obtained in one EU country will be recognised in all the other EU countries. If you are qualified as a doctor in Romania then you're qualified as a doctor in Britain.

In reality, things haven't worked out quite like that. The

EU never allows anything to be simple when it can make things complicated and expensive.

Consider, for example, the EU's Financial Services Action Plan (FSAP).

FSAP consists of 42 separate measures and the idea is that it enables all EU companies to offer banking, insurance and trading services everywhere within the EU. It is creating chaos and fury.

One of the measures given to us by FSAP is the Markets in Financial Instruments Directive (Mifid). The aim of this directive is to increase cross-border competition between fund managers, stock exchanges and investment banks and to allow financial service companies to market their products throughout the EU. However, in practice the new laws haven't been implemented equally across the EU. Some countries (such as Spain and Italy) have obtained exemptions to protect their national stock markets. Other countries have embellished or amended (gold plated) Mifid's provisions.

The European Union's Markets in Financial Instruments Directive contains 73 articles and is now law throughout the EU. (Remember that although Mifid contains 73 articles it is one of 42 separate measures. Remember too that the theoretical aim of this whole exercise was to simplify things and make them easier and cheaper for ordinary people.)

It seems to be generally agreed that the price investors and companies will pay for Mifid will be far higher than the value of the benefits. And, as always with the EU, the costs are significant.

Britain's Financial Services Authority (FSA) estimates that the one-off cost of implementing Mifid will be between £870 million and £1 billion (which means that the real cost will probably be five times that much) and that the annual running costs will be in the region of £100 million a year (which means that it will probably be five times that much). An independent organisation called Open Reach reckons that the total costs implementing Mifid could reach £6.5 billion.

One result of the new directive will be more paperwork. Mifid will also mean that British investors who have complaints about investments they have been sold may need to deal directly with foreign authorities. So, for example, if a British investor buys an investment from a Spanish firm and then wishes to complain and seek compensation he will have to deal directly with the Spanish authorities. Since there are well over a score of financial authorities to deal with, operating in over a score of different languages, the practical result will be that the British consumer will be far less able to obtain compensation. The end result is that the EU directive will reduce confidence in investment products still further.

Mifid isn't the only bit of FSAP which is a failure, of course. The Takeovers Directive was designed to create a single set of rules for takeovers within the EU. But that too has been a disaster. France, Germany and Italy all opted out of the key clauses and experts agree that the EU's directive is less effective than the UK's now redundant and out of date takeover code. The Takeovers Directive leaves British companies with a worse regime than they had before the EU got involved.

Another miserable, but expensive, failure for the EU.

The European Union is described as a 'dream state' by federalists. It may be a 'dream' to them. To the citizens who have to put up with EU rules and red tape it is a nightmare.

★★★

The EU has ordered Britain's Merchant Navy to fly the EU flag in place of the red Ensign.

★★★

Gordon Brown claims that Britain needs to match America and 'unite around the next round of enterprise reforms and the drive towards a more dynamic entrepreneurial culture'.

(Who the hell writes the man's speeches and articles?)

'During the Industrial Revolution,' says Brown,' 'Britain led the world in innovation, science and enterprise. It is time to rediscover that spirit and genius in the world of the Internet and digitalisation.'

Can Brown really be so out of touch that he doesn't know that his Government has (with the aid of the EU) more or less destroyed entrepreneurial activity in Britain? Is Gordon Brown really as stupid and out of touch with reality as he seems to be? (Can anyone, even a politician, be that stupid and that out of touch?)

Can Brown really be so stupefyingly stupid that he doesn't

understand that the miles of red tape which his Government has produced (and the kilometres of red tape which the EU has foisted upon us) have strangled many small companies – and are destroying thousands more?

Can Brown really be so complacent, so arrogant and so utterly divorced from the real world that he doesn't realise that his Government has, under the leadership of the EU, created a bureaucracy-heavy world in which knowledgeable and ambitious young people realise that the only sensible career path lies in employment in a Government or local authority department?

Can Brown be so blind, and busy patting himself on the back, that he doesn't listen to anything anyone else says?

On the very day that he was crying out for more new businesses in Britain, the Association of Taxation Technicians, giving evidence to a House of Lords committee reviewing the Finance Bill, pointed out that the tax rises made in that year's Budget (and authored by Gordon Brown himself) meant that small firms' owners would find themselves going around in circles.

The Chancellor's small business tax policies have been described by accountants as 'hideously complex'.

Thanks to the help they have received from the EU, Brown and Labour have destroyed the entrepreneurial spirit in Britain.

Gordon Brown will only help Britain recover its position as a home for entrepreneurial spirits if he resigns and leaves public life as quickly as possible. But what else could he do for a living? I wouldn't trust him to cut my lawn. If he promises never again to interfere with any aspect of English business life I will put on my doctor's hat and happily send him a sick note to last until he claims his pension. Brown is one person I'd like to see on permanent sick leave.

★★★

The bible might have managed with ten.

But there are now an estimated 111,000 EU laws.

At least there were when I was writing this page.

The one thing I can tell you with certainty is that there are now more than 111,000 EU laws.

14

The Damage Done By The British Government 'Gold Plating' EU Legislation

Anyone who has ever lived in France or Germany will confirm that the French and the Germans have always been keen on paperwork and on officials. Ever since forms and uniforms were invented the French and the Germans have led the world in both. It is, therefore, hardly surprising that the EU (a creation of the new Franco-German alliance) should thrive on paperwork and officialdom.

We, in Britain, have never been quite so keen on bits of paper or on people in uniform. We like queuing (something that neither the Germans nor the French know how to do properly) but we regard administration as an unavoidable evil rather than a purpose in life.

But there is something else, too.

The French and the Germans don't take the administrators seriously. They fill in forms by the dozen but no one takes any notice of them. Their streets are packed with officials in uniform but no one takes any notice of them either.

We, on the other hand, tend to take officials and paperwork very seriously. We don't have so much of either and so we treat both with a good deal more respect.

An English functionnaire will insist that the rules be followed to the letter. A French functionnaire will show you the loopholes. English citizens are brought up to play by the rules. French and German citizens are taught that the rules are merely a starting point for negotiations.

It is these fundamental variations in our history, and our outlook, which help explain why Britain is simply not suited for membership of the EU.

★★★

There is firm evidence available now that small businesses in Britain are suffering more from red tape and bureaucratic interference than their counterparts in the rest of Europe. Legislation produced by the European Union has been shown to be implemented more stringently than is necessary in the UK.

The Foreign Policy Centre (FPC) and the Federation of Small Businesses (FSB) have shown that the 'gold plating' of EU legislation is holding back the growth of small businesses.

The FPC and FSB found that gold plating (defined as the practice of over-implementing a directive passed by the European Union) occurs in a variety of forms which invariably take up time and involve significant additional costs.

Sometimes the British Government has been far too enthusiastic about applying EU legislation (in an attempt to curry favour with the EU's leaders). For example, in the autumn of 2007 the EU revealed that it had never wanted to stop Britain using imperial measurements such as pints, pounds, feet and miles and that it had been the British Government rather than the EU which had forced the pace of metrication and which had encouraged the conviction of small businessmen for selling, or offering for sale, produce in pounds rather than kilograms.

The British Government and various trading standards officials had argued that the EU had ruled that it was against the law to use scales which didn't display metric measures.

But, towards the end of 2007, the European Commission's Vice President Gunther Verheugen claimed that it was never the EU's intention to ban imperial measures and that as far as the Commission was concerned 'there is not now and never will be any requirement to drop imperial measures'.

Supporters of imperial measures and opponents of enforced metrication assumed that this meant that Britons would be 'allowed' to use imperial measures as a generous dispensation from our masters in Brussels. I suspected that the apparent softening was a result partly of the campaign by the courageous and determined organisers of the Metric Martyr Defence Fund and partly a result of the fact that large parts of the rest of the world, including the USA and a number of other countries, continue to use imperial measurements. Faced with the fact that a complete ban on imperial measurements would be irrational and ultimately unworkable, the EU had apparently found itself in something of a bind. It was a victory of sorts – both against the EU (which was assumed to have introduced the legislation banning imperial measures) and the British Government (which had gold plated the legislation).

And then two things happened. One was bad and one was staggeringly good.

The bad news was that a market trader had two sets of imperial scales confiscated by Hackney Council. The implication was clear: the British Government (and British local government officials) weren't going to abandon their gold-plating of the legislation even if the EU, which was responsible for the legislation, said that wasn't what they wanted or intended.

The good news was that the European Commission's Enterprise and Industry Directorate-General went much further in defence of imperial measures. A spokesman writing on behalf of the European Commission's Vice President Verheugen stated that: 'The Commission does not consider it necessary to change the current provisions on the use of pre-2000 weighing instruments in imperial-only units because the Directive does not prohibit the use of such instruments.'

As Neil Herron of the Metric Martyrs Defence Fund points out: 'What he (the Vice-President of the EC) is saying is that imperial equipment already in use when the directive came into force on January 1st 2000 is not/was not illegal under EU law.'

And this means that the traders who had been prosecuted (and found guilty) in Britain on the grounds that they were in breach of EU legislation were using scales which were not banned by the EU and so they must, presumably, have been wrongly accused and wrongly convicted. (I suspect it also means that the value of pre-2000 imperial scales will rocket.)

Neil Heron points out that the Metric Martyrs Defence Fund has exposed the enforced metrication programme as an 'absolute shambles'. It is surely difficult for anyone (even the most enthusiastic supporter of the EU) to argue with that. It seems to me that the Government (and a variety of local government officers) have misinterpreted EU legislation in their over-zealous attempts to do what they thought the EU wanted. It's all rather reminiscent of those nasty kids at school who will do anything to suck up to teacher.

The one remaining metric curiosity is that, as far as I've been able to find out, the law which will make it a criminal offence even to refer to imperial measures after 2009 has not been revoked. This means, for example, that any book which mentions inches, feet, miles, ounces, pounds and other imperial measures will become illegal in 2009. It presumably also means that rather a lot of road signs, maps, diaries and conversion tables will become illegal.

Oh, and there's one final puzzle.

Just who decided that our petrol had to be sold in litres?

Maps and signposts still give distances in miles. And car manufacturers and motorists still talk about cars doing so many miles to the gallon. So, why is petrol sold in litres?

As usual with the EU, it makes no sense whatsoever.

★★★

Sometimes civil servants in Whitehall extend the scope of the original EU directive by adding extra legislation which creates an additional and unnecessary burden for British industry. This was done with the money-laundering directive from the EU and with the directive involving landfill regulations. It was also done with the 1991 European Union regulation 2092-91 which deals with organic food. In EU law, organic food requires certain basic standards of animal husbandry. These are the standards which apply throughout most of the rest of the EU. In the UK, however, the Government has 'gold plated' the regulations. And so, for example, meat in the UK is only 'organic' if the animal from which the meat was taken was born into an organic system. For the rest of

Europe the regulation, as provided by the EU, allows 'organic' meat to be taken from intensively reared baby animals.

With other directives, British civil servants introduce extra targets (targets were enthusiastically introduced by Gordon Brown when he was Chancellor) and deadlines. Frequently, the new rules are confusing.

And, in many instances, the British Government has accepted and implemented new EU rules long before other countries. Although this may not seem to be particularly onerous, and perhaps not technically 'gold plating', it is nevertheless enormously damaging.

So for example, when the EU decided that EU citizens from the new accession states which joined in 2004 would have full working rights in all EU countries, only two countries in the EU accepted the legislation and implemented it in full. The Governments of the UK and the Republic of Ireland said that all citizens from all countries could come to their countries to seek work. Other EU countries (such as Germany, France and Italy) refused to implement the new legislation until 2011 when the EU's delay on full working rights is due to end. Even though they could have waited, or allowed immigration to accelerate slowly, the British Government chose to implement the new legislation immediately.

The immediate problem with this policy was that since other countries were not implementing the EU policy, immigration into Britain (with its free National Health Service and over-generous benefits policy) was disproportionate, creating an unsustainable burden on the country's infrastructure and arousing anger and resentment among the native population. The end result will, of course, be a rise in the incidence of racism. (When you add this huge mistake to the Government's long history of encouraging multi-culturalism, the consequences become even more frightening. In practice, multi-culturalism produces ghettoes of immigrants who are discouraged from assimilation by the provision of services designed to cater for the cultures they have, theoretically, left behind.)

Here's another example of gold plating.

Although some genetically modified food – such as maize – has been cleared for sale in the EU, a number of political leaders of member states of the EU have listened to their voters, ignored the eurocrats and banned GM foods. Austria, Hungary and France have, for example, banned all genetically modified foods. But despite the fact that repeated opinion polls show that a vast majority of the population do not want to eat genetically modified food, the British Government has decided to obey the EU and allow GM foods to be sold in Britain.

★★★

As a result of 'gold plating', many British businesses have been deterred from expanding or taking on new staff. One half of small British firms say that excessive regulation is a barrier to growth.

Our membership of the EU entitles us to trade freely with other countries in the EU. But because the British Government applies EU regulations more stringently than other governments do, British businesses operate at a great disadvantage. As a result, we buy far more than we sell to EU countries and have, and have always had, a negative trade balance with the rest of the EU. Thanks to the EU, and to the British Government's gold plating of EU laws, we are out of pocket by hundreds of billions of pounds, and millions of British jobs have been lost.

15

It's The EU That Insists We Carry ID Cards

'Every man should know that his conversations, his correspondence and his personal life are private.'
LYNDON B JOHNSON

'We are fast approaching the stage of the ultimate inversion: the stage where the government is free to do anything it pleases, while citizens may act only by permission; which is the stage of the darkest periods of human history, the stage of rule by brute force.'
AYN RAND

Britons are going to have to carry ID cards if we remain in the EU. The British Parliament no longer has the right to decide whether or not Britons are forced to carry identity cards. The EU has the right to force the British Government to impose identity cards on its citizens. ID cards are EU policy. The Italian Government, for example, has stated that ID cards will strengthen 'the feeling of unity within the EU'. (We will, presumably, all have matching EU ID cards in the same way that we now all have matching EU passports.)

The EU is demanding 'harmonised solutions' on biometric identification and data. In practical terms this means that the bureaucrats in Brussels are demanding an EU wide population register and ID cards. It is demanding national ID cards which will be used to store health, school and benefit records. Each card will carry either the fingerprints of the owner or an iris scan, and a European identity register will be set up. There will be biometric readers in doctors' surgeries and in hospitals. (It will be impossible to get treatment without your card being scanned.) Oddly enough, the Labour Party suddenly became keen on ID cards at the same time as the bureaucrats in Brussels said that they had to be issued. (As is often the case, English politicians are reluctant to admit that ideas like this come from Brussels. There are two reasons for their reluctance: first, they know that the public will be even more unwilling to accept the proposal and second they don't like to admit just how little power they have.)

To begin with, individual countries arranged to satisfy the EU's requirements in their own ways.

Back in 1994, when it was announced that Britain would be introducing new pictorial driving licences from July 1996, it was denied that this was an infringement of personal liberty. The Government did, however, admit that it was planning to include one or two other bits of information on the driving licences. When pressed for details, the Government admitted that driving licences would contain a computer chip which would contain: details of the driver's next of kin, address, occupation, place of employment, all previous driving details (including court appearances), insurance details, blood group, fingerprints, medical details, retinal pattern, DNA profile and national insurance number. All this information will, of course, be available to Government employees and to anyone else equipped with the requisite scanner and, of course, to anyone prepared to pay for it. In addition, it was acknowledged that the photographs on driving licences will be readable by surveillance cameras installed to track the movements of cars and their occupants around England.

ID cards are heaven sent for a fascist organisation like the EU. They will enable the EU to spy on us and to make money. Your personal financial and medical records will be readily available to all Government employees. Your tax inspector will know what illnesses you have had, and the receptionist at your local medical centre will know how much you earn and how much tax you pay. Every few years we will all have to line up at identity registration centres to be fingerprinted or to have our eyeballs scanned. We will have to be fingerprinted again if we want to buy a house or register with a doctor. (Is there any evidence that the eyeball scans they are planning to use are safe and won't make us blind?)

★★★

Our movements are already tracked by cameras in the streets and on the roads. Britain has more closed circuit television cameras per head than any other country – and yet the worst crime rates in the Western world. The cameras are allegedly there to prevent crime but have yet to be shown to have prevented crime at all. And just how much do all these cameras cost? And how much does it cost to hire people to watch them? Wouldn't our streets be safer if the people watching the cameras were, instead patrolling the streets? If the money spent on buying, erecting and running cameras, and hiring people to watch them, was spent on hiring policemen to patrol our streets we would, without a doubt, have the safest nation in the world. The official obsession with prying into our lives is, quite simply, putting us all at risk.

We will soon have 'black boxes' in our cars which will enable the EU to track our journeys mile by mile (in case our progress is missed by the cameras) and many Government employees are being fitted with hidden microphones disguised as name badges to record our conversations.

★★★

*'Most Governments want secrecy for themselves
but don't want you to have any.'*
HARRY D. SCHULTZ

★★★

It is clear, in retrospect, that the driving licence was the precursor of the ID card which the Labour Government is now determined to force us to carry. The high-tech driving licence was introduced in 1994 – some years before September 11th 2001. There was no mention of the need to introduce ID cards to combat terrorism. Nor indeed, were these early ID cards promoted as a method of combatting identity theft.

It is important to remember that ID cards (similar to those which will be introduced throughout Europe) were introduced in Germany under Hitler (and had to be available at all times for inspection by the police). And ID cards were introduced in the USSR under Stalin. They were required for internal travel.

The new ID cards proposed by Labour and the EU are also similar to, but more intrusive than, the identity cards which were utilised in South Africa some years ago. The South African identity cards stated the name of the bearer and where he came from. If the police stopped anyone he had to show his identity card. If he was in an area prohibited to him he could be arrested. If he didn't have his card he could be arrested. If arrested he would be taken to a police station and interrogated and perhaps imprisoned. The people who suffered most from these laws were quiet, decent, law abiding folk who were trying to go about their normal daily business. Those who were not quiet, decent and law abiding rarely got stopped by the police. They moved around quietly, keeping a good look out and making a quick getaway if spotted. The police, largely being bullies and cowards, much preferred to harass normal, law abiding citizens rather than chase the genuine bad guys.

If the EU and the Labour Government have their way we will all have to carry our ID cards at all times. If stopped and asked for identification we will have to show our cards. We will be arrested if we dare go out without our cards. ID cards will be used to enable the authorities to find, imprison and exterminate those who cause too much trouble (such as writing books like this one).

★★★

'Privacy protects us from abuses by those in power, even though we're doing nothing wrong at the time of surveillance. We're not deliberately hiding anything when we seek private places for reflection or conversation. We keep private diaries, sing in the shower and write letters to lovers. Privacy is a basic human need.'
HARRY D. SCHULTZ

★★★

The only people who can rely on their lives being kept private are senior politicians such as Gordon Brown – who rely on people whose wages are paid for by us to provide them with the sort of privacy we would like to enjoy if it had not been taken away by people working for the Government and, again, paid for by us.

In January 2008, it was revealed that the British Government's tax collecting department, HM Revenue and Customs, considered its online computer system, used by millions of taxpayers to file their tax returns, to be insufficiently secure for use by MPs, celebrities and members of the Royal Family.

Because of fears that their confidential details – such as bank details, addresses, national insurance numbers, earnings, investments – would be put at risk, thousands of high profile people had been secretly barred from using the online tax return system.

(HMRC had, a little earlier, lost private data for 25 million individuals.)

A Treasury minister admitted that 'There are categories of individual for whom security is a higher priority.'

In early 2008, it was announced that the EU was introducing new regulations requiring all non-Europeans 'to submit biometric data' (presumably including the registration of fingerprints and other personal data) before crossing Europe's frontiers.

The EU announced that it was introducing the new rules to combat terrorism, organised crime and illegal immigration and that there would also be a new European Border Surveillance System which would use satellites and unmanned aircraft to track unwanted visitors (and wanted ones too, no doubt).

It was revealed, however, that the rules would allow 'low risk frequent travellers' to pass through automated, fast-track frontier check points without coming into contact with the border guards. It wasn't made clear who would be classified as 'low risk' but it isn't difficult to guess that whereas little old ladies probably won't be on that list American politicians probably will be. The European commissioner for justice and home affairs also suggested that non-Europeans on short-stay visas would be checked against a Visa Information System which was already under construction. The commissioner called for a new database to store information on non-European nationals.

★★★

'Tyranny, whether it arises under threat of foreign physical attack or under constant domestic authoritative scrutiny is still tyranny. Liberty requires security

without intrusion, security plus privacy. Widespread police surveillance is the very definition of a police state. That's why we should champion privacy even when we have nothing to hide.'
BRUCE SCHNEIER

★★★

Our new ID cards will contain far, far more information than the cards which were used in South Africa or Nazi Germany. The KGB and the Stasi would have loved ID cards like these. The information on our compulsory cards will be passed to MI5 and MI6.

There will, in future, be many new offences relating to ID cards. It will, for example, be a criminal offence not to tell the authorities if your card (which you will have paid for) has been damaged or does not work properly. It will be a criminal offence to fail to tell the authorities of any change in your personal circumstances. Remember, there has never been any serious public debate about this fascist surveillance system which is supported only by fascist bureaucrats and by businesses which will make billions out of supplying the cards and out of the information they will be able to extract from them.

But I don't believe anyone seriously thinks that ID cards will stop crime or terrorism. (Anyone in a position of authority who genuinely believes that, should be relieved of his or her post immediately, led away quietly and placed in a padded room where he or she can sit quietly, avoiding bright lights and noises.) Spain has ID cards but these did not prevent the Madrid bombings. The September 11, 2001 hijackers all travelled on legitimate papers. And the introduction of ID cards will most certainly not improve the security of individual citizens in any way. The more people who have access to your personal information, the greater the risks of you being a victim of identity theft. The actions of the EU and the Government will positively encourage identity theft. The incidence of identity theft has already increased dramatically as the amount of information demanded from individuals by the authorities has increased. Every time personal information is put into the public domain the security of the individual diminishes. ID cards will make life worse – and infinitely more dangerous – for all of us.

There is no doubt that the distribution of ID cards will dramatically increase the incidence of identity theft. What will happen when people lose their ID cards? What happens when they are stolen? How do you go about getting a new one when you move house or change your name or job? The EU says that we will need to produce our ID cards when opening bank accounts. But many new bank accounts are opened over the Internet. Does this mean that we are expected to entrust our ID cards to the mail?

The extent of the risk to our personal security is perhaps best exemplified by the rise in personal identity theft which has taken place recently. Identity theft is currently estimated to cost American consumers more than $50 billion a year and it is a problem which is rapidly spreading to Europe.

There are, without doubt, two simple reasons for this.

First, a vast amount of personal, confidential information is now floating around in banks and public offices. (The introduction of ID cards will simply increase this phenomenon.)

Second, the people with whom we are forced to share our private and confidential information do not seem to regard it, once they've got it, as private or confidential. They certainly don't seem to take a great deal of care with it. The FT reported in autumn 2004 that fewer than a quarter of computers disposed of by companies have been properly cleansed of their data. Of 350 leading companies interviewed, 75% had recently sold or given away unwanted computers but only 23% had wiped the memories sufficiently to make the data on them unrecoverable. The companies who were interviewed included leading financial organisations that hold sensitive customer information and have a legal requirement to ensure that it remains confidential.

A large American bank is reported to have 'lost' computer tapes containing the personal tapes of 1.2 million American Government employees. A data collection company revealed that criminals had gained access to the social security numbers, addresses and other personal data of around 1,450,000 people. A fraud ring had infiltrated the company (which said it maintained strict security standards). One of the company's rivals then followed suit, revealing that 'unauthorised users' had compromised the identities of 310,000 of its customers. A shoe retailer admitted that its stores' credit card data had been breached. The US Secret Service said that at least 100,000 valuable numbers had been accessed. Later it turned out that the number of credit card holders whose security had been breached was, in fact, 1.4 million.

Banks and insurance companies and government bodies constantly demand and accumulate personal information. It only needs one crook working in a bank or Government office to make thousands of people vulnerable to identity theft. Can the big banks really assure us that they never have disgruntled or greedy employees?

The only people who will benefit from ID cards will be those running large corporations which can buy our personal information from the Government and use it to target us more accurately, (did the Government forget to mention that the private and confidential information on ID cards will be sold to multinational corporations for commercial purposes?) and those running the Government who will have more power over us. There is a finite amount of power in the world: as they get more power so we get less.

★★★

'If you don't have anything to hide, why would you object to carrying an ID card?'

'Tell me your income, your bank account number, what diseases you have had, when you last went to see the doctor, your home address, all your telephone numbers, your pin codes and your passwords.'

'No!'

'Why not?'

'Those are private. I'm not telling you stuff like that.'

'If the EU gets its way and forces us all to carry ID cards I will be able to buy all your private and confidential information. And every EU and Government employee will have access to all your personal information.'

★★★

'He that would make his own liberty secure, must guard even his enemy from oppression; for if he violates this duty he establishes a precedent that will reach himself.'
THOMAS PAINE

★★★

The eurocrats don't like us using cash.

Cash offers privacy and freedom. You can spend your money on whatever you want to spend it on without large international firms and the EU keeping a tab on your spending habits. Credit cards enable the authorities to keep a very careful watch on everything you spend, where you go and what you do.

(There are other advantages to you and I in using cash. We are protected against ID fraud. And, of course, we can see what we are spending and are far less likely to be reckless).

None of these things please the authorities who dismiss cash as a tool of tax evaders, terrorists, money launderers, fraudsters and drug smugglers.

Cash is being phased out. It is now illegal in the EU to try to pay for anything other than a modest purchase with cash.

★★★

'How many of us have paused during conversation in the past (few) years, suddenly aware that we might be eavesdropped on? Probably it was a phone conversation; maybe it was an e-mail or instant-message exchange or a talk in a public place. Maybe the topic was terrorism, politics or Islam. We stop suddenly, momentarily afraid that our words might be taken out of context, then we laugh at our paranoia and go on. But our demeanour has changed, and our words are subtly altered.'
BRUCE SCHNEIER

★★★

The news that scientists are planning to insert microchips into people has been received with enthusiasm by EU bureaucrats.

The uncritical enthusiasts for this latest miracle of the modern age point out that instead of having to carry around lots of pieces of plastic (credit cards, bank cash cards, membership cards and so on) we can all have a single microchip stuck under the skin on our arms.

It will be a case of 'chips in everyone'.

'Credit cards, bank cash cards — all redundant!' said one expert to whom I spoke. He was positively aglow with enthusiasm. 'Every bit of information you need to carry around with you will be on your own personal microchip. If you want to get cash out of a bank you just stick your arm into a hole in the wall. The bank's scanner will check your microchip and then, if you've got enough money in your account, simply dispense the cash!'

'It sounds very convenient,' I said, extremely cautiously. The alarm bells were already beginning to ring.

'Never again will anyone have to worry about having their credit cards stolen!' said the enthusiast for all things new.

'Ruthless thieves might just chop off people's arms,' I pointed out.

'Oh come on! Don't make fun!' protested the enthusiast rather crossly. 'This is a serious breakthrough which is going to revolutionise people's lives. No more money-belts when travelling abroad, no more credit card insurance. No more worry about what to do with your wallet when you go for a swim. No need to carry cash around with you at all. Every shop, every hotel, every petrol station will have a machine to read your arm.'

I told the enthusiast that I agreed that this would in some ways be extremely handy.

'What's more,' said the enthusiast, ignoring the pun, 'personal information can be stored on the same microchip.'

'What sort of personal information?' I asked, suspiciously.

'Birthdate, driving licence details, passport number, income tax records, national insurance number,' said the expert. 'Just imagine! You could travel abroad without worrying about whether or not you had your passport with you. And you could even have details of your airline bookings recorded on your microchip. You could walk through customs in your bathing costume! There would be no need to carry a fistful of documents with you. It would be easy to put in voting registration details too! When you visited your local polling station you'd just stick your arm into the box and vote. What's more, confidential medical information could be stored on the same microchip!'

I looked at him. 'Medical information?'

'The way things are at the moment the chances are that some of your medical records are stored with your general practitioner and some with whichever hospital consultant you've been seeing. This new system will mean that any doctor you see will have instant access to all your medical notes! And if you change doctors there will be no long delay while your medical records follow you. If you are knocked down in an accident, the casualty doctors who look after you will simply stick your arm into a machine and find out what drugs you're taking, what allergies you have, whether you are diabetic, epileptic or whatever else!'

'How feasible is all this?' I asked the enthusiastic expert.

'Oh it's entirely possible now,' he replied. 'Tests are under way and schemes like this will be available to the public very shortly.'

'And I bet the authorities will be very enthusiastic,' I said. 'People who agree to have the microchips implanted will probably get tax rebates.'

'Absolutely!' agreed the expert. 'Splendid idea. That would be a great encouragement.'

'Presumably these microchips use the same sort of technology as the subscriber cards used by satellite television?'

'I think so,' agreed the enthusiast

'That's interesting,' I said. 'If you have trouble with your subscriber card and want to have a channel unscrambled, you just telephone the company. They will then send a message to your card to unscramble the channel.'

'Yes?' said the enthusiast, obviously not quite understanding what I was getting at.

'They can send a message through the air directly to your own very personal subscriber card,' I pointed out.

'Yes,' agreed the enthusiast. 'It's very quick and very convenient.'

'And so what is there to stop the authorities sending messages to the microchip implanted under the skin of your arm?'

'I don't see what you're getting at.'

'The authorities will be able to edit the information on your microchip any time they want to. They can not only find out anything they want to know about you but they can also cancel your passport, your driving licence and your bank card whenever they like.'

'So?'

'In a perfect world where bureaucratic errors were unknown and bullying governments didn't exist it might be OK,' I said. 'But we don't live in a perfect world. We live in the EU.'

'You're paranoid,' protested the enthusiast.

'They could decide how they wanted you to vote. And make sure that you voted in the approved manner. If you complained or protested or caused a lot of trouble they could turn you into a non-person in seconds.'

'Don't be so silly!' snorted the enthusiast.

'And what about errors?' I asked. 'At the moment if one doctor makes an error when putting something into your medical records there is a chance – albeit a slim one – that another doctor might spot the error. And you can, of course, always ask to see your own medical records to check that everything they contain is fair and accurate. I suspect that open access will become a thing of the past when medical records are hidden away on a microchip underneath your skin. The non-availability of open access will simply mean that it will become even more difficult than it is at the moment for an ordinary citizen to check what the experts have written about him or her.'

The enthusiast didn't say anything but, for the first time, I detected some slight anxiety in his face. Maybe he will now think more carefully, and temper his enthusiasm for this new technology.

★★★

'Civilisation is the progress towards a society of privacy. The savage's whole existence is public, ruled by the laws of his tribe. Civilisation is the process of setting man free from men.'
AYN RAND

★★★

The 'Big Brother' rules so beloved by the European Union and the Labour Party are 'sold' to us on the basis that they are essential for catching terrorists. This is, to put it politely, a bare-faced lie. Big Brother rules (such as banks demanding copies of passports and the Government threatening to introduce identity cards) punish everyone and catch no one. Money is wasted and nothing is achieved – apart from the loss of our liberty and the increase of identity theft.

Does anyone in Brussels or Whitehall really, really believe that terrorists will be thwarted by being unable to open bank accounts unless they provide two recent gas bills? Does any bureaucrat anywhere genuinely believe that terrorists will halt their activities if it becomes illegal to go for a walk in the park without an ID card in your pocket?

If anyone believes that they should be certified insane.

★★★

'Progress might have been all right once, but it has gone on for too long.'
OGDEN NASH

★★★

British passports are being changed ready to be converted into identity cards. The changes are already under way.

As bored travellers (reduced to reading their passports) will know, British passports have always contained a stern message to foreigners.

'Her Britannic Majesty's Secretary of State requests and requires in the Name of Her Majesty all those whom it may concern to allow the bearer to pass freely without let or hindrance, and to afford the bearer such assistance and protection as may be necessary.'

Back in 1414, passports were personally signed by the monarch (the latest personally signed passport in existence is dated 1778 and was signed by George III for Sir John Stepney)

Sadly, the guff on your passport is meaningless piffle these days. Any airport employee in a uniform knows that whatever the Secretary of State may request and require his status as a 'security employee' entitles him to hold you up for hours and to make you stand on your head in a bucket of custard if the fancy takes him. All in the name of stopping terrorists and money launderers, of course.

But the wording is rather nice and it's been there a long time. And it's a pleasant reminder of the days when the British could make such demands of mere foreigners.

So, naturally, the EU plans to get rid of it and to have it replaced with some bureaucratic gobbledegook.

Here's the planned replacement text as included in the Treaty of Lisbon which Brown signed in 2007:

'Every citizen of the Union shall, in the territory of a third country in which the members of state of which he is a national is not represented, be entitled to protection by the diplomatic or consular authorities of any member state, on the same conditions as the nationals of that state.'

What this means in practice, of course, is that citizens of countries such as Estonia, Bulgaria, Romania and Latvia will be entitled to be represented by British consular and embassy officials in those parts of the world where their own countries don't have any officials.

This is not, of course, the first time that the EU has interfered with the British passport.

From 1920 onwards, Britons who wanted to travel abroad were issued with a smart, solid-feeling dark blue book with the Royal Coat of Arms on it. Known as 'Old Blue' the British passport was undoubtedly the most distinctive looking passport in the world. While other nationals pushed scruffy bits of cardboard at customs officers and airline staff, Britons could present their 'Old Blue' with a distinct sense of national pride.

And then in 1988, the EU replaced 'Old Blue' with the shrunken and rather tawdry little burgundy booklet which defines us all as citizens of the new European Union.

But Britain somehow managed to retain the right to keep the original wording in the new passport.

Now, thanks to the treaty Gordon Brown has signed (without the referendum he promised) the traditional wording will be changed.

Britain has made no objection to the change.

Not that it would make any difference if we did protest.

The change is enshrined in the Lisbon Treaty.

'A country and its government are not the same thing.'
RICHARD MAYBURY

16

The EU's Policy On Immigration – A Ticking Time Bomb

The Home Office predicted that 13,000 people from the eight former Soviet bloc countries which joined the EU in May 2004 would move to England. The Home Office got it wrong (as usual). In fact, more than 176,000 East Europeans arrived in England in the year following the controversial expansion of the EU. (The figure of 176,000 is the official figure. The real figure will be more than this, a lot more than this or a massive amount more than this.) Around 100,000 came from Poland.

The Home Office also predicted that after the initial 13,000 immigrants had arrived from the Soviet bloc countries, the influx of new residents would fall off. Once again they were wrong. Official figures show that the number of East Europeans still arriving in the UK in the summer of 2005 was running at between 13,000 and 14,000 a month. That's as many new residents each month as the Home Office predicted would arrive altogether. The whole nature of Britain has been changed dramatically by this influx of newcomers. Today, the official figures show that over six million UK residents were born abroad. In reality the number is much greater than this. Many of those coming into Britain are illegal immigrants. Others claim to be here as visitors or students. EU laws allow people to wander freely throughout Europe. Not surprisingly, many make a beeline for the part of the EU that provides the richest supply of benefits.

The social and financial cost of all these people has been phenomenal. The police report that the dramatic increase in the number of immigrants is responsible for an increase in crime. One Chief Constable blames the surge in immigration for a 35% rise in violent crime in his county. Migrants are eight times more likely to commit a crime than indigenous people. The NHS is struggling to cope with the vast increase in the number of people demanding investigations and operations. And the financial cost is further damaging an already weakened economy. There are, for example, reports of immigrants claiming child benefit even though the children they are claiming for don't live in the UK. It is, of course, nigh on impossible for the authorities to prevent this sort of deceit. The official figures show that migration has not been an economic benefit to Britain. On the contrary, immigration costs us money.

The Home Office has also estimated that an additional 60,000 people arrived illegally before May 2004. Since they had arrived illegally they could not, of course, work legally or pay income tax.

Is it any wonder that our crowded roads are getting ever more crowded and that hospital waiting lists are getting longer by the week?

Why haven't the Home Office civil servants who were responsible for this massive underestimate been sacked? Anyone with a real job who made an error of such magnitude would be invited to spend more time with his or her family. But English civil servants never take responsibility for their cock-ups. The idiots responsible for this particular variety of chaos are doubtless looking forward to index-linked pensions (paid for by taxpayers) and knighthoods.

(As an aside it is worth mentioning that over half of all the public sector jobs created by Labour since 1997 have been taken by migrants – over 600,000 in total.)

★★★

The Labour Government is keen on immigration for several reasons.

The big reason is that the State pension scheme which the

Government runs is a Ponzi scheme. If anyone else but the Government ran it they would be in prison. Many taxpayers assume that the money they hand over (in tax and national insurance payments) is put away in a safe place on their behalf (and possibly even invested for them) so that when they retire they can collect a pension which will, even if not generous enough to pay for Caribbean cruises, pay for the necessities of life. However, as I have been pointing out for several decades, that isn't the way the Government runs things. The money you hand over is not put on one side for you. Instead, it is used to pay pensions for today's pensioners. When you retire, your pension will be paid by whoever is around paying tax and national insurance at the time. It's an old fashioned, simple financial scam: an illegal Ponzi scheme. Governments have recently started getting worried about this particular piece of financial sleight of hand because they have realised that when tomorrow comes there won't be enough taxpayers to pay out all the pensions. This is why the loathsome politician David Blunkett warned English taxpayers not to expect the Government 'to dig them out of poverty in their old age'. The repulsive Blunkett ignored the fact that the money that would be used to dig them out of poverty is their own and not the Government's.

★★★

In the EU today, the average age is around 39 years. By the year 2050, the average citizen will be around 50 years old. Over half the population will be over 50 and nearly a third will be over 65. A survey conducted by Deutsche Bank reported that by 2050 there will be 75 pensioners for every 100 workers in the EU. (There will, of course, also be many people who are younger than this but who are, for a variety of reasons, unwilling or unable to work.)

These fundamental demographic changes are being produced by reduced infant mortality rates and, most importantly, by falling birth rates. Back in the 1960s, there were many scare stories about the population time bomb and couples were encouraged not to have more than two children. More significantly, however, the cost of raising more than two children has become an intolerable burden for those who have to earn a living and pay taxes. In modern Britain, and indeed in much of modern Europe, only those who live on State handouts are able to feed and care for more than two children. (The State is, therefore, ensuring that future generations will largely be composed of the lazy, the feckless and the incapable.) Women are having children later and are leaving longer gaps between children.

This dramatic ageing of the European population will have a dramatic impact on the potential for economic growth and on the demand from pensioners for financial support and for health care.

Since state pensions are paid for out of current tax revenues either taxes or national debts will have to rise steeply. Standard and Poor's (a credit-rating agency) has predicted that France and Germany, the two EU countries with the most serious pension problems, could see their public debt grow to more than 200% of GDP by the year 2050. This would clearly be unsustainable. (It is hardly surprising that the other EU countries are loathe to see Britain leave the EU. Far more private pension money has been saved by the British than by any other nationality. The EU wants to share those savings and Britain's accumulated pension funds are likely to be raided by other European countries on the grounds that when the EU is a single State so savings will become community property.)

Our politicians don't seem to have grasped the awful significance of the changes that are coming. We will need fewer schools and more old people's homes but our politicians are busy building more schools and, because of EU regulations, we have fewer old people's homes than ever. Youthful spenders will be replaced by middle-aged savers desperately trying to accumulate a little money to help ease their way through old age and to help pay for medical and dental care. The number of workers struggling to pay the costs of all those receiving sickness benefits and all those receiving pensions will fall lower and lower. The working classes who had become the middle classes will become the working classes again; they will work harder than ever, earn less than ever and pay more tax than ever. (State employees don't count as contributors since they too are a drag on the economy. Their salaries and pensions must be paid out of the earnings and taxes paid by the diminishing number of private sector workers.)

I first warned of this problem in 1988 (in a book called *The Health Scandal*) but European politicians either didn't see what was coming or else they kept their eyes averted because they couldn't bear to look.

Now, however, it is no longer possible to ignore the impending crisis. Actually, it's too late. It is now up to each and every man and woman to look after themselves. Anyone other than an ex-MP or ex-civil servant who relies on the Government to provide for them in their old age will spend their final years cold and hungry. If we stay in the EU, taxes are going to have to rise dramatically as British taxpayers struggle to help pay the pension deficits in France and Germany.

Sudden (and belated awareness) of this looming disaster helps to explain much of what is now going on in Europe.

It is because of this problem that European governments are desperately (though unsuccessfully) trying to reform their pension schemes. And it is even because of this impending crisis that legislation has been introduced giving older workers more protection. The EU needs private sector employees to carry on working well into their seventies. The new legislation is designed to ensure that employers cannot discriminate against employees on the basis of age. State employees and public sector workers will, of course, still be entitled to retire as early as 55 and will continue to receive generous taxpayer-funded pensions. Many, having time on their hands, will take up part-time jobs. They will be able and prepared to accept low wages and will threaten still further the financial security of many, particularly the self-employed.

The EU's way of holding off chaos for another few years is to dramatically increase the number of young people in Europe.

There are only two ways to do that.

The obvious, quick solution is to encourage immigration. So-called 'asylum seekers' fit this bill perfectly. (I say 'so-called' because the phrase 'asylum seeker' suggests that someone is escaping from a threatening, totalitarian regime. The phrase would, I suggest, be more accurately applied to the hundreds of thousands of middle-class Britons currently leaving England than to the hundreds of thousands of immigrants moving in.)

The other solution is to encourage women to have more babies. Loads of babies.

And they have tried to do this by a massive piece of social engineering designed to penalise taxpayers who don't have children.

- They have introduced absurdly over-generous programmes of maternity and paternity leave. (The scheme has backfired to a certain extent because thousands of employers are now wary about hiring young women of child-bearing age.)
- They have introduced a means-tested scheme enabling parents to claim chunks of money just for having children. (This scheme is so absurd that even couples earning over £60,000 can claim this hand-out.)
- They have dramatically improved the quality and availability and accessibility of child care so that young mothers can have loads of children and still go out to work.
- They have devised a bizarre scheme of benefits which encourages teenage girls to have as many babies as they like. The State pays them and provides them with housing. It can be no surprise that pregnancy is now seen by many teenage girls as a career path. In effect the State has turned into a giant pimp: encouraging young girls to have sex and become pregnant in the (probably vain) hope that their children will grow up to be productive tax-paying members of society.

This scheme enables the Government to encourage population growth without there being any conflict with the official policy of discouraging marriage – an institution which has never been favoured by statists who believe the institution must always take precedence over the individual. It is much easier to control a population when you break down family units. The result of Government policy is that people who live on state benefits have more children so that they can claim the extra money, whereas couples who work cannot afford to have more than one or two children because of all the taxes they pay. The Government has not yet realised that when a child grows up in a (probably one parent) family where there is no working parent, the chances are high that the child will follow the same parasitical path when it reaches adulthood.

The EU, and the British Government, are guilty of massive (and appallingly incompetent) social engineering.

Their hubris and determination to interfere seems to know no bounds. Before the 2005 election, Labour announced that the 'first few months are so important in the life-chances' of children (the politicians presumably have access to information denied to the medical profession) that the Government must take responsibility for providing 'learning experiences' in the cot.

I'd like to think I dreamt that last bit.

But, sadly, I didn't.

★★★

'By the year 2020, one third of the population in the developed world will be over the age of sixty-five. One quarter of the population will be diabetic. In every home where there are two healthy parents and two healthy children there will be four disabled or dependant individuals needing constant care. Diseases such as diabetes and schizophrenia (which are genetically transmitted) and blindness (which is ten times as common among the over sixty-fives and thirty times as common among the over seventy-fives) will be as common as indigestion and hay fever are today. Unemployment will be normal. Stress-related diseases will be endemic. Developed countries around the world will face bankruptcy as they struggle to find the cash to pay pensions, sick pay and unemployment benefits.

Resentment, bitterness and anger will divide the young and the old, the able-bodied and the dependant, the employed and the unemployed. There will be anarchy, despair and civil war. There will be ghettoes of elderly and disabled citizens abandoned to care for themselves. There will be armed guards on our hospitals. Those with jobs will travel to work in armoured cars.'

The paragraphs above were taken from the Prologue to my book *The Health Scandal* which I wrote in the mid 1980s and which was first published in 1988.

When the book was being prepared for publication, the publishers (Sidgwick and Jackson) were wildly enthusiastic about its prospects and expressed themselves eager to promote the book as widely as possible. But suddenly, and without explanation, things changed. The book came out without even a whimper – let alone a bang. There was so little publicity that I sent out a press release myself – and was told off by the publishers for doing so. The book was remaindered very quickly and no real effort was made to sell the paperback rights. When Sidgwick and Jackson insisted that the paperback rights could not be sold my agent took back the rights. She sold the paperback rights very quickly. This was curious because it meant that we did not have to share the financial proceeds from the paperback sale with Sidgwick & Jackson. Not for the only time in my life I got the impression that a book of mine had been effectively suppressed by its own publisher. It was the way this book was treated which was one of the triggers for me to start publishing my own work.

The fears I first expressed in the mid 1980s do not now seem quite so outrageous. Many of the predictions I made in that book are coming true. And rather than doing anything to help prevent the coming crisis, the bureaucrats of the EU have made things worse. Their miles of red tape have created a sclerotic economy and their desperate attempts to lower the average age in Western European countries by encouraging immigration is creating social unrest and a right wing political backlash.

Rather than doing anything to prevent my forecasts coming true, every action of the EU seems to have been designed to ensure that my worst fears come true.

The EU believes that by forcing European countries with 'maturing' populations to accept huge numbers of immigrants these problems can be avoided.

★★★

The EU realised some time ago that the more mature nations within the EU are declining. A falling birth rate meant that Europe wasn't making economic progress. Now, there is nothing at all wrong with not making economic progress in itself but the people behind the EU were never going to be satisfied with a stagnant superstate. And they did have one huge problem. All the individual member states of the EU have for decades been operating pension schemes which are Ponzi schemes.

The theory was that if young, vibrant Eastern European

countries could be brought into the EU, their much higher birth rates would help to solve this problem. It was, of course, true that many of these nations were Muslim and since the resident Muslim populations of the original member states tend to have larger families than Christian families, the two factors together would mean that Europe would become dominated by Muslims. But the eurocrats didn't care about that. They just wanted power and realised that if they simply took control of the policy making it wouldn't matter whether the voters were Christian, Muslim, Jewish or Buddhist. Their theory was that the rapidly growing Muslim populations would pay the taxes needed to keep the Ponzi scheme going for a little while longer.

Obeying EU instructions, Britain's Government now believes (or pretends to believe) that expanding the EU and encouraging immigration will get them out of the mess they have created. They are wrong. The new countries which are joining the EU have low birth rates and their demographic structure is even less attractive than that of Western Europe. The enthusiasm for allowing Turkey into the EU is largely led by those who suspect that Turkey's younger population will help to delay the date at which Europe's ageing population becomes a real problem. They don't seem unduly concerned about the fact that allowing Turkey into Europe will help change the EU from a predominantly Christian State to a predominantly Muslim State.

(Anyone in doubt that this will happen should remember that early in 2008 the Archbishop of Canterbury, Rowan Williams, theoretically the spiritual leader of the world's Anglicans and head of the Church of England, suggested that Britain should 'constructively accommodate' certain aspects of Sharia law. He told the BBC that the application of Sharia law in certain circumstances 'seems unavoidable to achieve social cohesion'. Sharia law is, of course, a body of Islamic law based on the Koran, the words and actions of the Prophet Mohammed. The introduction of Sharia law would destroy for ever the traditional theory that there is one law, and one law alone, for all Britons and that all Britons are equal before the law. It would be an extraordinary defeat for the traditions of British freedom and a victory for those who favour multiculturalism and the end of Britain.)

And, of course, this theory only works if all the young immigrants who are allowed into the country become contributors rather than takers; they have to become active, tax paying workers rather than people living on benefits.

Second, the Labour Government believes that if it lets lots of people come into the country (and gives them chunky handouts to welcome them to Britain) they will be so grateful that they will vote Labour for evermore.

Third, the aim is to water down the local population and to make sure that the English are soon in a minority unable to make much of a fuss when their country disappears. As immigrants pour into England (and most of them stay in England, rather than travel to Scotland or Wales – both of which are at best unwelcoming and at worst downright hostile to the English, let alone to Rumanians) the percentage of English voters who have even heard of William Shakespeare and Winston Churchill will soon become a minority. The rest of the English, the proud middle classes, will have all gone to France and Spain, diluting the local populations there. This is, make no mistake about it, all part of a doomed plan to make sure that the United States of Europe can be created without any real protest.

★★★

The Government lies about immigration (just as they lie about everything else). They claim that immigrants are of enormous value to Britain and that they are making the country richer – increasing our wealth and prosperity. This is a blatant lie. There is not one shred of truth in it. The huge numbers of immigrants who have poured into Britain in recent years have lowered wage rates, created unemployment among native Britons, created a black economy which sucks money out of the economy without paying anything back in taxes, claimed vast amounts in benefits and used up massive amounts of infrastructure (putting a huge and intolerable burden on health and education services). They are also responsible for a massive increase in crime rates. Immigrants have failed to integrate (in fact we have spent huge amounts of public money adapting our society to their requirements and their cultures in a way that no other country on the planet would consider necessary or appropriate). Our Government and councils have printed official leaflets in dozens of languages, and civil servants of all varieties have bent over backwards, forwards and sideways to avoid any chance of political incorrectness. In becoming the ultimate multicultural society and in abandoning (and apologising for) our history and our own culture we have lost virtually every scrap of dignity and self-respect. The final straw is the fact that many of the immigrants our Government is forcing us to welcome send most of their earnings back to the country they still think of as home. Poles working in the UK are estimated to have sent back £1.8 billion in 2007. Money that could have been used to boost the British economy has instead started a boom in Poland. And when they have taken what they want from us they go back to whichever part of the European superstate they came from. That is the sad reality of the immigration policy the Government defends because it has been foisted upon us by the EU, and British politicians can't say no to the European Union. The result has been dramatic. One third of people living in London were born abroad. Another 10,000 foreigners settle in the English capital every month. And the numbers arriving are likely to continue to increase. Constantly increasing numbers of illegal immigrants are crossing the EU's eastern border and, once in the EU, find it absurdly easy to travel to the UK.

★★★

'Ask the American Indians what happens when you don't control immigration.'
ANON

★★★

The people who run the EU are keen to have Turkey as a member.

Why?

Turkey is very large and very poor and will have to be given billions of pounds of aid. Turkey's gross domestic product (GDP) per head is less than a third of the average GDP in the enlarged EU. A third of all the Turks work as farmers and the cost to the EU agricultural subsidies will be vast.

Turkey already has a population of over 70 million. It is

growing much faster than Western European countries and will, within less than a generation, be the biggest member of the EU. It will then have even more votes in the European Parliament than Germany.

Those are the drawbacks.

So what's in it for the EU?

Why are our masters in Brussels so determined to bring Turkey into the EU?

Well, first and foremost, the Americans want Turkey in the EU. (The Americans were effectively the founders of the EU and have long believed that a large EU is a 'good thing' for America.)

The Americans want Turkey within the EU for two reasons: first, it is partly in Europe and partly in Asia and second, it is a Muslim country. The Americans believe that if Turkey is in the EU then other Muslim countries (particularly Asian ones) will feel linked to the West. They believe that this will make it easier to 'sell' the idea of liberal, Western, democracy to Muslim countries. (I didn't claim it was a logical reason. I just said it was what the Americans wanted. The Americans do not understand anything much outside Detroit.)

The EU bureaucrats, and the politicians who 'lead' Western European governments (I use the word 'lead' in a general sort of way) know that millions of Turks will move to England, France and Germany in search of higher wages. (If they come to England the Turks will, of course, go back home if they fall ill. The health care in Turkey is infinitely better than it is in England.) The idea is that the immigrating Turks will have loads of children and help solve the coming pensions crisis.

★★★

Supporters of immigration point to the fact that huge quantities of Britons are leaving to live in other countries (sometimes within the EU) and suggest that this proves that having a global market is a 'good thing'. Indeed, around 14 million Britons have already decided that the Britain of today bears no resemblance to the Britain in which they grew up and have decided to quit.

What the supporters of immigration don't seem to realise is that the Britons who are leaving the country aren't going to look for work in another country – they are invariably leaving Britain because they can't stand what their country has become. The majority are not going abroad to work, they are going abroad to retire. Others are young professionals and skilled workers – leaving because they are fed up of living in a fascist State which takes from them but gives nothing back. The majority of those leaving are people who have an income – either from earning money or from their pensions – and they pay taxes.

Think about it.

And think about the consequences.

★★★

Every year hundreds of thousands of people are entering Britain. Many are claiming benefits. Very few are paying much tax. The majority are low-skilled. They have little knowledge of the language or the country. They demand that Britain provide them information in their own language. They expect to preserve their own cultural rules while living in Britain. Since 2003, a staggering two million foreign nationals have obtained British national insurance numbers – and are entitled to benefits paid by British taxpayers.

The EU's policy on immigration is designed to apply to all countries within the EU. The EU forces Britain, and other member nations, to employ (and pay for) expensive teams of lawyers and translators to speed up migration. (Translation costs are huge for all parts of Britain's infrastructure. Local councils spend £100 million a year on translation services, the NHS spends £55 million and the police spend over £30 million.)

And so, for example, the EU encourages Poles and Bulgarians to leave and move elsewhere. And why would they not want to? If a Pole has the choice of living in poverty in Poland or of living in comparative luxury in England what is he going to do? On the other hand how many Britons want to move to Poland or Bulgaria? The whole system is very one-sided. But it suits the EU. Because the people who run the EU want to destroy Britain in general and England in particular.

And then there are the asylum seekers.

For the vast majority of asylum seekers, England is the country of first choice. Tens of thousands arrive each year. For hardly any of them is England (or Britain) the first safe country in which they landed. Asylum seekers travel across the rest of Europe to get into England where the benefits are best.

And there are the illegal immigrants. The Government's own experts have admitted that they don't have the foggiest idea how many illegal immigrants are living in Britain. Most of the known 450,000 illegal immigrants in England will probably be granted amnesty because the British Government admitted at the end of 2007 that it didn't have the resources to investigate every case.

British taxpayers spend over £1 billion a year on legal aid and other costs generated by asylum seekers and illegal immigrants.

And it's going to get worse – much worse.

The European Commission has announced that another million economic migrants are now about to be welcomed from Asia and Africa. Guess where they will want to go? Poland or England? Difficult choice. And the EU is also introducing a Blue Card visa which will offer permanent residency to workers and their families anywhere in the EU (e.g. they can choose between England or Bulgaria) after five years. It is expected that over 20 million Asians and Africans will apply for Blue Cards.

The cost of dealing with all these immigrants is phenomenal. Four out of five Somali immigrants in Britain live in social housing, as do nearly half of all Turks. More than half of all Turkish immigrants do not work. (And, remember, it is extremely likely that Turkey will soon be a full member of the European Union. How many of Turkey's estimated 67,000,000 inhabitants will choose to move to Britain?)

At the same time as this happening, hundreds of thousands of people are leaving Britain. Hardly any of those leaving are claiming benefits. The vast majority are paying tax. Most are paying top rate tax. Over one million British graduates now live and work abroad. No other country in the world has lost so many of its most highly educated citizens. According to Ashley Mote MEP, writing in his monograph *J'Accuse...!* there are now 14 million Britons living abroad. Ashley Mote also points out that the number of British citizens emigrating has risen by 45% since Labour came to power in 1997 and is now at its highest ever. Many who are leaving are doing so to escape the growing intrusiveness of the European and

British political and legal systems. The most popular destination for those leaving is Australia. Naturally, the Australian Government only accepts Britons who are skilled professionals. (Those Britons who leave for other EU countries say, with justification, that it is the 'gold plating' of legislation in the UK which makes life unbearable.) Wherever they are going the Britons who are leaving are the ones with skills, the professionals and the ones with money. The Britons who are remaining are mostly the ones who are living on benefits.

You don't need to be an economic genius to work out that the infrastructure of Britain is going to get much, much worse and taxes are going to have go much, much higher.

It's so obvious even Gordon Brown could work it out.

Oh, and by the way, according to Ashley Mote MEP, British taxpayers are now contributing £2.5 billion towards an EU programme to treble social security benefits in Romania and Bulgaria.

Nice of us, eh?

★★★

There is another reason why immigrants are changing the whole nature of Britain.

Birth rates.

In order to sustain itself, a country needs to reproduce at a rate of 2.1 children per woman.

But because many better off and better educated women are choosing not to have children, the indigenous British are currently reproducing at a rate of just 1.5 children per woman.

Meanwhile, the birth rate among Muslims stands at five children per woman.

In London in 2006, more children were born to immigrant women than to British women.

In another generation or so, immigrants will be in a majority in many towns and cities in Britain.

(Better off women are choosing not to have children – or to limit the size of their families – because as taxpaying earners they cannot afford large families. Many, distressed by the way the country is deteriorating, prefer not to bring children into the world.)

17

The EU Will Encourage
A Swing To Right

A massive swing to the political right is coming in Europe.

This is now inevitable. Indeed, it is already happening.

The swing to the right, unwittingly encouraged by EU policies, is threatening to destroy the EU even before the EU enlargement has been completed.

Voters all over Europe are frightened by unemployment and poor pension payments. They blame the rise in the number of immigrants from poorer countries. As a result, ultra right wing nationalist groups have already risen in Austria, France and Switzerland and they will continue to grow in size and power. In Switzerland, fear of the EU and of asylum seekers has helped Christoph Blocher and the Swiss People's Party to do well.

There is no doubt that EU policies have led to a rise in the success of right wing parties whose supporters object to the formation of a new European superstate.

In my book *England Our England* (published in 2003) I predicted the rise of nationalism throughout Europe. It seemed pretty obvious at the time. The EU wants to destroy the identity of individual nations. It wants to take away culture and history and replace them with, well, nothing. Inevitably, there are many people who object. Occasionally, of course, the EU is happy to encourage some nationalism. Scottish and Welsh nationalism are acceptable because Scotland and Wales are due to be new EU regions. The EU has long intended to break up the United Kingdom. Encouraging the Scots and the Welsh to demand their independence suits the EU's purposes very well. (They won't get their independence, of course. But the EU wants them to think they will.)

Today, nationalism is rife throughout Europe. In every EU country there is now at least one powerful and rising nationalist party. The EU dismisses all these parties, and their supporters, with a single word smear: fascists. In truth, of course, the EU is the most fascist organisation ever created.

Can it still really be any surprise to anyone that right wing national parties are currently doing well throughout the European Union?

In France, Jean-Marie Le Pen came second in the Presidential election of 2002. In Austria, the Freedom Party led by Jorg Haider became part of a coalition government. (The EU said that this was unacceptable and refused to accept the Government chosen by the Austrian people.) In the Netherlands, Pim Fortuyn ran on an anti-immigration ticket in the 2002 election and was very successful until he was assassinated. In Germany, the neo-Nazis made huge gains in the 2004 elections. In England, the British National Party (BNP) is now the fourth most successful political party – and is rapidly gathering support.

Anger at the loss of their national identity and a concern that their country would be swallowed up by the EU has aroused the French – who fear for their nation's culture and social stability. It is only a matter of time before Jean-Marie Le Pen (or someone like him) takes power in France. (The ban on the wearing of headscarves in schools by Muslims is just a start and a sign that politicians there are getting worried.) In Germany, soldiers in the army have been seen giving Nazi salutes.

The revolution is taking place quietly. Opposition to the EU, and to immigration and the free movement of people around Europe, is creating strong waves of nationalism.

It will happen in Britain. And it will happen soon.

New Labour has already moved so far to the right that the Tories have nowhere to go. (If anything, some of Labour's policies are probably further to the right than even the Tories would dare propose.)

The impact made by the vast number of immigrants surging into Britain (and living on benefits) is already creating a groundswell of opposition to immigration and an upsurge in the feeling that 'charity begins at home'. Anger and resentment are building fast.

As taxes rise and pensions fall so the anger and resentment will grow. As Britain's infrastructure continues to crumble (and it will) so the anger and resentment will reach a critical point. Ordinary middle class citizens who are paying out large amounts in tax will become angry at having to buy private medical insurance and at having to pay to have their children privately educated.

All three parties will respond to the fears created by the boom in immigration by moving further to the right. Politicians need power and they will soon realise that the only way they can get it is by becoming more right wing.

Like everything in public life, the move to the right will overshoot and reach dangerous extremes. (Stockmarkets always go up and down too much. Currencies always rise and fall too far. Political movements always become extreme.)

The political party which gains power will, in the end, be the party which moves fastest and most unapologetically to the right. This will happen within a few years.

In Britain there will be a rise in nationalism and a rise in the amount of racism. Politicians who used to equate nationalism with racism will quickly change their tune. Opposition to the EU and its fascist bureaucrats will grow rapidly.

(Don't believe that politicians won't adapt. Before he got into power Blair wanted to take Britain out of the EU. Expediency is the only rule the modern politician obeys.)

The EU has laws in place which are designed to prevent the growth of any opposition to the EU. But you can't suppress millions of people who feel angry enough to turn against the system.

These days, major regime changes can and do take place without a bloody revolution. Look at what happened in the USSR. One day the Berlin Wall was firm, strong and apparently impregnable. The next day hippies were tearing bits off it and flogging them off to souvenir hunters. The leaders of the Soviet Union probably didn't think the Berlin Wall would ever have hippies dancing on it, tearing out stones and selling them as souvenirs. They probably thought their powerful laws would squash dissent. They were wrong.

In the last decade there have been two dozen countries in which similar things have happened. In Georgia, for example, the people simply rose up, said 'enough' and took over. In the end even armies won't support oppressive governments.

What happened to the USSR will happen to Europe. There will be a demand for freedom and a surge to the right.

The changes in Europe will be as painful as they are inevitable. The collapse of the economic infrastructure of the EU will cause real chaos and genuine financial hardship for millions. Fortunes will be lost and State benefits and pensions will be dramatically reduced – they may disappear completely.

The pain which will accompany this massive swing to the right will be more palatable if we are outside the EU when the move takes place.

The europhiles will deny this but neither the EU nor the euro have a future.

The idea of Europe surviving as a superstate may be fine in theory but in practice it just won't work. And when the European superstate collapses the fallout will be considerable. France and Germany will, as always, look after themselves. The other countries in the EU will be badly damaged for decades. The economic problems caused by the collapse of the euro will lead to crisis after crisis in many European countries.

Those who claim that it is impossible for the EU to collapse should look around.

For years the trend outside the EU has been towards the localisation of power and resources. The USSR and Yugoslavia have split up. Canada may break up. And even the American States don't seem quite as United as they once were: Hawaii is on the verge of becoming independent again and Texas is considering leaving the Union.

Even within the EU there has been pressure for the break-up of some countries and for the formation of smaller states. Andorra has become independent (with a population of 58,000). In Spain the Basques want independence. Germany and Belgium have both given more power to regions. In France, there has been a powerful movement towards dividing the nation.

Tomorrow's Europe will be broken up into scores, maybe hundreds, of much smaller, independent regions – linking together very loosely for defence and trade. The citizens of all these small countries will be much better off – and much more capable of controlling their own destinies – when political power is in the hands of local or regional politicians who are accountable to the electors.

18

Global Warming and the EU And The Stupidity Of The Carbon-offsets Programme and the Biofuels Directive

The EU has stated that 5.75 per cent of transport fuel must be biofuel by the end of 2008 and that a fifth of all energy must be 'green' by 2020. The targets are as absurd as they are arbitrary.

We must, say the eurocrats, have green fuel, green cars, green rubbish collections, green homes, green factories and green aeroplanes. The EU even says that we must soon generate 20% of our electricity from renewable sources. (It is this nonsensical policy which will result in our countryside being covered with wind turbines.)

Naturally, in order to ensure that their goal is reached, the EU is subsidising the growing of biofuels. This makes global warming worse, results in a lot of people starving to death and makes big money for a few people. So, for example, in February 2008 a major global agricultural conglomerate, which is involved in growing crops for biofuel, reported that its annual profit rose by 75% in the last year. Oh goody, that's why we pay so much for membership of the EU.

It isn't just the eurocrats whose efforts are laughably inept. In an attempt to ensure that the 'go green' targets are met, some local councils in Britain are now insisting that households have green wheelie bins as well as the old-fashioned black ones. Perhaps they think that these new green bins will save the planet. I don't really want to know how much more energy it takes to make green wheelie bins than to make black ones, or the number of households which now have two bins (where before the new 'green regulations' they had only one).

The organisation Ofgem, which regulates gas and electricity markets in the UK (or, at least, does so at the moment though I have no doubt that the EU will replace it with one of its own trans-EU organisations soon) has said that the European Union's various 'energy' schemes have already added 6% to the average energy bill in Britain.

★★★

The European Commission, father and mother of the straight banana and the perfect cucumber, and a safe but wildly overpaid working environment for many of the world's most blindingly stupid bureaucrats, has called for biofuels to replace 10% of all petrol by the year 2020.

To reach its target, 25% of all European arable land will be turned over to ethanol production.

The consequences of this madness are seemingly unending.

Farmers who used to grow soybeans are now growing corn because they can either sell it as food or sell it to the oil companies to mix in with their petrol. Rapeseed crops are now seen everywhere in Europe as farmers abandon growing barley and wheat. (The disappearance of barley is, of course, a reason why beer prices are rising. And will continue to rise.)

I wonder how many farmers know (or care) that rapeseed oil produces lots of nitrous oxide gas – which creates even more global warming than carbon dioxide? I wonder how many eurocrats know that you can't send ethanol along the usual gasoline pipelines because it is corrosive and picks up impurities? (Don't ask what it does to petrol tanks.) But I'm prepared to hazard a guess that not many know that this means the darned stuff has to be transported in tanks by rail. And that means building more suitable containers and more trains. The energy cost of all this construction is phenomenal. And then, of course, energy is required to move the train from one place to another. To accurately assess the energy value of biofuels we need to consider a whole raft of extra costs – including the cost of growing the food to feed the farm workers growing the biofuel.

Those who believe that ethanol offers answers to all our problems are magnificently, technicolour stupid. Those who believe that ethanol offers any answers to some of our problems are just plain stupid.

The lunatic belief in ethanol has increased the price of food around the world and is boosting the price of farmland. The makers of Italian pasta, Mexican tortillas, American corned beef and German beer have all warned that the price of their products will have to rocket. Food conglomerates have issued a series of profit warnings. The ethanol promoters don't seem to care, but their bright new idea will result in a massive increase in worldwide starvation. Forty per cent of the population in Swaziland are starving as I write and yet their Government is allowing agricultural land to be used to grow enormously profitable biofuels.

The pro-ethanol strategy (as they like to think of it) is eye wateringly wasteful. It's so stupid that it's difficult to say how stupid it is. But I will try.

It's like trying to replace the world's shrinking glaciers by making ice cubes in a series of refrigerators, carting the ice cubes by lorry to the site of the shrunken glaciers, and then hoping that the ice cubes will repair the damage.

★★★

Here are several good reasons why biofuels won't work.

First, Creating ethanol from corn will use up vast amounts of our corn supply. The corn needed for one tankful of ethanol could feed one person for a year. In Iowa in the USA, 25 ethanol plants are now operating, and 30 being built or planned. Once built, these plants will consume half the State's crop of corn. The prices for sugar, corn and wheat are rising because we are using these foodstuffs for fuel. A huge chunk of world grain consumption is now going into American petrol tanks. (At a time, it should be noted, when America has already become a net importer of food.) This will result in greater starvation in a world where there is a continuing and (because of global warming) developing food shortage. The global lack of fresh water (caused by the increase in the number of bathrooms being built, the increase in the number of people on the planet, the increasing demands of providing water for increasing numbers of cattle, the increasing pollution of our water supplies and global warming) will make growing crops even more difficult. And will also result in higher prices for basic foodstuffs.

Using rapeseed and sugar beet instead of corn doesn't help because (and this will doubtless come as something of a surprise to politicians and bureaucrats) you still need land to grow rapeseed and sugar beet.

And when you've grown the stuff you still need to use lots of energy to harvest it, transport it and turn it into ethanol. (The dullards at the European Commission probably imagine that you plant some sugar beet seeds and wait for a nice neat row of petrol pumps to pop up a few weeks later.)

Second, it costs more in terms of energy to get the fuel than it delivers. There are energy costs in building and running tractors, and moving the corn around. You have to include the energy needed to plant the corn, water it, harvest it and turn into alcohol. Oil is needed to make the fertilisers and pesticides the farmers use.

Numerous experts have shown that producing ethanol actually costs energy. According to David Pimentel, a professor of ecology and agricultural science at Cornell University in the USA, 129,600 British thermal units of energy are used to produce one gallon of ethanol. And one gallon of ethanol provides just 76,000 Btu of energy.

Another expert has worked out that around 131,000 BTUs are needed to make a gallon of ethanol but that gallon will only produce 77,000 BTU.

These figures mean a loss of over 50,000 BTU for every gallon of ethanol produced.

The most important thing to remember about fuels is the energy output to energy input ratio. This measures the amount of work you have to do in order to obtain the fuel. The energy output to input ratio for oil is magnificent. It varies between 30 to 1 and 200 to 1 depending on where the oil is. If it's easy to get at then the ratio is probably closer to 200 to 1. Ethanol is very different. It depends on plants which have to be grown afresh every year. To grow plants to turn into ethanol you have to plant seeds, harvest the crop, take the crop to the refinery and then start work on it. You need a tractor to plant the seed, a tractor to harvest the crop and a lorry to take the crop to the refinery. It takes fuel to create the fuel. Oh, and then there's the fertiliser, the herbicide and the pesticide the farmer uses. Where do those come from? Oil. I repeat: to obtain ethanol we have to use up energy to make energy. We get less out than we put in.

Third, burning plant-based ethanol still contributes to global warming. Almost all biofuels cause more greenhouse gas emissions than conventional fuels if the pollution caused by producing these so-called 'green' fuels is taken into account (which it obviously has to be). In February 2008, two studies published in the journal *Science* took a broad look at the effect of converting huge amounts of land to grow biofuels. Scientists concluded that destroying natural ecosystems – whether they are rain forests in the tropics or grasslands in South America – increases the release of greenhouse gases into the atmosphere because the ecosystems are the planet's natural way of dealing with carbon emissions. Plant-based fuels were originally claimed to be better than fossil fuels because the carbon released when they are burned is balanced by the carbon absorbed when the plants grow. But even that was simplistic and wrong. The process of turning plants into fuel causes its own emissions because biofuels have to be refined and transported before they can be used.

The reports in *Science* showed that the clearance of grassland releases 93 times the amount of greenhouse gas that would be saved by the fuel made annually on that land. The scientists concluded that it doesn't really matter if you clear rainforest or scrubland – you are making things worse. In its usual pitiful way the EU has attempted to deal with this problem by proposing regulations stipulating that imported biofuels cannot come from land that was previously rainforest.

Brilliant.

What the eurocrats obviously didn't work out is that when the EU buys biofuels which have been grown on ordinary farmland, the price of food prices will rocket and so rainforest will be cleared to grow food.

Even if the EU gets really clever and insists that Europeans can only buy food that has been grown on ordinary farmland, the situation won't be helped one little bit because rainforest will still have to be cleared so that people in Third World countries can have a little something to eat occasionally.

The stupidity of eurocrats sometimes leaves me open-mouthed with amazement.

Fourth, pollution from ethanol could create worse health hazards than gasoline – especially for sufferers from respiratory diseases such as asthma. Ethanol-burning cars increase the level of toxic ozone gas in the environment. This will mean that the atmosphere will become much more dangerous. Pollution from ethanol is more dangerous than petrol because when it breaks down in the atmosphere, it produces considerably far more ozone than petrol does. Ozone is corrosive and damages the lungs. (Ozone is so corrosive it can crack rubber and destroy stone statues). Other substances released from use of ethanol as fuel include benzene, butadene, formaldehyde and acetaldehyde. All these are carcinogens.

Fifth, the search for so-called green fuels, with which we can all prevent climate change and save the environment, is resulting in some strangely destructive behaviour. So, for example, the rising demand for palm oil (an ingredient in biodiesel) has led to tropical forests being cleared in vast areas of South East Asia. People are now chopping down hardwood forests in Asia in order to grow palm oil to take to the USA for the biodiesel industry. This is being done in order to keep petrol prices down so that Americans don't have to change their way of life. The end result, of course, is the speeding up of global warming.

Encouragement (and subsidies) from the USA and the European Union means that farmers all around the world are now creating more farmland on which to grow sugar beet and rapeseed and corn. Higher prices for their produce means that there is an incentive to clear land and plant crops.

That surely cannot be a bad thing, say the empty-skulled bureaucrats in Brussels.

Oh dear.

It is.

Because, in order to obtain fresh farmland, the farmers of Brazil and Asia are chopping down vast tracts of rainforest. This, surprisingly enough, means less rainforest.

And, in turn, means that there are fewer trees to get rid of all the carbon dioxide being produced by the tractors and lorries used by the farmers planting the corn, the sugar beet and the rapeseed.

Clearing rainforests to increase the land available for the cultivation of palm oil is bringing ecological disaster for countries such as Indonesia and Malaysia. And it is adding to the global warming problem. Indonesia, a key palm oil producer, now has the worst carbon emissions level per head of population thanks to the fact that forests have been cut down to make room for palm oil production.

The United Nations has predicted that the natural rainforest of Indonesia will have disappeared in just 15 years time, because of the planting of palm oil to turn into biodiesel so that Europeans (and Americans) can keep on driving their motorcars and taking long flights. Plantations of oil palms for biodiesel have been held responsible for 87% of deforestation in Malaysia. The oh so bloody goody goody fuel planters are ploughing up the planet. As I write, their bulldozers are busy in Africa and South America as well as Asia. The environmental damage seems endless. Sugar cane being grown in huge amounts degrades soils, causes pollution when fields are burnt to get rid of stubble, and destroys wildlife.

The United Nations has also reported that biofuels use up vast amounts of water (a commodity that is becoming increasingly scarce). And monocropping (growing the same crop year after year) increases pests and has a negative impact on soil quality.

The bottom line is that bioethanol and biodiesel are a huge scam which will increase not reduce greenhouse gas emissions. Indeed, biofuels may well be the final nail in the planet's coffin.

It's about time the self-righteous nonsense preached about ethanol was put to rest. There is nothing remotely green about biofuels such as ethanol. It is a grotesque myth that biofuels are carbon neutral and will help with the oil shortage.

Biofuels are promoted as planet friendly. But ethanol (from corn or sugar cane) and biodiesel (made from soybean or palm oil) are no answer to any of our problems. The only people benefiting are the motorists who are able to keep driving their cars, the governments who are able to keep collecting the taxes raised on those fuels and the corporations growing and selling the crops which are being used to make biofuels.

The only good thing to come out of all this is that OPEC has threatened to cut oil production if the West continues to use more ethanol. This will increase oil prices but it may help ensure that the oil lasts a year or two longer. Anyone who thinks that biofuels are an answer to our problems is certifiable. The American Government and the EU are spending billions of taxpayers' dollars and euros subsidising the biofuel industry. And yet the OECD has calculated that it would take 70% of all Europe's farmland to supply enough biofuels to save 10% of the oil currently used in transport.

Will anyone take any notice of all these truths? Will the EU and the Americans stop their mad race to replace oil with biofuel?

Of course not.

For one thing the American and European farming lobbies are far too powerful to be ignored. And they are enjoying massive profits from the biofuel boom.

And for another the Americans are desperate to weaken the economies of oil-rich countries such as Iran, Russia and Venezuela.

★★★

The EU Commission's absurd proposal that biofuels should account for 10% of road transport fuels may please the farming lobby but it has been questioned by many experts – including by the Commission's own in-house science institute.

A London based economic consultancy, Europe Economics, has argued that biofuel targets amount to a 'form of state support for an environmentally and economically harmful activity designed to consolidate existing price support mechanisms for vested interest groups, mostly farmers'.

The economists say the target would lead to annual subsidies to the biofuels industry of £8.2 billion and possibly as much as £17 billion by 2020. This compares with the £30 billion spent each year on the EU's Common Agricultural Policy.

'It is clear that a European biofuel industry cannot be viable without political support by means of tariffs and a very high level of subsidy,' say the economists, whose study was commissioned by Open Europe, a UK think-tank campaigning for a loosely structured, economically liberal EU.

★★★

Then there are the EU's new light bulbs.

In another of its crazy attempts to 'save the planet' and prove itself to be stuffed full of environmentally-conscious bureaucrats and politicians, the EU has decided to ban the sale of traditional incandescent light bulbs – the ones which have the tungsten filaments which dangle uselessly when the bulb has blown (or been dropped). Banning our old-fashioned light bulbs will, they seem to think, help stamp out global warming and save the planet. We will be forced to replace our old-fashioned light bulbs with new compact fluorescent bulbs (known as CFLs to the average acronym-happy eurocrat). These, they claim, use only a fifth of the energy needed by the shortly-to-be-made-illegal bulbs.

There are, inevitably, a few problems.

First, according to the UK's Government, the immediate cost to the UK alone of this latest absurdity is likely to be around £3 billion.

Second, the lighting produced by the new bulbs will be so dim that most people won't be able to read by them. Angela Merkel, the German politician who put forward the proposal that we should all use these new bulbs has admitted that because the 'energy-saving' bulbs she uses in her flat take some time to warm up she often has 'a bit of a problem' when she is looking for something she has 'dropped on the carpet'. The result will be lots more people falling over and breaking limbs and lots more people suffering from headaches. The consequence will be that many people will simply buy more lamps and use two or three bulbs where they previously used one bulb.

Third, the new bulbs must be kept switched on for far longer if they are to run efficiently. That means using up more energy.

Fourth, the new bulbs are much heavier than old-fashioned bulbs. This means that they will take more energy to transport. Lorries carrying them around the EU will use up more petrol.

Fifth, the new bulbs are much larger than the old ones. They will take up more storage space.

Sixth, they cost up to 20 times as much as the old bulbs. Vastly overpaid eurocrats probably won't care. Ordinary people will notice a huge rise in the cost of their bulbs bill.

Seventh, the CFL lightbulbs produce a much harsher, less relaxing light. Moreover, they often don't produce a nice, steady light (like an incandescent bulb) but flicker. They flicker at 50 times a second. If you try to read with one of the new bulbs there is a chance that your head will start to swim. Will the new bulbs trigger fits? I have no idea but I wouldn't bet against it. They will, at least, cause 'discomfort'. It seems pretty certain that the new EU-approved bulbs will cause migraines and dizziness.

Eighth, because they flicker, the new bulbs can make fast moving machine parts look stationary. How many limbs will be lost as a result of this? Your guess is as good as mine, and since I'm a qualified doctor my guess is probably as good as any guess made by an EU eurocrat.

Ninth, normal CFLs cannot be used with dimmer switches or electronically triggered security lights. Dimmer switches and electronically triggered security lights will have to be thrown away – wasting vast amounts of energy.

Tenth, the EU-approved bulbs cannot be used in ovens, freezers or microwave ovens because they don't work if the temperature is too low or too high. So, no more bulbs in ovens, freezers or microwave ovens.

Eleventh, the new allegedly low energy bulbs take ten times as much energy to manufacture as the old bulbs. You, unlike the eurocrats, may consider this rather significant.

Twelfth, according to the British Government, less than half of all the light fittings currently installed in British homes will take CFLs. So 24 million homeowners will, between them, have to throw out hundreds of millions of light fittings. The redundant light fittings will, of course, have to be replaced with new light fittings.

Thirteenth, CFLs need more ventilation than standard bulbs and so cannot be used in any enclosed light fitting.

Fourteenth, the EU approved light bulbs use toxic materials including mercury vapour. This is a bit of a problem because the EU has banned products containing mercury vapour from landfill sites. Used CFLs will, therefore, have to be collected and disposed of separately. Experts advise that you telephone your local sanitation or refuse department if you wish to dispose of a used CFL bulb. The British Government has admitted that the bulbs contain mercury which is a deadly poison and has warned: 'If a low-energy bulb is smashed, the room needs to be vacated for at least 15 minutes. A vacuum cleaner should not be used to clear up the debris, and care taken not to inhale the dust. Use rubber gloves, and put the broken bulb into a sealed plastic bag, which should be taken to the local council for disposal. Unbroken used bulbs can be taken back to the retailer if the owner is a member of the Distributor Takeback Scheme. Otherwise, many local waste disposal sites now have the facilities to safely collect and dispose of old bulbs. But, this advice is not printed on the packaging.' You will, of course, probably have to drive to the disposal site (which will take up fuel and energy as well as time). You will have to do this every time a bulb is broken. There will almost certainly be a disposal charge because getting rid of dangerous light bulbs without being able to bury them will be quite a problem. The EU will doubtless look into this problem at some time in the future.

Fifteenth, the more CFLs are turned on and off the shorter their life will be. To work at their best, CFLs must be kept on pretty well continuously. This means that if you are going to get the best out of your new EU-approved light bulb you will have to get used to sleeping with the light on. (If you don't keep your CFLs turned on permanently your very expensive light bulbs will need replacing very often and the energy they use will be pretty much the same as the energy used by an incandescent light bulb.)

Sixteenth, the new light bulbs which the EU is forcing us to use will aggravate a variety of health problems. Patients with lupus, an auto-immune disease, will suffer from many symptoms, including pain. Patients with light sensitive disorders will suffer more. The new bulbs could trigger eczema-like skin reactions and could produce skin reactions that lead to cancer.

Seventeenth, some CFLs need breaking in for about 100 hours before their brightness level stabilises. So, every time you instal a new bulb you may have to put up with potentially serious health problems (headaches, tripping over) for 100 hours or so.

Eighteenth, CFL bulbs may interfere with the remote control for your television or other equipment – and may cause static noises on your radio or cordless telephone. One expert advises that if this happens you should switch off the light. Another has found that a cardboard tube fashioned from an old lavatory roll centre and glued onto the relevant, sensitive part of the television will minimise or eradicate the problem. (I do not recommend that you try this at home. Electrical appliances get hot. Bits of cardboard tend to be flammable.)

The EU prefers to ignore this extraordinarily damning list of drawbacks and to consider its new legislation a really good idea. The British Government, loyal and stupid as ever, plans to have all traditional bulbs replaced by the new, more dangerous ones by 2011. Other countries will doubtless take a rather more leisurely approach to this particular legislation.

Of course, people will find ways to get round the EU's new nonsense. When I visited a local store to buy a couple of old-fashioned bulbs the other day the assistant told me that they'd run out. 'People have heard of this daft new EU law,' he told me with a shrug of indifference. 'Bulbs don't go off so a lot of my customers are stock-piling the old ones that are due to be banned. I don't suppose anyone will ever know unless the EU gets round to sending inspectors round to people's homes.' He thought for a moment. 'Come to think of it,' he added, 'it wouldn't surprise me if they did do that.'

★★★

When politicians fly off on their latest freebie holiday they respond to critics (who want to know why they are polluting the environment and adding to global warming, instead of staying in a tent in Cornwall) by claiming that they have purchased 'carbon offsets' to balance their carbon 'footprints'.

In 2007, the British Government said that everyone should have their own carbon swipe cards forcing them to take more care of the environment. (This will presumably not apply to Government departments. Figures from the Sustainable Development Commission show that the emissions produced by Government departments are rising dramatically.)

Al Gore uses the 'carbon offset' excuse as he flies around the world promoting the film which explains why people who spend all their time flying around the planet are destroying the planet. When Gore found himself under fire for using 20 times as much electricity in his Nashville mansion as the average American, he defended himself with the same argument. He claimed he offset all his carbon dioxide emissions by buying green credits.

Public figures all like to portray themselves as 'green' and 'environmentally aware'. When asked about the fact that he has three Hummer vehicles the Governor of California, Arnold Schwarzenegger, announced that two of the vehicles had been converted to take ethanol. Managing to say this with a straight face must have required more acting skills than I realised he had.

And how does all this fit in with other Government policies to close down 300 local schools and countless thousands of rural post offices? When village schools and post offices are closed the people living in those villages must spend huge amounts of time, money and energy driving into town. When rural schools are shut children have to be taken into town every morning and taken home again every evening. When post offices are shut, villagers must drive into town to buy a stamp, post a parcel or collect a pension. The cost in energy terms is vast.

You will not be surprised to hear that the whole daft business of trading carbon emissions is an EU project. Offsetting carbon emissions is a sick joke; a perfect example of hypocrisy. What is the point? Surely we should be reducing emissions?

Politicians and millionaire pop stars buy carbon emission offsets in order to 'balance' their flying around the world in private planes.

But this doesn't help the planet at all.

Carbon trading is practical hypocrisy.

No wonder the EU is an enthusiastic supporter.

It will by now come as no surprise to you that the European Union, has, set up its own carbon trading programme. The EU's programme is called the Emissions Trading Scheme and, as you might expect, the European Union's scheme is of no benefit to the environment, the planet or you and me. As you might equally expect it is, on the other hand, of enormous benefit to the large companies which are responsible for global warming.

Officially, the EU's carbon trading scheme was set up to encourage dirty power stations to switch to cleaner forms of energy. The British Government was, as it always is with anything which comes from Brussels, an enthusiastic supporter. Either because they are corrupt or amazingly stupid (or possibly both, of course) Britain's Government of war criminals made European carbon trading an integral part of their drive to reduce greenhouse gas emissions.

The two are not related, of course.

And in practice the scheme has allowed the dirtiest polluters, the companies really responsible for global warming, to push up their bills and increase their profits without lowering the level of their greenhouse gas emissions.

Even industry experts admit that the EU's carbon trading scheme has been a windfall which has allowed the big power companies to increase their profits by £1.5 billion a year. In January 2008, it was announced that, thanks to the EU's scheme, energy suppliers would be given a bonanza windfall of £9 billion.

You might have thought that if the EU really wanted to cut pollution, it would have introduced strict fines for companies which produce a lot of carbon dioxide. But the EU bureaucrats didn't want to do anything quite so logical, sensible, simple or effective.

The EU's scheme gives permits to major electricity producers and manufacturers, allowing them to produce a fixed amount of carbon dioxide every year.

Any company which reduces its allowed ration of pollution can sell its unused permit to pollute on the open market. A company which exceeds its allowed level of pollution must buy an extra permit to pollute.

Barmy?

Absolutely.

But it gets barmier.

You will not believe how barmy it gets.

Anyone with functioning brain tissue between their ears would have forced companies to buy their permits to pollute. This would have given them a real financial incentive to reduce their level of pollution.

But, oh no.

Not the EU.

The EU (supported and endorsed let me remind you by all three major political parties in Britain) succumbed to pressure from the polluters and handed out the permits free of charge.

In case you thought that might be a misprint I'll repeat it: the EU gave the power giants their permits (and the billion pound windfall payments) entirely free of charge.

Unbelievably, the EU actually gave free permits to pollute to some of Europe's largest companies.

What the witless idiots at the EU presumably hadn't realised was that the minute the big electricity producers had their permits, they would cut their output of electricity in order to reduce their level of pollutants. They would then be able to sell their spare polluting capacity to other companies. Having cut the amount of electricity they were producing the big electricity companies were then able to put up their prices.

Double whammy!

A bunch of the world's biggest polluters made extra money by charging more for their electricity. And they made extra money by selling off part of their permits to pollute. (Permits which, remember, the EU had given them free of charge.)

The result of the EU's policies will, according to the European Commission, mean that electricity prices will need to rise by 10% to 15% across Europe. The costs in the UK are likely to be much higher than that. And the capital commitment costs of meeting the EU's renewable energy targets are around £3,000 per household. (This, of course, has to be added to the fact that oil and other natural fuels are becoming more expensive as the stuff runs out.)

And, as if that wasn't enough, the EU policy on biofuels will drive food prices up even faster than they are already rising. It is estimated that the EU's biofuel policy will add £750 a year to the average family food bill.

So, that's how the EU is protecting the environment and preventing global warming and looking after its citizens.

More bureaucracy and higher bills.

★★★

Do carbon offsets really give politicians a good excuse for continuing to do whatever they like?

The idea of carbon offsets is that when you fly to Bermuda to stay in a pop star's home you invest in a project which either removes some carbon dioxide from the atmosphere or prevents some carbon dioxide being put into the atmosphere. There are now many small, and rapidly growing firms, offering a variety of such schemes (mainly, I suspect, to embarrassed politicians).

The British Government has announced that it is spending £3 million offsetting the environmental damage caused by the flights of Labour Ministers. (They have not explained why they didn't just keep them at home.)

Most of the people who 'offset' are air travellers.

This is probably because it's fairly easy to define the damage done by a flight and probably because it is a fairly inexpensive way to feel good about yourself.

The truth, however, is that flying is a relatively insignificant factor in the production of carbon dioxide in the United Kingdom – producing only 5.5% of the nation's carbon dioxide. However, the companies which sell carbon offsets have targeted people who fly because they're easy to isolate and easy to make guilty.

Do these schemes work? Are they really going to make a difference?

The answer, I fear, is a fairly loud 'No'.

Some projects (planting trees for example) would have taken place with or without someone paying a carbon offset 'guilt' fee. As far as the planet is concerned nothing whatsoever is gained by giving the tree planter an extra fee for the right to his 'carbon offset'. (There are persistent rumours that some unscrupulous individuals may sell the carbon value of their trees to numerous buyers.)

Since there is no register of who is paying for what it is perfectly possible that some slightly bent Arthur Daley character in some far off land could be selling and reselling the carbon offset value of the tree he planted many, many times.

No one knows.

Nor does anyone really know the damage done by a flight or the value of a tree.

When the magazine *Nature* asked four offset firms for the carbon dioxide emissions per person of a return London to Bangkok flight, they got four different answers – varying from 2.1 tons of carbon dioxide to 9.9 tons of carbon dioxide.

And, in practice, of course, the damage done per traveller depends on the number of people who were on the flight.

Fly by private jet and you are obviously doing far more damage than if you are crammed sardine-like into a charter flight.

Other projects which produce carbon offset brownie points (such as making biofuels) are at best worthless.

The other problem is that it is pretty well impossible to carbon offset all the terrible things we are doing.

To offset the UK's annual emissions total of carbon dioxide we would have to plant and maintain for ever a forest the size of Dorset. Every year. And whenever a tree was cut down another one would have to be planted.

The Labour Government claims that other solutions include paying for energy efficient wood burning stoves to be exported to Nicaragua. (How, pray, do they get there? By kite?), installing energy efficient light bulbs in Kazakhstan, refitting low-flow shower heads into showers and putting solar panels into houses.

Friends of the Earth is sceptical, pointing out that you might as well try 'stopping sea levels rising by drinking a glass of water'.

The bottom line is that buying carbon offsets is just an easy way for well off politicians to feel good about themselves without having to give up their freebie holidays abroad.

And, it's a great way for people to make money.

There are now a number of carbon trading companies which make a living out of acting as agents for the industry.

In practice, the whole scheme is a load of worthless and irrelevant baloney which isn't going to make a damn of difference to anything. It doesn't make any difference to carbon emissions, global warming or peak oil. The only beneficiary is the daft sod who wrote out a cheque so that he didn't have to sell the Hummer or cancel the holiday to the Seychelles.

It's all a bit like the system of 'indulgences' which was in vogue during medieval times. Sinners haggled with and then paid a corrupt priest a fee to absolve their sins.

Nothing changes.

Except that the planet is screwed.

And we did it.

The EU's carbon emissions trading scheme (ETS) has been severely criticised by economists who have pointed out that the most cost-effective way of reducing carbon emissions is to introduce an economy-wide carbon price and that the best way to do this would be to abandon ETS and to tax the consumption of primary fuels in proportion to their carbon content. That would, of course, be far too simple for the EU to consider.

Naturally, all this nonsense comes at a price.

The EU has admitted that their crackpot policies will cost every household in Europe an average of another £520 a year. 'But that's OK', said a spokesman spinning madly. 'It's just the cost of three tankfuls of petrol a year.' I don't know about you but I've yet to see a motorcar that takes £173 worth of petrol. But I expect eurocrats are used to driving round in very large, very expensive limousines.

Makes you feel warm inside doesn't it?

★★★

Carbon trading isn't the only daft energy policy the EU has devised.

Despite the fact that the experts agree that wind power and wave power are unlikely ever to contribute a noticeable amount of energy to our needs – and will be costly in both energy and economic terms – the EU has stated its enthusiasm for windmill generated electricity. (There's more about why alternative energy sources won't work in my book *Oil Apocalypse*). Naturally, the Labour Party is therefore also keen on wind power and has publicly expressed its determination to expand the number of wind farms in England.

But not always.

In December 2004, it was reported that Britain's then Prime Minister Tony Blair (now a keen EU supporter) had helped block plans to build a wind farm near his Sedgefield constituency home.

More than 3,100 homes would have been supplied with 'green' electricity if an energy company had been allowed to build four wind turbines a mile from Mr Blair's house.

But when the plans emerged, Mr and Mrs Blair used their not inconsiderable influence to support the opposition. The Sedgefield wind farm was rejected despite that fact that there had been 'strong professional recommendations in support of the project'.

★★★

As an aside, it isn't difficult to find examples of Government policies which make it clear that neither politicians nor civil servants take global warming (or energy conservation) very seriously.

My latest favourite example of this is a television advertisement which has been created on behalf of the Government. The advertisement shows a couple watching unhappily as their seemingly brand new car is crushed. This threatening and unhappy sight is accompanied by a voice-over telling us that if we don't pay our car tax the Government can crush our cars.

I couldn't believe this when I first heard it. But the advertisement has been repeated endlessly. A little research showed that the British Government is now crushing around 50,000 vehicles a year – and making a significant profit from selling the crushed vehicles as scrap. The official figure, provided by the Driver and Vehicle Licensing Agency, is that in 2007 the Labour Government crushed 46,126 vehicles, a rise of 34% over the 34,369 which were crushed in 2006. This is a huge rise over the 8,000 cars a year that were destroyed from 1997 to 2001. (The policy of crushing untaxed cars was first introduced by Tony Blair's Government in 1997. Naturally, the cars which are crushed are usually those belonging to poorer members of society who cannot afford high car taxes.)

Apart from its threatening nature the thing about this advert which astonished me is that the Government is boasting that it has the power to crush brand new cars if and when it wants to – and that it does! The DVLA even urges the public to shop offenders and to tip them off 'online, by telephone or by post'.

Just where, I wonder, does this fit into the policies of a Government allegedly campaigning to save energy and to prevent waste?

Does no one in Government know how much energy will be wasted in making and then crushing motorcars? Does no one in Government realise just how pointless, inappropriate and utterly reckless this is?

By all means confiscate cars if people don't, can't or won't pay their tax. It's a tough policy but most tax collecting is done in a pretty ruthless way. I have no real problem with the Government confiscating and selling cars (though it's probably a bit over the top if your cheque genuinely got lost in the post) but deliberately crushing cars in a fit of authoritarian pique seems a perfect illustration of the way our Government now behaves.

The message is clear.

'We can do what we like because we have all the power. And you can do nothing to stop us.'

Pure fascism.

★★★

The bottom line is that we really can blame the EU for climate change and all its awful consequences.

If there was ever any point to the EU it would have been to bring different countries together to deal with the climate change problem, and to bring pressure upon other countries around the world.

And, if the EU had been serious about dealing with climate change it would have run massive campaigns encouraging its citizens to become vegetarian (growing grain to feed animals to provide meat is a major cause of starvation in the Third World now that biofuels are being used to replace oil as a fuel) and it would have done its utmost to stop the unnecessary climate-damaging wars being fought by Britain. Such simple but positive actions would have done infinitely more good than forcing citizens to put biofuels into their petrol tanks.

But the bottom line is that the EU's efforts to deal with climate change have been negative.

It's difficult to believe but this huge, expensive and unalterably bureaucratic organisation has actually managed to make things worse.

19

The Failure Of The Media To Inform Us About The EU

'A really efficient totalitarian state would be one in which the all-powerful executive of political bosses and their army of managers control a servitude. To make them love it is the task assigned, in present day totalitarian states, to ministries of propaganda, newspaper editors and schoolteachers.'
ALDOUS HUXLEY

We have access to more information than any other generation. Ever. But the quality of the information, and its relevance to our needs, is of some considerable doubt. The only certainty is that a good deal of it has been deliberately distorted and manipulated and bears little resemblance to the truth. We are overladen with information about celebrities. Our news is served up in pre-digested bite-sized chunks which have had all the goodness removed from them.

This isn't a phenomenon which is unique to Britain. A survey conducted in the United States of America showed that over half of American citizens have no idea where Canada is situated. You can understand Americans not knowing where Europe or China can be found on a map but you'd think that a few more of them might be able to find Canada. A survey in Spain (conducted just before the Spanish voted overwhelmingly to accept the ill-fated EU constitution) showed that 88% of Spaniards admitted that they knew nothing or very little about the EU and had no idea what the constitution contained or what significance it had. That didn't stop them voting for it.

But it is a phenomenon which affects us too. I suspect that an honest and properly conducted survey would show that 99% of Britons have no idea how much the EU affects their lives and just how it was mis-sold to us.

This general ignorance about crucial issues is, of course, a fault of the media. It is no accident.

When debating the issue of vivisection many years ago (you can tell it was a long time ago because for a decade or so now vivisectors have refused to debate the issue with me in public) a leading supporter of animal experiments admitted that most animal experiments are misleading and provide false information if the results are extrapolated and applied to human patients. He admitted that he and his colleagues did not know which experiments might prove useful to doctors and which might be so misleading that they might actually be of negative benefit to doctors and patients.

I pointed out that if the experimenters themselves don't know which experiments are valid, and can be relied upon, then all experiments are useless. If you have 10 pieces of information and know that six of those pieces of information are inaccurate and that four are accurate – but don't know which six are bad and which four are good – then all 10 pieces of information are useless and aren't worth the effort of obtaining them.

The same is true of the information you obtain from newspapers, from television and from the radio.

So much of the information available to us is biased, prejudiced, bent and planted that it is nigh on impossible to determine which information is of value and which is not.

This is true of almost all so-called 'news' but it is particularly true of 'news' about the European Union.

Trying to find out what is going on in the EU (or trying to find out what the EU is doing and why) by reading the papers or watching television is like trying to tell the time by watching the second hand of a watch. It looks as if it should be useful and it keeps you busy. But, however long you spend on it, you will never be any closer to the truth. Television is particularly useless as a medium for providing news. One problem is that those who produce and present it are obsessed with making news 'fun' and 'sexy'. Another problem is that television news editors give priority to news items which can be illustrated with moving pictures. These two factors mean that the news agenda is decided not by which stories are truly important but by which stories can be illustrated – and illustrated well.

As a result, how much of the stuff in this book had you heard about on the TV or read about in your daily newspaper? Very little, I suspect. The big problem is that editors, producers and journalists rarely blame the European Union for things which are the fault of the European Union. The legislation which results in absurd politically-correct decisions dominating our lives comes from the EU. The legislation which results in nonsensical rules about the disposal of rubbish comes from the EU. The dramatic rise in drunkenness on our streets is the fault of the EU. The mass of anti-discrimination legislation which has done so much damage to small and large companies comes from the EU. Identity cards are being forced upon us because of the EU. But rarely, if ever, do journalists put the blame where it should lie. If more people knew the extent of the damage done to our lives by the EU then more people would want us to leave the EU.

And even when the EU is mentioned in news stories, the chances are that the information we are fed is 'spun' to favour the EU. As a general rule you can rely on the fact that any information about the EU which you obtain from a newspaper, a television station or a radio station is worthless. This is, in my view, particularly true of information provided by the BBC which is, as a purveyor of news, infinitely untrustworthy and infinitely unreliable. The BBC exists solely because it is supposed to be an independent source of news and information. Its supporters say that citizens in a democracy should pay the licence fee because of this. But the BBC is patently not an independent source of either news or information. On the contrary, on a number of crucial issues (including the EU) the BBC is a source only of biased news and prejudiced information. One of the BBC's main faults is that it never challenges (or allows anyone to challenge) the establishment-accepted 'wisdom' of the day as far as serious issues are concerned. You are unlikely to hear anyone on the BBC arguing that eating meat causes cancer (it does but this is a truth which upsets the farming lobby), that vivisection is scientifically unsound (it is but this is a truth which upsets the pharmaceutical industry) or that the EU is a fascist organisation (it is but this is a truth which upsets the EU). It is an outrage that citizens should be forced to pay for this propaganda machine even if they don't want to watch or listen to any of its programmes.

★★★

The English press has, by and large, remained pathetically and inexplicably loyal to the European Union. I don't think any newspaper has remained more absurdly loyal than the *Financial Times*. On the 3rd June 2005, the same week that the people of France and Holland had dramatically and clearly rejected the new EU constitution (and, indeed, made it clear that they didn't have much enthusiasm for the EU either) the *Financial Times* made an extraordinary attempt to defend the EU.

'...the EU has become a victim of its own success,' the newspaper argued. 'War has receded into the distant memory – in Western Europe at least – and means little to two generations. Meanwhile, the economic prosperity and comfortable lifestyles of Europe's social model, underpinned by the EU's single market, have already been banked by Europe's citizens.'

So, according to the *Financial Times*, the people of Europe rejected the EU's proposed constitution because the EU has been too successful.

Such ignorance almost beggar belief.

Does the *Financial Times* really not know that unemployment levels in Europe are now between 10% and 15% (in Britain they are lower only because the Government has fiddled the figures)? Does the *Financial Times* regard really the euro as a success? Does the *Financial Times* genuinely believe that the Common Agricultural Policy is successful and sensible? Does the *Financial Times* approve of the activities of the European Central Bank? Or does the *Financial Times* simply feel obliged (for some reason of which I am not aware) to support the EU and to search for explanations and excuses for its obvious unpopularity?

★★★

The EU hands out prizes to book authors and journalists. (You will probably not be surprised to hear that although I have written extensively about the EU there has never been any suggestion that any of my work might be rewarded by the EU.)

It does seem odd to me that journalists should be rewarded in this way – and then expect to continue to be trusted by their readers.

Would anyone trust a political journalist who received a special prize from the Labour Government for his or her work?

★★★

Anyone who relies on mainstream newspapers, television or radio for news about the EU will have a very superficial and one-sided view of what is going on. What masquerades as news is simply a mixture of lies, half truths, spin, counterspin and propaganda. The aim of the media today is to misinform, to manipulate and to make you afraid.

The strangest headline I've seen for many a year appeared in the *Daily Mail*. It was: 'Brown offers Britain a moral compass'

This is the same Gordon Brown who has impoverished millions of hardworking pensioners and who supported the illegal invasion of Iraq. The same Brown who described Blair as 'the most successful PM of all time'. The same Brown whom even Blair's wife is alleged to have called a liar.

'There is,' said the *Daily Mail*, 'a decency and integrity about Mr Brown that the *Mail* admires.'

★★★

Just in case the media doesn't behave properly, and in order to control the news about the EU, the EU commission has created an in-house news agency. The EU project 'Europe by Satellite' will provide pre-packaged news reports for television stations. Broadcasters will no longer have to pay for cameramen and reporters to provide news about the EU. The EU will provide television stations with pre-packaged news reports which can be presented as their own 'independent' bulletins.

★★★

In addition to his view about the size of a lie being important,

Hitler also believed that if a lie was repeated often enough it would, eventually, be confused with the truth by the greater part of the population.

★★★

'(People) more readily fall victims to the big lie than the small lie, since it would never come into their heads to fabricate colossal untruths, and they would not believe that others could have the impudence to distort the truth so infamously.'
ADOLF HITLER

★★★

Quite rightly, distrust of the press is becoming widespread. A major recent survey in the USA showed that 45% of Americans believe little or nothing that they read in newspapers. Twenty years ago only 16% of readers expressed such profound scepticism.

Apart from newsletters and small publishers there is no free press in America.

And with the exception of newsletters and small publishers there is no free press in Britain either.

In most countries where there is no free press it is because the government has used brute force to censor the media. Tyrants from the dusty depths of history right up to the Nazis and the communists knew the importance of controlling the press.

But things are different now.

The difference with the 21st century despots is that they know how to manipulate the media. Instead of dipping journalists in boiling tar, they hire tame journalists to spread their message. Labour's spin-doctors were, in a spiritual sense, fathered by Hitler and Goebbels.

Today, politicians may not own the media and they may no longer need to chop off the arms and heads of troublesome scribes, but they can control the media with ever-increasing subtlety. News used to be defined as information someone didn't want to see in print. These days the opposite, is true.

The result is that although we may seem to have a free press, we don't. And that's worse than having a despot who boils disobedient journalists in oil. What you read in your newspaper, and what you see on television and what you hear on the radio are, by and large, the accepted messages. People believe what they see and what they hear and what they read.

But today's journalists are muzzled not by the threat of violence but by the promise of wealth and fame and success. The statist elite of the EU and the Labour Government don't kill journalists – they buy them.

Today's journalists have given up their spirit in return for money, fame and honours. Journalists used to pride themselves on their freedom and independence. Today's journalists are too often servile, weak and greedy. They are also too easily bribed.

The people who should be protecting our freedom are helping our tyrannical rulers to take it from us. The rulers tell the journalists that what they are doing is 'inevitable' and 'necessary' and they talk of threats from terrorism and the need for progress.

Today's news journalists have no sense of history, no ability to think for themselves; they have become part of show business. They are not in the slightest bit interested in truth. They will blow whichever way the wind takes them.

Too many journalists and editors have chosen popularity with their bosses, gold and fame, above principle. They want to be 'in' with the 'in crowd', they want to be liked. They are sycophantic quislings not journalists. They grovel at the feet of third rate politicians and businessmen and they suppress the truth in return for an invitation to Chequers and a company car (preferably with chauffeur).

It is the role of journalists to harry, criticise and question politicians. Always. Whoever is in power. Journalists should never have friends among politicians and should never accept favours. It is as bad for a journalist to accept hospitality from a politician as it would be to accept a bribe from an industrialist.

Today journalists are regularly wined and dined by politicians (at taxpayers' expense).

Now, if any of those journalists had been writing a story, say, on the oil industry and had spent a weekend dining and wining at the expense of an oil company chief, do you not think there might have been raised eyebrows?

Journalists should avoid the hospitality of the people they are supposed to be investigating as determinedly as they should (but don't) refuse honours or awards or prizes. Any journalist who accepts a peerage, a knighthood or even an MBE has betrayed his readers. Dammit, journalists shouldn't even be on first name terms with the people they write or broadcast about. They shouldn't eat with them or drink with them.

Niccolo Machiavelli recommended that a prince could make someone a puppet by 'dignifying him, enriching him, binding him to himself by benefits, and sharing with him the honours... of the State.'

What all this means is that those who rely upon the press and upon TV and radio for their news, and for an interpretation of the news, will be unable to see what is happening or form useful judgements.

You cannot possibly rely upon your daily newspaper or news programme for anything approaching the truth about the EU. Indeed, I would go further. Every time you read an article about the EU in a national newspaper you should assume that the writer is lying. And every time you listen to a programme about the EU on the BBC you should ask yourself not whether the broadcaster is telling the truth but why he is lying.

★★★

I used to work for the BBC regularly – presenting programmes on both radio and television. But I don't get invited to appear on the BBC these days. Review copies of my books are sent to programme editors and presenters but, on the whole, we would get as much response if we sent copies to the Man in the Moon. When representatives of the BBC do ring up it is usually to invite me to appear on something in which I have absolutely no interest and which is unlikely to give me any opportunity to embarrass any part of the official establishment. The last time the BBC called it was to offer me a fee of £2,000 to appear on a 'celebrity' issue of a BBC quiz programme. I doubt if I will be invited to discuss this book on any BBC programme.

I have never heard a BBC programme (on radio or television) which dealt with the EU fairly, or which treated English culture and traditions with respect. (Actually, although the BBC appears to me to loathe England and the English, the BBC doesn't seem to have much time for anything British. I imagine the EU was delighted when BBC Radio 4 axed its traditional early morning medley of patriotic songs including Rule Britannia, Men of Harlech and Scotland the Brave.) There is a BBC Scotland and there is a BBC Wales but there is not, never has been and is never likely to be a BBC England.

The BBC usually only gives airtime to politicians and other establishment figures and gives little (or preferably no) time to anyone threatening the establishment with contrary or original thoughts. The whole darned organisation spins more than a top.

I am not the only person to have noticed that the BBC takes an unusually partisan line on the EU. This pro-European bias has been evident to many listeners for many years and few people were surprised when, in June 2004, a study conducted by the Centre for Policy Studies revealed that the BBC gave twice as much coverage to pro-EU speakers as to eurosceptics. (I'd like to see, but am unlikely ever to obtain, a list of any direct and indirect grants and financial inducements the BBC has received from the European Union.)

Naturally, representatives of the BBC are invariably quick to defend their organisation. I suspect that some of them really believe that they are impartial and it is certainly a fact that they often fail to realise just how much their bias is showing. People who work for the BBC don't think of themselves as being part of the establishment (in fact many of them like to think of themselves as being rather radical) but with the possible exception of the British Medical Association I don't think I've ever known a more pro-establishment body than the BBC. The BBC has a hierarchy based on the civil service and certainly doesn't reflect the diversity of opinion in England. Very few BBC employees have ever experienced life in the free market (the ones who have, have usually failed).

The problem is that the BBC's internal environment, their in-house culture, is terribly biased towards Labour and all its best-established enthusiasms. Any honest broadcaster would have left the BBC in disgust years ago. The European Union is important to Labour and so it is important to the BBC too. (The BBC's uncomfortable, and for it rather embarrassing, position over the illegal invasion of Iraq was merely a reflection of the Labour Party's own internal schism.)

Most BBC staff members are recruited through advertisements which appear exclusively in left-wing pro-Labour newspapers such as *The Guardian* and the organisation grows and grooms its own managers instead of recruiting from outside. Inevitably, most of the people who work for the BBC are *Guardian* readers. There are uncomfortable and unacceptable links between BBC staff and the Labour Party.

Is it really surprising, therefore, that the BBC ends up supporting the EU and refusing to allow the critics of the EU fair access to its airtime? Is it surprising that BBC staff invariably seem frightened of producing anything likely to upset the establishment? Was it really surprising when one well-known presenter referred to the Labour Party as 'we'? Most BBC staff may not be stupid enough to endorse one party in public but they don't even realise that their prejudices are prejudices. They simply regard their views as 'right'.

The BBC organisation is plump, complacent and infinitely pro-establishment; full of people looking over their shoulders, terribly pleased with themselves and scared witless that their comfy sinecure may end. Is it any result that young BBC broadcasters do nothing original or daring or likely to upset any part of the establishment, unless it is acceptably original or daring (in which case, of course, it is neither) and unthreatening to the establishment within and without the BBC.

The ultimate insult, of course, is that it is impossible to listen to the radio or watch television in England without paying a hefty annual fee to the BBC. Where else in the world do the citizens have to pay to be indoctrinated? Does no one outside the BBC realise that any broadcaster which is totally dependent upon the establishment and the government of the day for its very existence must end up as no more than a tool for both.

Although the BBC gets its income from a tax on the public (whether they watch its programmes or not) the BBC is effectively a state-owned broadcaster. It certainly acts like one. No one with a brain would expect to turn on the BBC to listen to the news. The BBC is a good old-fashioned state broadcaster. It would have been comfortable operating in the USSR in the 1960s.

OFPIS

★★★

*'The most consistent and ultimately damaging failure of political journalism
in America has its roots in the clubby/cocktail personal relationships
that inevitably develop between politicians and journalists.
When professional antagonists become after-hours drinking buddies,
they are not likely to turn each other in.'*
HUNTER S. THOMPSON

★★★

It is widely believed that when the Labour Government's proposal for a regional assembly was rejected by voters in the North East of England in 2004, the whole idea of regional assemblies was abandoned.

'The deputy prime minister's big idea was shelved in 2004 after voters in the north-east decided four to one that they did not want an expensive talking shop,' wrote *The Economist* in July 2006.

I sent the following letter to the editor of *The Economist*.

'It is true that after the voters rejected John Prescott's proposal for elected assemblies the idea was shelved in 2004. But the English still have the unelected assemblies which existed before the idea of elected assemblies was rejected. Each region (including the North-East) has its own regional assembly crammed full of Tony's cronies. Naturally, the voters weren't given that as an option.'

The Economist did not publish my letter.

But the regional assemblies existed then and they exist today.

★★★

The British people have never been told the truth about the European Union. The people have never been given a chance to have their say about our membership of the EU.

If their role in our society is to share news and to spread the truth, editors and journalists have failed miserably.

I have no doubt that if these omissions were ever rectified the people's answer would be clearly and decisively in favour of leaving this wretched, harmful and doomed organisation.

Sadly, and to the shame of the media, when the EU collapses and we are eventually freed of it, journalists will not be able to claim any of the credit.

20

The Lisbon Treaty, The EU Constitution, The Queen, A Good Many Lies And The End Of Britain

In the summer of 2003, several huge polls showed that 90% of the British people wanted a referendum on the proposed new EU constitution. But the Prime Minister at the time, Tony Blair refused to give one, claiming that the constitution would make little difference to Britain or the British people.

He was pretty much alone in this claim. Senior politicians in France, Germany, Italy and Spain all agreed that the constitution involved the creation of a superstate and had huge implications for individual countries within the EU.

The new EU constitution was designed to make the EU a legal entity, with its own Foreign Minister and law that would take total precedence over UK law. The constitution which Blair claimed would make no real difference to the British people was designed to make the UK a series of provinces or regions within a superstate.

Those hoping that the Queen might stand firm and refuse to sign the papers assenting to the new constitution (which is effectively her own constitutional death warrant) were devastated when Buckingham Palace replied making it clear that the Queen would 'roll over' and surrender.

The Monarch has a right and a duty to advise, counsel and warn her Government. But, sadly, Queen Elizabeth II has said and done nothing to stop what is happening to her country. Despite receiving many letters from her subjects explaining how they believe they have been tricked and lied to by politicians, the Queen seems amazingly happy with the fact that England is about to disappear.

Here is the standard reply sent out by the Queen to those who write and complain about the rise of the EU and the disappearance of England.

Since the reply is a 'standard' rather than a personal letter (indeed, it is more of a statement than a letter) I do not feel that it is wrong to republish it here.

'The Queen has received your recent letter on membership of the European Union and a possible referendum on the proposed EU Constitutional Treaty. As Her Majesty receives many letters on this subject, it is not possible to send an individual reply to every one.'

'The Queen appreciates the thoughtfulness of correspondents who take the time to write and give her their views. Her Majesty follows, with interest, developments in the European Union and recognises that the United Kingdom's membership of the European Union is governed by treaties that were freely entered into, following all normal constitutional procedures.'

'Her Majesty does have prerogative and statutory powers. However, policy on the United Kingdom's membership of the European Union is entirely a matter for The Queen's Ministers. As such, Her Majesty's own powers are exercised, by convention, on and in accordance with advice from those Ministers. As part of this important constitutional convention it is customary for Her Majesty to grant Royal Assent to Bills duly passed by Government.'

'A copy of your letter is being forwarded to the Foreign and Commonwealth Office for the Attention of the Secretary of State for Foreign and Commonwealth Affairs.'

'By providing my Ministers with a full list of those who write to me to complain about the EU, I can help ensure that when the new Constitution has been ratified, armed members of Europol will come round to your house and drag you off to a maximum security re-education facility in Poland.'

OK I admit it. I made up the last paragraph. The rest is real.

How sad it is to have to report that it seems to me that the English people have been betrayed by Parliament, by Government and by their Monarch, Queen Elizabeth the Last.

I've always rather liked the Queen.

There used to be an old Act of Parliament which entitled her subjects to wander into Buckingham Palace to sign the visitors' book. When I was a kid I used to go there whenever I was in London. I'd totter up to the policeman on the gate, tell him I wanted to sign the visitors' book and saunter through, across the gravel. The tourists admiring the guardsmen (this was in the days when they were on the outside of the railings) would stare in awe. I mention this merely to show that I'm no anti-Royalist.

But I have to say that our Queen has let us all down rather badly. I've no doubt that she has been advised that it isn't her place to disagree with her Ministers. But the Queen will, I suspect, greatly regret her decision one day. By then it will be too late. Meanwhile she can, I suppose, console herself with her EU subsidies. In 2007, the Queen's Sandringham farms made £408,970 in subsidies from the EU's Common Agricultural Policy.

Compare the rather weedy way our Queen has responded to today's very real threat to our nation's independence and sovereignty and compare it with her namesake's response.

The piece below is the speech Elizabeth I made when addressing her troops who were, at the time, awaiting the arrival of the Spanish Armada in 1588. I think you'll agree that Elizabeth I showed a rather more feisty determination to defend her country than her namesake has exhibited.

'My loving people, we have been persuaded by some that are careful of our safety to take heed how we commit ourselves to armed multitudes for fear of treachery, but I assure you I do not desire to live to distrust my faithful and loving people. Let tyrants fear; I have always so behaved myself under God, I have placed my chiefest strength and safeguard in the loyal hearts and goodwill of my subjects. And therefore I am come amongst you, as you see, at this time not for my recreation and disport, but being resolved in the midst and heat of battle to live and die amongst you all. To lay down for God, my kingdom and for my people, my honour and my blood even in the dust. I know I have the body of a weak and feeble woman, but I have the heart and stomach of a King and a King of England too and think it foul scorn that Parma or Spain or any Prince of Europe should dare to invade the borders of my realm; to which, rather than any dishonour shall grow by me, I myself will take up arms, I myself will be your General, Judge and Rewarder of every one of your virtues in the field. I know already for your forwardness you have deserved rewards and crowns; and we do assure you, on the word of a Prince, they shall be duly paid you.'

★★★

Blair's refusal to allow a referendum on the EU constitution wasn't much of a surprise. EU politicians don't like giving voters a chance to air their views on the EU. The standard argument is that voters have a chance to air their views at the ballot box when selecting political representatives. Some EU supporters refuse to hold referendums on the grounds that Hitler gave the voters referendums. Quite why this makes referendums unacceptable it is difficult to see. Hitler also drove around in big cars but this doesn't seem to have stopped EU leaders from following his example.

In November 2007, new French President Nicolas Sarkozy stated that referendums on the EU constitution (which had by then been turned into the Lisbon Treaty) would be 'dangerous'. Sarkozy admitted that his fellow countrymen (whom he is paid to represent) would reject the new treaty if they had the chance. He also admitted that the constitution would be rejected in the UK if Britons had a chance to vote on it. 'A referendum now would bring Europe into danger,' he said. 'There will be no Treaty if we had a referendum in France, which would again be followed by a referendum in the UK.'

Sarkozy said the referendum would be rejected because there was a 'cleavage between the people and governments'.

Maybe someone needs to remind the arrogant Sarkozy that in democratic countries, governments are elected to serve the people, not to rule them.

Vernon Coleman

Meanwhile, it is, of course, a nonsense to say that European voters have any real choices. For years, none of the three main parties in England has offered any variety; all have supported the EU wholeheartedly. The same has been true for much of the rest of Europe. This isn't terribly surprising. The EU disapproves sternly of parties which oppose European integration. The EU spends vast amounts of taxpayers' money on making sure that the EU gets the results it wants.

And parties which disapprove of the EU will soon be illegal.

★★★

The new EU constitution was written by former French President and committed federalist, Giscard d'Estang. He was helped by a 12 member praesidium chosen by him and it was created without even a nod in the direction of democracy. The constitution means that Britain, hardly independent now, will cease to exist. Scotland and Wales and Northern Ireland will become regions of the EU. England will no longer be an independent country but will be broken up into a number of regions.

The new EU constitution creates a mega state and makes the two World Wars of the twentieth century a waste of time. What used to be Britain (but will become a collection of regions) will no longer have control over its own finance (and so the euro will be inevitable), foreign policy, taxation, defence, social security, criminal justice, immigration, asylum seekers, transport, communications, health, commercial policies and energy. The EU will control everything.

Was Blair lying when he said the new constitution was of no significance and didn't merit a referendum?

Or is he really that stupid?

It's impossible to say.

But it was widely suspected that Blair wouldn't have a referendum because he knew that if he did he would lose.

★★★

'Some committed Europhiles frankly acknowledge that, at times, they have deliberately disguised quite profound changes as mere technical adjustments to avoid causing popular alarm. Jean-Claude Juncker, the Prime Minister of Luxembourg and the EU's longest- serving head of government, explains:

OFPIS

'We decide on something, leave it lying around and wait and see what happens. If no one kicks up a fuss, because most people don't know what has been decided, we continue step by step until there is no turning back.'
THE ECONOMIST 25.9.04 (ALWAYS A STAUNCH SUPPORTER OF THE EU)

★★★

Prior to the General Election in May 2005, the British Government allocated £495,000 of taxpayers' money for a PR drive to promote the planned new EU constitution. (The same constitution that Blair said wasn't significant enough to merit a referendum.) Some of the money was allocated for signing up celebrities as 'champions of the EU Constitution'.

The European Commission funded a series of seminars, theatre activities, leafleting campaigns and 'celebration days' in schools, public libraries and local government buildings.

Vast amounts of public money were spent promoting the EU and the EU constitution.

Since then huge amounts of EU money have been directed to pro-EU organisations.

A team of accountants working for OFPIS recently concluded that the total amount of public money spent questioning the value of the EU and supporting organisations, think-tanks and publishers providing the public with honest information about the European Union project had, by early 2008, reached the staggering sum of 0 euros (£0 in real money).

★★★

Labour Minister Jack Straw claimed that Britain had won 'each and every one' of its negotiations over the EU constitution. He claimed that supporting the EU constitution was a sign of patriotism; guaranteeing liberty, prosperity and sovereignty.

The fact is that British ministers tabled 275 essential amendments to the EU constitution. They lost 248 of them.

★★★

Individual countries could not agree on what the planned new EU constitution did or did not say. British Ministers seemed to think it said one thing. Ministers of all other countries seemed to think it said something else. The British Government said that the constitution's new Charter of Fundamental Rights did not limit the rights of managers to sack workers. But the French and the Belgians said the charter of Fundamental Rights did limit the rights of managers to sack workers. The British Government said that the Constitution would end all speculation about a common EU tax.

'The Constitution shows that there are no plans for a common EU tax,' said the British Government.

This is not quite what the Belgian Government (and others) said. They said they believed that the EU was heading for a common tax.

On February 25th 2005, Germany's Foreign Minister confirmed that the new EU constitution was intended to create a United States of Europe. Hans Martin Bury said the treaty was the 'birth certificate' for a giant superstate, and a 'framework for an ever closer union'.

Two weeks earlier, English Foreign Minister Jack Straw had said that the treaty would bolster England's sovereign rights. The Labour Government claimed that the new EU constitution was merely a 'tidying up' exercise.

The EU constitution has been described as the 'birth certificate of the United States of Europe' by Hans Martin Bury, whose words should be taken seriously for he spoke as Germany's Europe minister. In sharp contrast to New Labour's claim that the EU constitution was just a tidying up exercise, Herr Bury said that the constitution was 'more than just a milestone'.

'It is...', he said, 'the framework for – as it says in the preamble – an ever closer union.'

In 2003, German Foreign Minister Joschka Fischer said that the new EU constitution was 'the most important treaty since the formation of the European Economic Community'.

The EU constitution was not about changing xenophobic European nations into a multicultural superstate (though that was part of it). It was about getting rid of free markets, small governments and freedom and replacing them (because they are seen by the EU federalists as 'messy' and 'inefficient') with a centralised, protectionist state managed by bureaucrats.

★★★

*'The EU constitution is 'an expression of Europe as a union of nation-states...
the rejection of Europe as a federal superstate'.'*
TONY BLAIR, WAR CRIMINAL AND FORMER PRIME MINISTER

*'Member States shall actively and unreservedly support the
European Union's foreign and security policy.'*
FROM THE EU CONSTITUTION

*'The Union shall have exclusive competence over...monetary policy,
commercial policy, Customs Union.'*
FROM THE EU CONSTITUTION

'EU law shall have primacy over the law of member States.'
FROM THE EU CONSTITUTION

*'This constitution marks a shift from a primarily economic Europe
to a political Europe.'*
JOSEP BORRELL, SPANISH PRESIDENT OF THE EUROPEAN PARLIAMENT

*'The EU constitution represents 'a great step forward for the EU to
become a true political union'.'*
JEAN-LUC DEHAENE, BELGIAN VICE-PRESIDENT OF THE CONVENTION
WHICH DRAFTED THE EU CONSTITUTION

★★★

During the campaign to persuade us of the value of the new
EU Constitution, the British Government fought constantly on
behalf of the EU (frequently supported with money provided by
the European Commission). The campaigning wasn't about truth
or fairness or providing information so that voters can make up
their own minds. The Government's campaigning was simply
about winning. And in order to win, the Labour Government was
prepared to lie. Here are some of the lies the Labour Government
told about the EU during the campaign to persuade us to accept
the EU constitution:

*1. Labour claimed that during the last 30 years we haven't lost any
power to Brussels.*

As lies go this one was about as big as the one told in 1975
when Britons were tricked into voting to stay in the Common
Market and were promised that 'no important new policy can be
decided in Brussels or anywhere else without the consent of an
English Minister.'

2. Labour claimed that the new EU constitution (the one the French and the Dutch rejected) would make Brussels more accountable to Sovereign parliaments.

Er, did I say the last lie was a big one? Wrong. Compared to this lie the last lie was a small one. This new constitution was designed to introduce a system enabling the European commission to ignore objections from the British Parliament completely.

3. Labour claimed that the new EU constitution 'literally limits the power of the EU'.

Another corker. They got more or less the right words. But they got them in the wrong order.

In fact, the new EU constitution 'literally gave the EU unlimited powers'. The constitution contained a general Flexibility Clause enabling the EU to adopt new powers not set out in the constitution whenever it wanted to.

It was a bit like signing a contract which allowed the other party to revise the clauses of the contract whenever it wanted to. And gave you no power whatsoever.

Actually, it wasn't a bit like that. It was exactly like that.

4. Labour claimed that the new EU constitution was a victory for Britain.

They say that all of the Labour Government's 'red lines' had been obeyed.

Well, that's not quite exactly true.

Actually, the Labour Government tabled a total of 275 amendments to the constitution and won 27 of them. That means that the Labour Government agreed to let the Brussels bureaucrats ignore 248 of their red lines.

Labour lost out on the creation of a European Mutual Defence Pact, the creation of a European Foreign Minister and a common foreign policy. They lost out on common asylum and immigration systems, a provision that Britain must give up her seat on the UN security council if the EU Foreign Minister wants it and the appointment of a new European Public Prosecutor.

That's six of the ones the British Government lost.

They lost another 242 of those.

5. Labour claimed that Britain had a veto and could, therefore, say 'no' to any EU development the Government didn't like.

I'm not sure whether that counts as a lie or a joke.

It's so far removed from the truth that calling it a lie is like describing the sea as wet. A bit too obvious.

We gave up our veto years ago. Various Prime Ministers gave away bits of our power and Tony Blair surrendered our veto in 66 areas in the two previous treaties he signed without a referendum.

6. Labour said that the new constitution would result in the EU handing back some of its power to England.

Er, oh no it won't. It doesn't say that.

At all.

Anywhere.

The EU bureaucrats will just get ever more powerful.

7. Labour said that being in the EU has made us more prosperous.

All together now.

'Oh, no it hasn't.'

The red tape pouring out of Brussels is destroying British industry.

The truth is that the EU (which allegedly champions free market reform) is obsessed with legislation. And the cost of this legislation to British industry is billions a month (pounds or euros) and is rising rapidly.

EU legislation is a major cause of the fact that British is now enjoying a record number of personal bankruptcies and bankruptcies among small companies.

★★★

When the new Iraqi constitution was being drawn up, Sir Kieran Prendergast, the UN's political affairs chief, was reported as saying that constitutions only work when there is a broad base of input and consultation.

How true.

What a pity the EU didn't follow this line of thought.

The EU constitution which Blair merrily signed in October

2004 was drawn up by a French aristocrat and a small, hand-picked team of people no-one (except perhaps their parents) had ever heard of.

★★★

It is now generally accepted by everyone (except Gordon Brown and the British Government) that the Treaty of Lisbon which Brown signed in December 2007, is the EU Constitution which the French people rejected in 2005, and which the British people were never allowed to vote on.

When he signed the EU Lisbon Treaty, on December 14th 2007, Britain's Scottish Prime Minister, Gordon Brown, claimed that he could break Labour's Manifesto pledge to hold a referendum on the EU Constitution because the new treaty was 'different' from the original.

The Foreign Secretary, David Miliband, went further. He claimed that the Treaty was 'completely different'.

On the other hand, Valery Giscard d'Estang, former French President and the architect of the EU Constitution, said that the substance of the Treaty that Brown signed was 'absolutely similar' to the original document. Giscard d'Estang should know. Mr d'Estang said that although the treaty was 'legally new' it was essentially the same as the old one.

When interviewed about the Lisbon Treaty, Valery Giscard d'Estang said: 'Let us be very precise about it. You know, the text in Lisbon was written in a different way than the text called Constitution for Europe. When we wrote it, the Constitution, we wrote it directly, article one, article two, article three and so on. What they did in Lisbon is a different work. They took our text, they started from our text and they tried to introduce the different articles or notions into the existing treaties. So of course the approach is materially and intellectually different...it's just another presentation and combination of presentation but the text is word to word the same one.'

In 2005, the Labour Manifesto pledged to put the EU constitution to a public vote – a referendum. Since the author of the Constitution (and other authorities within the EU) regard the two documents as identical for practical purposes (though they are presented in a different way and they have different titles) it was politically dishonest for Brown to say that a referendum wasn't necessary.

The Lisbon Treaty amends, rather than replaces, existing EU treaties. But, as *The Economist* agreed, 'the content is little different' and 'other European heads of government seem sure that the treaty is a constitution in all but name.'

The German Chancellor Angela Merkel said: 'The substance of the constitution is preserved. That is a fact.' The leaders of Spain, Ireland, Czechoslovakia and Luxembourg (for example) all acknowledged in public that the Treaty was substantially the same as the rejected Constitution.

MPs on the House of Commons EU Scrutiny Committee studied the Constitution and the Lisbon Treaty and concluded that only two of the 440 provisions differed substantially. (Of the two that differed, one related to the EU's flag and the other to the EU's anthem.)

And, in 2008, after the Lisbon Treaty had been signed, a report by the Labour dominated House of Commons foreign affairs select committee concluded that the Treaty had ceded vital powers to Brussels and that ministers were misleading the public by saying that it did not. The committee accused the Government of downplaying the importance of the provisions in the treaty and said: 'We conclude that there is no material difference between the provisions on foreign policy in the Constitutional Treaty which the Government made subject to approval in a referendum and those in the Lisbon Treaty on which a referendum is being denied.'

The committee said that the signing of the treaty was the culmination of a process which had 'little scope for UK public or parliamentary debate and engagement'.

★★★

There is no doubt that the Lisbon Treaty diluted (yet again) UK sovereignty.

The Lisbon Treaty formally gave the EU the characteristics that international law recognises as the usual attributes of statehood. Thanks to Gordon Brown and the other signatories, the EU now has a head of state, a foreign office, a criminal justice system and the right to sign international treaties.

The Treaty also gave the EU the authority to abolish any controls on individuals, whatever their nationality, when crossing internal borders. If 20 million Russians manage to enter the EU then the British Government will be powerless to stop them from entering Britain and staying there. The Labour Government, headed by a Scotsman, broke its promise to hold a referendum because it would have had to reveal just how much of our sovereignty had been ceded to Brussels and how much more it was giving away. Brown knew that if he had a referendum he – and the EU – would lose. And so, just as he had chickened out of holding an election in the autumn of 2007 because he had been frightened that he would lose, so he broke his promise about a referendum.

The new Treaty which Brown signed in December 2007 extended the powers of the EU in every conceivable direction. The treaty gave the EU 'primacy' over the laws of the member states, it gave the EU power over Britain's economic and employment policies (despite the fact that we are not in the euro) and it abolished national vetoes. The Treaty created a full European criminal justice system, with a European public prosecutor and an EU legal code. (The new EU legal codes run directly counter to our own common law traditions.). The treaty Brown signed gave the EU jurisdiction over transport, energy, public health, trade, employment, social policy, competition, agriculture, fisheries, defence, foreign affairs, space exploration, and asylum and immigration. The EU now has ownership and command of our police, army, Royal navy, RAF, currency reserves, North Sea oil and nuclear weapons. Serving officers in the forces will have to take an oath of allegiance to the EU instead of the Queen. It is now illegal to criticise the EU.

Oh, and the Lisbon Treaty gave the EU the right to make up any new laws it wants and to change the Treaty that Brown signed if it wants to do so. The Lisbon Treaty is 'self-amending'. It can be altered for any purpose, at any time. Neither you nor Gordon Brown can do anything about it.

On the day that the Lisbon Treaty was signed, the EU stopped being an association of states and became a State in its own right.

Gordon Brown is not just a moron; he is a bad, bad man. He

and the rest of the Labour Government should be thrown out of public life in disgrace.

★★★

The Lisbon Treaty created a permanent Presidency of the European Council. (The European Council is the rather expensive little get-together of European heads of government which meets every three months.) The idea behind creating a permanent Presidency was that this would get rid of the rotating Presidency whereby each of the member nations got to sit in the President's chair for six months at a time. But the idea of replacing the rotating Presidencies didn't prove too popular with politicians who saw their chance of being a rotating President slipping through their fingers. And so, the EU being what it is, they decided to have a new permanent President as well as the old rotating one. The new permanent President would chair the four annual meetings of the European Council and the rotating President would try to sit still long enough to chair the monthly ministerial meetings. But the more they thought about it, the small, select group who decide what happens within the EU decided that if they were going to double the number of jobs for the boys they might as well triple them while they were at it. And so they decided that a third Lord High Executioner, to be called the High Representative, would chair the monthly General Affairs Council of the EU and, at the same time, be Vice-President of the European Commission.

★★★

Heath, Thatcher, Major and Blair all gave away bits and pieces of our sovereignty. Heath, who was bribed to take Britain into the Common Market, and who brazenly lied about the consequences to the British people, will eventually be remembered as the worst traitor Britain has ever had. Margaret Thatcher, who had originally been an enthusiastic supporter of the EU, eventually came to realise just how much the voters had been deceived and tricked and just how dangerous the EU really was. In her last book she wrote that the attempt to create a European superstate would be seen in the future as having been 'the greatest folly of the modern era' and that for Britain to have become part of it would eventually be seen as 'a political error of the first magnitude'. By then, of course, it was too late. She was out of office and she'd signed the documents which had helped destroy the nation she'd been paid to lead. About Blair it is difficult to say anything. The man was, and is, beneath contempt. But Brown, the Scotsman, will be remembered as the man who plunged the knife into the still beating heart of the United Kingdom and finished the job that Heath had started. Tony Blair should be executed as a war criminal. Gordon Brown should be executed as a traitor. Thatcher and John Major may have been confused and ignorant. It is difficult to believe that Gordon Brown did not know what he was doing.

★★★

When he signed the Lisbon Treaty, Brown broke a solemn manifesto promise and denied the British people the right to decide their future.

He hinted that he might hold a general election shortly after the Labour Party appointed him Prime Minister (without any public approval) and that this would count as a referendum on the EU constitution treaty. But when it became clear that he would almost certainly lose he lost his nerve and changed his mind. No election and no referendum.

The whole history of our sordid relationship with the EU is littered with lies, broken promises and betrayals. Brown's was perhaps the most cynical betrayal of all.

The Lisbon Treaty, which Brown signed, handed over huge amounts of power to a bunch of unelected eurocrats, quangocrats and lawyers.

'The manifesto is what we put to the public. We've got to honour that manifesto. That is an issue of trust for me with the electorate,' said Gordon Brown in June 2007, shortly after he was appointed Prime Minister.

Six months later he broke that trust. He broke it because he knew that he would lose a referendum. And he put his loyalty to the EU above his loyalty to the British people who elected his party to power. He also put his loyalty to the EU above his own good reputation.

Oh, and there are a couple of other things.

As I've already pointed out, but will repeat because it is so important, the Lisbon Treaty gave the EU the right to add to its powers without further approval.

271

So there won't be any need for Gordon Brown (or any of his replacements) to sign any more Treaties. The EU now has 'self-amending' powers which mean that the EU can take whatever power it likes without having to ask member states for permission or authority.

And the Lisbon Treaty imposes a duty on member states to put their own national interests behind those of the EU.

When Brown finally asked MPs to approve the EU Treaty he had signed on the nation's behalf he asked them do so without even giving them a real chance to examine the Treaty.

Immediately before the crucial vote on the Treaty, it was revealed that only after the vote would MPs be able to read the full text of the Treaty. (Even then, the text would not be provided by the Government but by a private organisation.)

MPs were asked (or, perhaps the more appropriate word would be 'instructed') to give away the last vestige of our democracy without even being allowed to know precisely what they were giving away.

In a world where we are all warned against signing contracts and documents without reading the small print it seems utterly outrageous that our politicians should be prepared to sign away our freedom, our rights, our country, our culture, our heritage, our independence and our future without even bothering to demand a chance to read the relevant document.

★★★

The Lisbon Treaty purposes:
- Europe-wide taxes (probably on top of national taxes)
- Massive increases in workers' rights – even guaranteeing a job for life
- A Europe-wide minimum wage
- A common education curriculum throughout the EU (which must include pro-EU propaganda)
- A more powerful EU army
- The abolition of national sovereignty
- A huge rise in the EU budget
- Recognition that the new constitution is regarded as the first step towards political unity

I feel sure that the Labour Government meant to tell you about these things. Perhaps they just forgot.

The Lisbon Treaty is, according to EU insiders, the last EU treaty. It is the last EU treaty because it provides the EU with all the powers it will ever need.

Now that Gordon Brown has signed the Lisbon Treaty (the EU constitution which was rejected by the French and which would have been rejected by British voters if they'd had the chance) an EU foreign affairs spokesman will have the right to speak for Britain on the United Nations Security Council. A representative of the EU will state the position of the EU (and therefore Britain) at the United Nations.

An EU official put it quite clearly: 'We retain, except for the name of the minister, the Constitutional Treaty text of 2004 including the provisions on the UN. There is a provision which provides for the representative of the EU to state the position of the EU at the UN Security Council.'

★★★

The new EU Treaty, signed by Brown in Lisbon, gives the EU full control over Britain's immigration policy. The EU now allows asylum seekers the right to enter Britain and to claim full benefits. Moreover, the EU insists that migrants are free to enter the UK and that they must receive the same benefits as Britons. The EU now controls external borders to the EU and will take control of the UK's borders.

★★★

The three main political parties have betrayed the electorate. There was little or no public debate or discussion about the Lisbon Treaty. MPs should have been screaming in the streets. But the silence was numbing. And editors and journalists are just as guilty of betraying their reason for existence. Politicians, journalists and broadcasters all allowed our freedom to be handed over as though it was meaningless. Did they keep quiet because they think we are too stupid to care or because they fear that if we knew what was happening we would object? Do they not understand that when power is centralised it is the people who lose?

When the House of Commons first began to plan its debate

on the Lisbon Treaty, Gordon Brown wasn't even in the House of Commons for what was unarguably the most important debate in British history.

The original plan was that Parliament would have 20 to 25 days to debate the Treaty that Brown had signed. (Indeed, Brown had said that a referendum on the successor to the rejected EU Constitution was unnecessary because MPs would be given ample time to debate it in the House of Commons. Just after the text was agreed by EU leaders, Brown said he wanted the 'fullest possible parliamentary debate'.) But as it became clear that there was increasing discontent about the transfer of power to Europe (and that even Labour MPs who were keen supporters of the EU were feeling resentful about Brown's failure to uphold the pre-election promise the party had made) the Labour whips told MPs to expect just 12 days of Commons time to discuss the Treaty, with topics for each day's debate to be chosen by ministers – a trick apparently designed to avoid sensitive issues.

It's worth remembering, that during the 2005 general election the Government avoided any serious debate on the EU constitution by insisting that debate was unnecessary since the issue would be discussed fully during the referendum which was promised in its manifesto. So, the Labour Party has, at every possible opportunity, avoided debate and denied the British people any semblance of democracy. It is the standard EU story. The truth is suppressed, lies are told, promises are broken and the voters are denied any chance to have their say on the most important event in British history.

MPs debated the Government's plan to reduce the time available to debate Brown's betrayal, and to define the terms of the debate, on the 28th January 2008. The vote was taken at 10pm. It was, without a doubt, the single most important parliamentary vote in British or English history. It was the vote which allowed the Government to ensure that the British people never found out precisely how much they had been betrayed.

But it was nigh on impossible to discover the result of the vote. The BBC news programme I watched didn't mention it. The BBC's Ceefax didn't include the result of the vote on its list of the news stories. BBC News 24 seemed obsessed by President

Bush's State of the Union address in Washington. On its website the BBC's list of top stories included 'Man killed in row over football', 'Kennedy backs Obama', 'Diana feared Al Fayed bugging' and, top of the list, a 'Special report on Securitas robbery'.

In the end, I managed to find the result of the vote by searching the Internet. MPs had voted for the Government by 299 to 243.

Just 243 MPs realised the importance of this debate.

And, since there were 646 MPs in the House of Commons at the time, 104 didn't bother to turn up to vote. They had, presumably, found something more important to do.

★★★

In January 2008 it was revealed, in a confidential EU paper, that although Gordon Brown and other leaders had signed the Lisbon Treaty, the EU had not decided precisely what powers it would take.

'Much of the Lisbon Treaty is about giving the EU power to create new institutions and arrangements and to decide on how they will actually work in practice at a later date,' said Neil O'Brien of the think-tank Open Europe.

In other words, signing the treaty was the political equivalent of signing a blank cheque.

This isn't the first time signatories to an EU Treaty have signed a blank cheque. When the first Treaty of Rome was signed in 1958 by the leaders of Belgium, West Germany, France, Italy, Luxembourg and Netherlands, it consisted of a very impressive collection of blank pages. There was a frontispiece and a page for signatories. The rest was just plain paper.

★★★

When the House of Commons finally began to debate the Lisbon Treaty, the man who had signed it wasn't even in Europe. He was on a tour of the Far East. At the time when Parliament was starting the most important debate of Britain's history the Prime Minister had deliberately absented himself from the country. He had, according to *The Guardian* newspaper, timed his trip to show that 'the globe matters more than Europe'.

Despite the fact that 638 out of 646 MPs had been elected on the basis of a manifesto commitment to a referendum, two of the three main parties had retrospectively changed their minds. The Liberal Democrats had decided that Parliament was the proper place to consider such an important measure (rather than allowing 'ordinary' people to decide whether or not their country should be taken away from them) and the Labour Party were claiming that the text of the new treaty was different to the one that had been rejected by the French. (Some Labour MPs were claiming that they didn't agree with the idea of allowing the people to have a referendum anyway. The Foreign Secretary, David Miliband, apparently suggested that he never agreed with the Labour Party promising a referendum at the 2004 general election.)

To make sure that all Labour MPs voted for every aspect of the Treaty, the Government used daily three-line whips to keep members in line and even installed a text-messaging system to make sure that MPs could be summoned quickly to the chamber. Brown et al may have pretended that the Treaty wasn't terribly important, but their actions made it clear that they knew exactly how crucial the vote would be both for the nation and the future of the EU.

The suggestion that the Lisbon Treaty isn't the same as the rejected EU Constitution was, of course, just another Labour Party lie. Other European leaders had already admitted that it was the same in all but name.

Politicians had got Britain into the EU with a lie. And they were signing Britain's final death warrant with another lie.

The irony is that, in the end, this refusal to acknowledge democracy will provide us with an escape route. If Brown had organised and somehow managed to win a referendum (by, for example, dominating the media, submitting a loaded question or fixing the vote) he would have made it difficult for the silent majority to battle on. But by rejecting democracy and refusing to stick to his promise and have a referendum, Brown has made it much easier for us to continue to fight.

★★★

A postal ballot conducted and released in March 2008 and involving 152,520 people in 10 marginal constituencies in the UK, produced a result showing that 133,251 (88%) of the electors wanted a referendum on the EU's Lisbon Treaty.

Naturally, the Labour Government ignored this massive public vote and on Wednesday 5th March 2008 the House of Commons finally rejected calls for the referendum the Government had promised to the electors as part of its pre-election manifesto. MPs had denied voters a say on the treaty which will change Britain for ever.

It was, without a doubt, one of the most important events in Britain's history but most British newspapers didn't carry the news on their front pages. This vital and significant event was pushed aside by a variety of minor and ephemeral news stories.

'Everything seems to be following its usual course because even in terrible moments, when everything is at stake, people go on living as if nothing were happening.'
GOETHE

21

Why The EU Is Just Like The Old USSR

'All progress depends on the unreasonable man, since the reasonable man simply adapts himself to the world as it is.'
GEORGE BERNARD SHAW

Many people now believe that the EU is, in many critical ways, now indistinguishable from the old Soviet Union.

In a speech delivered at the House of Commons in 2002, Vladimir Bukovsky noted the following similarities between the old USSR and the EU.

1. Anyone who opposes or deviates from the socialist system will be ostracised. For example, when the Austrian people had the temerity to elect 'the wrong sort of Government' (it was considered too nationalistic and right wing by the EU) the EU pronounced the new Government unacceptable. With apparent magnanimity the EU announced that it would 'accept' an Italian President elected by the Italian people. All sorts of tricks are used to isolate and marginalise those who oppose the EU. Those questioning the EU are often portrayed as insular and parochial.

2. Like the USSR the EU is governed by a group of people who appoint one another, are unaccountable to the public, enjoy generous salaries, massive perks and huge pensions, are pretty much above the law and cannot be sacked. The EU, like any committed

socialist government, operates without any real feedback from the people, and certainly without any concern for what the people think. The State must always come first. The only people who benefit (as with all socialist and fascist organisations – and the two are, of course, interchangeable) are those who have put themselves and their friends in charge. The workers never really benefit from socialism. The profits of the hard-working, the creative and the thrifty are redistributed to the bureaucracy: the lazy, the unthinking and the wasteful.

The central planners (in the case of the USSR they were in Moscow, in the case of the EU they are in Brussels) insist on making all the judgements and decisions but their lack of experience means that they get everything wrong, so there are constant shortages and black markets.

State socialism in the EU has not led to affluence, equality and freedom but, effectively, to a one-party political system. (All three main parties in Britain support the EU and the destruction of Britain). The fascist EU has, inevitably, created a massive bureaucracy, heavy-handed secret police, government control of the media and endless secrecy and lies.

The socialist bureaucracy of the EU is run by people who arrogantly believe that they are the only ones who need to know and that they always know best.

3. There was one political party in the USSR (and no opposition) and the same is true of the EU. Political parties which don't support the EU are denied the oxygen of financial support. Politicians who do support the EU can look forward to good jobs (when they retire or get thrown out of domestic politics they may, like Neil Kinnock or Chris Patten, get jobs as EU commissioners). The system looks after its own. When the EU constitution was being debated the main sticking point among delegates was not the sovereignty of their individual nations, or the rights of the voters, but the number of delegates each country would be allowed to send to EU meetings. Each nation's individuality was pushed to one side as irrelevant and inconsequential, in favour of the rights of politicians to attend regular, all expenses-paid beanos.

4. Like the USSR, the EU was created with little or no respect for normal democratic principles. Much of what has happened within the EU has happened secretly and without the normal principles of democracy being considered or applied. What has happened over the last few decades has happened largely in secret.

5. Instead of information about the EU we have been fed a good deal of propaganda. The bureaucrats organise and control people and they try to control the availability of knowledge. The people are always controlled with lies and misinformation. (Today these are known as 'spin'.) Anyone who dares to oppose the EU or to promote England is likely to be described as a 'racist'. My book *England Our England* has proved enormously popular with readers (and was, within the first year, reprinted numerous times) but advertisements for the book were banned by a number of publications. Although the book is one of Britain's bestselling books on politics, it has never been reviewed in any national newspaper.

Very few Britons realise exactly what has already happened, how what has happened has already affected their lives and how things will now develop unless we do something very soon. A poll quietly taken for Britain's Foreign Office showed that a quarter of Britons did not know that their country was already a member of the EU. Astonishingly, 7% of Britons thought that the USA was a member. This ignorance isn't unique to Britain. A poll in Germany showed that 31% of the public had never heard of the European Commission.

The bureaucrats realise that until there is more awareness of and interest in what has happened, and what is happening, there are unlikely to be any protests.

6. The former USSR was renowned for its vast number of laws, rules and regulations. But the USSR was nothing compared to the EU. The EC has become a law factory covering everything imaginable and enabling small petty-minded bureaucrats to hound small businesses and flex their puny muscles. One law on fire regulations alone cost UK businesses £8 billion. New regulations have poured out, governing every aspect of our lives, and businessmen have been swamped by an avalanche of red tape.

Dairy farmers have been subjected, in the last few years alone, to 1,100 separate, specific new laws. Even teddy bear manufacturers have been targeted.

Huge numbers of new criminal offences have been listed.

It is true that these new laws have to be debated by MEPs but the debates are managed at such a frenetic rate – with MEPs voting on as many as 400 issues in just 90 minutes – that in practice, the laws proposed by the bureaucrats are just nodded through. Speakers in the European Parliament are allowed 90 seconds to read out prepared speeches. And then the voting begins.

There are so many new laws that the British Government cannot study them all. The Council of Ministers cannot even read the new laws which the EU passes. The real power now lies with faceless, nameless, unelected bureaucrats who have no accountability whatsoever.

The unknown bureaucrats in Brussels are so desperate to extend their own power and authority, that they have, through the production of miles and miles of unwanted red tape, effectively destroyed the European economy.

Our special tragedy is that Britain's economy has suffered more than most from these new laws.

The other big European nations (France, Germany and Italy) just ignore the rules they don't like. Both France and Germany have flagrantly broken the rules on government deficits but for these two countries there have been no sanctions, no fines and no penalties. 'These are for smaller countries,' said a French Government spokesman with typical gallic arrogance. The French have ignored hundreds of directives relating to the single market (directives which Britain, of course, has obeyed slavishly). Commenting on why he had, like so many other Britons, bought a home in France, one former Tory Minister said he'd bought it because it was such a relief to get away from the EU.

Britain, of course, obeys all the rules – even 'gold-plating' many. And British people and British businessmen pay the ever-increasing price.

7. It was a crime for individual countries to talk about quitting the USSR. Indeed, there was no official procedure to enable countries to leave the soviet union. The EU is much the same.

8. Corruption usually starts from the bottom and works its way up through the system. In both the USSR and the EU the corruption starts at the top and works its way down. Corruption was systemic in the old USSR and it is systemic in the EU. The EU is riddled with the standard socialist form of corruption where the protagonists live by the motto: 'what is yours is mine and what is mine is mine and I will chop your hands off if you try to take it'. This was the popular way of doing things in the USSR. Like the USSR, the EU operates in a way that ensures the redistribution of wealth. In both cases the system means that the wealth is redistributed from the workers to the bureaucrats.

9. Like a pyramid selling scheme the USSR needed to be aggressive and to continue growing in order to stay alive. If it stopped growing it would fail. The EU is the same. It makes absolutely no economic sense for the EU to take in small, poor countries. The countries which were recently encouraged to join the EU were welcomed for ideological economic reasons. The bureaucracy needs to grow to justify its existence, and its demands for increasing amounts of money. All bureaucracies like to grow. It is, in part, their raison d'etre. As they grow so they become increasingly important. Assistants can have assistants of their own. Secretaries can have secretaries. The politicians of the existing countries are persuaded that if the EU grows they will have bigger markets. No one bothers about the fact that the new countries which join the EU will want to share in the subsidies which the EU hands out. Countries like the UK, which pay money to be members of the EU, will have to pay more money for even less reason.

The new countries coming into the EU have many different cultures and laws. Just how they are going to fit into one superstate is something only the bureaucrats who have planned the whole thing can explain. (And, as always, they aren't talking.)

For example, consider Turkey, one of the proposed new EU members. Under Turkish law, if a rapist marries his victim he can walk free. The basis for this is that nobody would want to marry a girl who is not a virgin and so the rapist is doing the girl a favour.

Turkish law also allows a mother who murders her child to be given a reduced sentence if the baby was born out of wedlock. Another Turkish law rules that kidnapping a married woman is a greater crime than kidnapping a woman who isn't married.

The Turkish authorities arrested a young journalist simply on suspicion of being linked to a banned political party. For this she was sentenced to 12½ years in prison.

I mention all this not in criticism but simply to show just how much difference there is between Turkish culture and British culture. And yet the Turkish and the British are expected to be citizens of the same 450 million citizen country; supposedly sharing customs, mores and laws. Naturally, all governments want harmonisation to be organised on their own terms.

(The Americans are desperate for Turkey to join the EU. They believe that if this happens it will make it impossible for Bin Laden and others to claim that the EU is another 'Christian Superstate'.)

10. In the former USSR the citizens of individual countries were told that they should forget about their former national identities. They should, they were told, consider themselves members of the USSR rather than citizens of the Ukraine or Russia. Exactly the same thing is happening in the EU superstate. The EU is intent on destroying and absorbing national states. Britain and England will both disappear completely as the EU superstate develops its identity.

11. The USSR was an ideological dictatorship. That is what the EU is. The aim of the EU is the formation of a State, the preservation of socialism within the State and the expansion of the principles of political correctness. Most political groups which oppose the EU are small, and will remain small, because it is virtually impossible to obtain funding or publicity for any group which opposes the EU.

In the UK there are just three main parties – all of which are supportive of the EU. This is manifestly unfair since it means that a majority of the British population must inevitably remain unrepresented.

Organisations which represent national interests (particularly English interests) are denied power, money and publicity on the grounds that they must be racist. Anyone who supports Britain or England will find themselves branded a racist. (Supporters of Wales and Scotland are never accused of being racist since both these countries will still exist as regions in the new EU superstate.)

12. The USSR had a gulag and so does the EU. The EU has an intellectual gulag; if your views differ from the 'approved' views you will find it difficult to get them published.

Naturally, those who disapprove of the EU will find it difficult or impossible to obtain a job working for the EU. Making a speech or writing a book which criticises the EU (or the laws of the EU) may be regarded as a crime if it is considered subversive. (It is, of course, up to the bureaucrats of the EU to decide whether or not something is 'subversive'.) One Englishman made the mistake of standing up at a public meeting and defending the rights and freedoms of English country people. He started his speech by saying: 'If there is a black, vegetarian, Muslim, asylum-seeking, one-legged, lesbian lorry driver present, then you may be offended at what I am going to say, as I want the same rights that you have got already.'

As a result of this satirical comment, two police officers visited the speaker's home, arrested him (refusing to tell him why) took him to a police station and threw him into a cell.

When five Britons visited Brussels and drove around the city in vehicles which were decorated with posters which called for a referendum on the EU constitution they were arrested for 'disturbing public order' and 'demonstrating without permission'.

13. Citizens in the old USSR had to carry ID cards. The loss of civil liberties which this entailed used to be regarded with suspicion and some contempt by Western European democracies. In the new EU, citizens are losing their freedom and must soon carry ID cards. (It is a myth that ID cards contribute anything whatsoever to national security. ID cards always exist for one reason only: to take away the freedoms and civil liberties of the citizens who must carry them.)

It is very easy to lose your freedom, but very difficult to get it back.

14. Officers in the new EU police force have even greater privileges than officers in the much-feared KGB. All members of the new EU police force have diplomatic immunity. They can walk into your home, arrest you, beat you up and steal your property and you cannot do a darned thing about it.

'Individuals have a duty to violate domestic laws to prevent crimes against peace and humanity from occurring.'
Nurnberg war crimes tribunal 1945-6

22

Why The EU Will Fail

There are many in Europe who seem to believe that a genuine United States of Europe can be created out of a group of disparate nations (with entirely different cultures, histories, interests and enthusiasms) and that the result will be a single country along the lines of the United States of America.

This is, of course, baloney and only a complete idiot could believe it.

There are several reasons why it won't work.

The USA has a common language, a national identity, a shared (short) history, a national media and a population which feels comfortable about moving about from one part of the country to another. The separate countries of Europe have well-established identities and a lot of very different histories and cultures. The citizens of France, Germany, Italy and England don't want to be citizens of a European superstate. The vast majority still think of themselves as being French, German, Italian or English rather than 'European'. Find me someone who calls themselves a 'European' and I will show you an EU employee.

Political debate within Europe still remains primarily national (with individual countries looking out for their own interests) and although the EU has ensured that most of the barriers to free and easy movement have been lifted (on the mainland continent at least) most EU citizens still live in the country where they were born. Only just over one in a hundred citizens of the EU live in a country other than their own. Ninety nine out of every hundred 'Europeans' still live in the country of their birth. People remain loyal to the country of their birth and not to Europe. The French are worried that they are losing control of an organisation (the EU) which was created by the French. The vast number of regulations introduced to make the single market work have aroused resentment and contempt. In England there has been anger at the prosecution of market traders for selling produce in pounds and ounces rather than in EU-approved metric weights. But other countries have had their problems too. Dutch window cleaners, for example, were horrified and angry when they discovered that their ladders were too long to comply with EU health and safety regulations. Dutch houses are often higher than in other countries. How are the window cleaners supposed to clean the windows? None of this hatred and contempt for the EU is helped by the widespread belief that EU institutions, employees and spending programmes are both wasteful and corrupt.

But it is the language problem which will, above all others, ensure that there will be no United States of Europe.

Most European citizens speak only their native tongue. And any attempt to create a European language will fail. The original plan was to avoid national pride by replacing individual languages with Esperanto. That, of course, was a dismal failure.

As the number of EU nations grows so the language problems grow. The EU has become a bonanza for interpreters. The rules of the EU mean that every new law and every new piece of piffle has to be translated into every language and that there is an almost unquenchable thirst for translators who can translate Greek into Danish and Norwegian into Romanian. The EU should have been named Babel.

Does anyone honestly believe that the French will give up their language and accept English as the 'main' European language? Does anyone believe that the Germans or Italians will allow their languages to take second place to Spanish or English? Does anyone really believe that the good citizens of Leeds can be persuaded that in future they must conduct all their business in Greek?

Falsely forcing disparate communities to integrate will not create growth or peace or happiness. Have those who favour a

United States of Europe learned nothing from the human and economic disaster of the USSR?

For years the world has been moving towards flexibility, mobility and decentralisation. Both the USSR and the former Yugoslavia have broken up into individual states.

But Europe has been moving rapidly in the other direction – towards a system which bears more than a passing resemblance to the old USSR – with Brussels taking the place of Moscow.

Both the USSR and the EU can be described as fundamentally socialist or fascist organisations. (Socialists invariably accuse their critics of fascism but in practice extreme socialists are nearly always fascists.)The idea of a constitutionally limited government has sustained free civilisation since the days of the *Magna Carta*. But New Labour and the EU seem to believe that the law is simply what they say it is. To them the Government takes priority over the individual. And whichever way you look at it that's fascism.

The EU is like the old soviet union in many ways; a new and entirely artificial 'superstate'; a haven for corruption, coercion and aggression; an intellectual gulag which exists solely because it provides well-paid jobs for smug buffoons and preening, self-important thugs; political incompetents and dishonest bureaucrats. The EU is fascist and racist: everything it accuses its enemies of being.

The basic building blocks for a growing economy are incentives and personal interest and a controlled bureaucracy (because bureaucracy suffocates enterprise). The EU removes incentives and personal interest and stifles entrepreneurs with bureaucracy. Is it any wonder that European economies are stagnating?

The citizens of the EU can no longer remember why the EU was founded, they don't like what it has become and they are terrified of what it is likely to be in the future.

The USSR collapsed under the weight of a malignant and incompetent central planning bureaucracy. The EU will implode in precisely the same way and for the same reason. It will end quite suddenly and unexpectedly. But when it ends it will end for good.

The people supporting the EU claim to be progressive, liberal intellectuals. In practice, of course, they are not progressive, liberal or intellectual. There are only three types of EU supporter: the liars, the crooks and the fools.

The EU is committed to the idea that the State must always take precedence over the individual and the long-ago discredited notion that more and bigger are better.

The theory about more and bigger being better is out of date, dangerous, destructive and, quite simply, wrong. The USA was built on the philosophy of more and bigger and you don't need much of a brain, or much of a grasp of geopolitics, to realise that the USA is in terminal decline. The USA passed its peak at about the same time as the world passed 'peak oil'.

The EU was always an idea way past its time.

It was always doomed to fail.

The only questions now are how far will it get before it fails, how much will it cost and how much damage will it do.

23

Why English (And British) History Is Being Suppressed

'Despite the political, economic and cultural legacy that has perpetuated its name, England no longer officially exists as a country and enjoys no separate political status within the United Kingdom.'
ENCYCLOPEDIA BRITANNICA

If the EU's plans for Britain are carried through to completion it will only be England which will disappear. Scotland and Wales will retain their identity as regions of the new European superstate. England, however, will disappear and will be converted into nine anonymous regions.

There are plenty of Scottish and Welsh nationalists who are ready, very willing and able to defend the interests of their respective countries. Many seem content to see their nations reborn as part of the new, rapidly enlarging EU. If the future of England is left to the Scots and the Welsh then England will have no future. Fairly or unfairly, there would be few tears shed in Scotland or Wales if England disappeared. (It is worth remembering that many members of the current British Government are Scottish in origin.)

Whereas it is widely perceived as a 'good thing' when Scottish and Welsh nationalists fight for the identity and independence of their nations, English nationalists are neither thick on the ground nor well respected. To describe yourself as English (let alone an

English nationalist) is to risk being accused of being racist.

The sad truth is that if we don't do anything to save her then England is doomed. It will be no good saying 'We should have done something' when England has become a footnote in the history books.

Journalists and broadcasters take every opportunity to attack or be snide about the English; to sneer at English history, English culture and great Englishmen. Anyone who talks proudly of England is dismissed as a lunatic, an out of date buffoon who is almost certainly racist.

★★★

'There is a forgotten, nay almost forbidden, word which means more to me than any other. That word is England.'
WINSTON CHURCHILL

★★★

The word ethnic simply means a group sharing a common origin, culture or language. The English are an ethnic group but schools don't teach about the history of the English and makers of English wine have been told by the EU that it is illegal to sell English wine on the grounds that England doesn't officially exist any more.

Will the EU allow England to continue to have sports teams? I very much doubt it. There will be no place for England in the new United States of Europe. How long have the English cricket, soccer and rugby teams got if we stay in the EU? No more than a decade at most. In recent years it has repeatedly been suggested that English cricket teams be renamed after cities rather than the traditional counties. It is difficult to avoid the suspicion that the suggestion might have come from Brussels – where bureaucrats are doubtless keen to do anything they can to wean English citizens off their loyalty to their old-fashioned counties. The new regions will not, of course, take any notice of old county boundaries.

The EU is determined to kill off England (and the English) and so the English are the constant victims of rampant racism. They are, indeed, now perhaps Europe's most persecuted minority.

Does that not make the EU, and those who support it, guilty of racism and genocide?

England is being officially airbrushed out of existence. The last census form, distributed to all British homes at the turn of the millennium, allowed citizens to describe their nationality, heritage and ethnic background as Scottish, Welsh, Irish, Chinese, Pakistani – virtually anything you can think of.

But there was no space on the form for anyone to describe themselves as 'English'.

Why?

Simple.

The EU does not want England to exist.

This overt example of racism (the attempted destruction of an entire race is better described as genocide) continues on countless application forms (particularly ones where people are being invited to apply for official or quasi-official posts) where applicants are requested to indicate their ethnic background.

We are witnessing a silent holocaust of English culture; an EU inspired bout of racial cleansing.

When students at an English University wanted to start an English society they were told they couldn't.

To support or celebrate anything English is likely to result in a ban. English history has been airbrushed out of our education curriculum.

★★★

'This blessed plot, this earth, this realm, this England.'
WILLIAM SHAKESPEARE

★★★

A reader berated me for writing about France with such affection.

'If you love England and loathe the EU why do you love Paris?' he demanded.

Simple.

I love England. I like France. I like Germany. I like Spain. I like Italy. And so on.

But I want the individual countries of Europe to retain their individuality.

It is their individuality which makes them what they are.

For the same reason I prefer hotels and pubs which are run

by individuals who care – rather than owned by chains and run by managers.

★★★

It now seems to be official Government policy to sneer at or ignore British history and politicians and civil servants seem particularly determined to persuade us to forget about English history. England is, it seems, something of an embarrassment. The city of London happily spent £100,000 of public money celebrating St Patrick's Day but refused to spend a penny celebrating St George's Day.

At the Dome on Millennium night, Britons watched a bizarre celebration of the rest of the world. Whereas other countries remembered and took pleasure from their own particular ethnic glories the English were denied this joy. There was no maypole dancing and there were no Morris Dancers. There wasn't a brass band in sight.

Did no one even think of celebrating the end of the first 2000 years of our history with English musicians playing music by English composers? Why were our national values so grossly undersold?

The English have contributed so much to the world – why must we now be ashamed of our history? There are many things about England of which we should be proud. Why are we encouraged to forget them?

Sadly, our politicians have encouraged us to believe that anyone proud to be English must be racist. And so English interests, history and identity are vigorously suppressed.

This is all politically inspired nonsense, of course. There is nothing whatsoever racist about the English being proud of their nationality, or wishing to celebrate their past.

The fact is that it is essential to the EU's plan that England should disappear.

During the last football World Cup, English football fans at colleges in the UK were encouraged to display the flags of other countries but expressly forbidden to display the England flag. When England won the world rugby cup one British national newspaper dealt with the embarrassment of a soon to be non-existent country winning a major trophy by reporting the win as 'England Win It

For Europe'. When actor Daniel Day-Lewis won an Oscar it was reported as 'a triumph for Europe'.

The malignant influence of the EU gets everywhere these days.

It is undoubtedly a result of our Government's craven obedience to the EU that the 'how to be British' curriculum designed for immigrants who want UK citizenship contains little or nothing about English history. Immigrants who want to be English must show that they know: their rights as EU citizens, how to obtain legal aid, how to use legislation designed to outlaw discrimination, how to claim unemployment benefits, how to seek compensation for unfair dismissal, how to complain about police conduct, how to complain about sexual harassment and details of the minimum wage and holiday pay. They must also show a working knowledge of how Brussels institutions operate. There is, however, no need for would-be Britons to know anything about the Norman Conquest, the First World War, the Battle of Britain, Winston Churchill, Henry VIII, the English Civil War, the Battle of Trafalgar, the British Empire, the formation of the English Parliament or the Battle of Waterloo.

★★★

'England is perhaps the only great country whose intellectuals are ashamed of their own nationality. In left-wing circles it is always felt that there is something slightly disgraceful in being an Englishman and that it is a duty to snigger at every English institution, from horse racing to suet puddings. It is a strange fact, but it is unquestionably true that almost any English intellectual would feel more ashamed of standing to attention during 'God Save the King' than of stealing from a poor box.'
GEORGE ORWELL

★★★

Government Departments are particularly likely to find British and English history an embarrassment.

Consider, for example, the British Council.

The British Council was founded in 1934 by the British Foreign Office. It was originally known as the British Committee for Relations With Other Countries.

Today the British Council's mission is still to promote British culture, education, science and technology to the rest of the world. To this end the British Council gets through around £500 million a year. (Most of this is provided as a grant from the Foreign Office). But today's British Council is no longer selling a picture postcard Britain. On the contrary, the British Council seems keen to portray 'a warts and all Britain'. To do this they use 'cutting edge theatre groups, DJs and conceptual artists'.

One attempt to 'sell' Britain to the world involved decorating a British pavilion in Venice in the popular African colours of red, black and green. Even the Union flags hanging outside the pavilion were coloured red, black and green instead of the more customary red, white and blue. I cannot help wondering how many British taxpayers would feel that this was a good use of their hard earned money. Some might have felt that there might perhaps be a better way to sell Britain and the British to the world. I'm afraid that whenever I read about the efforts of the British Council the words 'irrelevant', 'wasteful' 'pointless' and 'pretentious' seem to circle around and refuse to go away.

Then there is the Post Office.

In 2006, the Royal Mail issued five stamps depicting a pair of performers allegedly representing different musical styles popular in Britain today.

The five stamps showed:

1. A Bollywood movie dancer and sitar player
2. A Reggae bass guitarist and African drummer
3. A Celtic fiddler and harpist
4. A Jazz and Blues saxophone player and guitarist
5. Latin American salsa dancers and a maraca player.

What a pity that the Royal Mail could not find any English music to represent on its stamps.

★★★

'We call our islands by no less than six different names, England, Britain, Great Britain, the British Isles, the United Kingdom and, in very exalted moments, Albion.'
GEORGE ORWELL

★★★

For years now men and women from Scotland have dominated

English politics and public life. Since the Scots now have their own parliament, their domination and control of our lives is impossible to justify. The Scots are hugely over-represented in the House of Commons, in the Government and in the Cabinet. And yet they have their own 'parliament' in Edinburgh. It's no surprise that the Scots sneer at the English living in a 'Jockocracy'. It certainly isn't a democracy any more.

Former Prime Minister Tony Blair is Scottish (though he does his best to conceal his roots). He was born and went to public school in Scotland. (He went to Fettes, often called the Scottish Eton). Gordon Brown is Scottish through and through. Ministers in charge of Transport and Health have been Scottish even though neither ministry has any responsibility in Scotland. Scots from Scottish constituencies have power in Westminster and vote on issues which affect England alone. Many English constituencies are held by Scots. (Though woe betide Englishmen or women who try to stand for election to represent Scottish seats). Three Scots in succession (Lords Mackay, Irvine and Falconer) led the English legal system (the Scots have their own). There have been four Scottish Archbishops of Canterbury leading the Church of England though there would, of course, never be an English Moderator of the Church of Scotland. The Scottish Parliament is very much a parliament of Scots. There are 400,000 English people living in Scotland but only a handful of English people sit in their parliament. Many English quangos, think tanks and pressure groups are run by Scots. Many were given their power by Blair. Large sections of the media are controlled by Scots. Many of the Scots who have abandoned their home country and come to England seeking, and acquiring fame, fortune and power are assertive, arrogant and violently anti-English. At the 2005 general election (effectively to elect a Prime Minister for England, since Scotland, Wales and Northern Ireland had their own Parliaments) the candidates for the three main parties included two Scotsmen and a Welshman of Transylvanian origins.

The Scottish Claim of Right states:

'We...do hereby declare and pledge that in all our actions and deliberations (the) interests (of the Scottish people) shall be paramount.'

The Scottish Claim of Rights has been signed and approved by Gordon Brown, Alistair Darling, Michael Martin and many other eminent Scottish politicians within the House of Commons.

It is difficult to see how any politician who has signed the Scottish Claim of Rights can possibly serve in the British House of Commons.

It is hardly surprising that in January 2008 it was revealed that Gordon Brown had ordered the removal of Britannia from our coins. Britannia was the Latin name for the largest of the British isles. Believed to have been based on warrior queen Boadicea she has appeared on British coins since Roman times and became an important national symbol after the unification of the parliaments of England and Scotland in 1707.

Gordon Brown is very much a Scot. A recent major survey showed that 25% of adults agree that Gordon Brown is 'a Scot who doesn't understand England'. The evidence suggests that Brown doesn't care much about England either. Now that Scotland now has its own Parliament it is, of course, appalling that a Scot should be Prime Minister and responsible for what happens to England and the English. Brown represents a Scottish constituency and should, if he wishes to be in politics, be sitting in the Scottish parliament, not making decisions which affect the English.

To an impartial observer it seems as though Brown must wake up in the morning planning a day of stuffing it to the English. Some observers might find it difficult to understand why some of Brown's decisions could not be described as racist.

For example, in the summer of 2007, it was revealed that in his final budget as Chancellor of the Exchequer, Brown had (in the words of the *Financial Times*) 'quietly slashed by a third this year's hospital building and equipment budget in one of his last acts as chancellor. Prompted by the tightness of the public finances, the new Prime Minister, who has placed the NHS as his 'immediate priority', cut the capital budget of the English NHS for 2007/8 from £6.2 billion to £4.2 billion. The move could delay the Government's hospital building and reconfiguration programme in England. However, Mr Brown avoided equivalent cuts to the Scottish and Welsh NHS budgets even though the funding formula for the UK suggests they should have shared the pain. That decision leaves him open to criticism that he favoured patients in his home country.'

Other media ignored the story which exhibited clear discrimination against those living in England and provided yet another example of English patients being denied the sort of basic hope and dignity made available to patients in Scotland (at the expense of English taxpayers).

For a decade, Brown presided over and approved a scandalously unfair system whereby hardworking English taxpayers supported and subsidised Scottish citizens. Astonishingly, the British Government currently spends between £1,500 and £2,000 more per head on Scottish citizens than it spends on English citizens – resulting in an absurdly generous annual subsidy of £22 billion a year.

It is because of this massive subsidy that all medical prescriptions are now free in Scotland. Moreover, Scottish cancer patients are given life-saving drugs which are denied to English patients. The English not only have to pay the taxes which make these free drugs possible, but they also pay on top for their own drugs. English university students must pay their tuition fees while Scottish students get their education free, even if they are studying at an English university. As an added insult to the English, the Scots will provide free tuition at Scottish universities for students from France, Germany, Greece or any other EU country. English students, whose parents' taxes make this free tuition possible, will be the only ones who have to pay the annual fees. I have no idea why this isn't in breach of legislation against racism but somehow, since neither of them like England or the English, I have no doubt that the Scots and the EU will have an answer.

The elderly in England must sell their homes to pay for nursing home care while the elderly in Scotland get free nursing home care. (Very few people in England yet realise how onerous nursing home care can be. A major survey showed that 55% of 45-65 year olds think that the basic Sate pension of less than £90 a week would cover the cost of their nursing care should they require it, even though the average weekly minimum fee for residential care homes is over £400 a week.) It is why 400,000 elderly people in England are being denied help with dressing, washing and preparing meals while elderly people in Scotland (where Gordon Brown comes from, remember) receive all these services entirely free of charge.

★★★

'I still remember watching the humbling of England,' wrote Gordon Brown about watching the Scottish football team play England. 'And if worst comes to worst, we still beat England sometimes.'

Note the word of the use 'we' in that final sentence.

'We still beat England sometimes.'

And this man is the British Prime Minister?

★★★

Scotland has a population of around five million. Of these only 163,000 are net taxpayers. In other words, of the five million Scots, an astonishing 4,837,000 are kept by English taxpayers. In Scotland, the State is responsible for 58% of all spending. Indeed, Scotland has one of the highest levels of public expenditure in the Organisation for Economic Cooperation and Development (OECD). Government spending in Scotland is 16% above the UK average.

If Scotland were ever to go it alone, and become truly independent the Scottish people would have to put up with huge cuts in public spending and services. The North Sea Oil revenues, which Scottish nationalists frequently talk about with exaggerated reverence, would go nowhere near paying for the luxurious Scottish way of life.

★★★

As one reader pointed out to me, he is allowed to advertise for a Scottish cook, a Chinese cook or a French cook. But he wasn't allowed to advertise for an English cook because that was considered racist (England doesn't officially exist and so, officially, there can't be any English cooks or any English cooking).

Local councils frequently demand that the English flag be removed from private flagpoles. When asked 'why?' they invariably answer that the English flag is racist and that anyone flying it must be racist too. It is not, of course, considered racist to fly a Scottish flag or a Welsh flag. And no council would accuse anyone of racism if they were demented enough to want to fly an EU flag.

A Government report concluded that school children have been sent home for wearing clothing containing the cross of St George, and that many politically correct school teachers have banned the English flag. The report concluded that parents felt it was no longer acceptable to be proud to be English.

★★★

As a result of the way the regionalisation of the UK was begun in 1998, Scottish and Welsh MPs can vote on matters affecting English constituencies but English MPs have no reciprocal rights over what happens in Scotland and Wales. Scottish MPs can (and do) introduce legislation on education and health in England while entirely different legislation is introduced in Scotland. And although English MPs have a vote on what happens in England (but are frequently outvoted by Scottish and Welsh MPs given instructions by Scottish ministers) they have no vote at all on what happens in Scotland or Wales. The Government and the main political parties in the UK have for years been dominated by Scots. England now has a Scottish Prime Minister who appears to have little interest in or enthusiasm for England as a nation. The English £20 note is now adorned with a picture of a Scottish economist. England is now the only part of the United Kingdom which is denied self-government. England is the only part of the union which is governed entirely by the Union Government and Parliament. This, of course, is undemocratic, unjust, unfair and entirely indefensible.

Even small islands around the UK (the Isle of Man, Guernsey and Jersey) have their own political and constitutional existence, their own parliaments and a degree of self-government. England has no political or constitutional existence and this will make it very easy for the EU to get rid of it.

Like many people (in Scotland and Wales as well as England) I believe that English laws which affect only the English should be dealt with only by English MPs – just as the Scottish Parliament deals exclusively with Scottish measures and the Welsh Assembly deals with Welsh matters.

If England didn't have to support Scotland, Wales and Northern Ireland, the English would have the best public services and the lowest tax rates in the world.

However, none of the three main parties will support an English Parliament because the EU won't let them. There can't be an English Parliament as long as we are members of the EU because the EU decided long ago to break up England.

★★★

The Scots receive more money from England because of the Barnett formula. Joel Barnett was Labour's chief secretary to the Treasury in 1978. Just before he lost his job, Barnett devised a formula designed to deal with differing levels of poverty and population across Britain. (Today, Lord Barnett now admits that the system is 'grossly unbalanced'.)

The Scots grab their annual subsidy cheque and then demand more. They behave like truculent teenagers. They live off their parents (the English) and yet are constantly rude to and about them. They receive huge subsidies but always want more.

Since Scotland acquired its EU regional Parliament and moved towards being an official EU region, public spending in Scotland has more than doubled from £14 billion a year to £30 billion. More than half of the entire Scottish economy is public spending. In 2005, according to the Office for National Statistics, public spending accounted for more than 50% of Scottish Gross Domestic Product (GDP) and yet Scottish tax receipts contributed just 75% of this sum – leaving a budget deficit of 13% of GDP. The deficit was, of course, met by the English taxpayers.

A quarter of employed people working in Scotland are working for the State and being paid by English taxpayers. To make things even worse, public sector wages in Scotland are so high that those lucky enough to work for the State earn, on average, £90 a week more than those who have proper jobs and are doing something useful for a living. The inevitable consequence is that those who are ambitious, and who want security and good pay, all work for the Government. This ensures that business start-ups struggle and that economic growth is stifled. Scotland's economic growth between 2000 and 2006 increased at a pitiful 1.9% a year.

301

Scotland is flooded with English money and this has created the worst benefits culture in Britain. There is no incentive to modernise or to work. There are whole families in Scotland who regard living on benefits as a career choice. (It is, perhaps, hardly surprising that the Scots have the poorest health of any industrialised nation. On average, they die much earlier than anyone else. But when you have no real reason to live there is no reason to stay alive.)

Meanwhile, the money that is wasted on a hideously bloated and unhealthy public sector in Scotland is desperately needed in England where the vital infrastructure is crumbling and collapsing at a frightening pace.

The only practical solution is to give the Scots what they think they want: the chance to become a fully-fledged separate region within the EU. (Politicians in the Scottish National Party will doubtless think they are getting independence. They'll eventually learn the truth.) The English would save the billions they currently give to the Scots in subsidies. The Scots can, of course, have the revenue from that North Sea oil which is off their coastline (this is by no means all of it, though the Scots invariably talk about North Sea oil as though it all belonged to Scotland). Scottish politicians talk about the oil as though it will enable them to live like Arab sheiks. The truth, sadly, is that the revenues from the oil are declining rapidly (the oil fields there went past their 'peak oil' status years ago and stocks are running out) and will go nowhere near balancing the money the Scots currently receive from the English in wildly over-generous subsidies.

If they choose independence (of any variety) the Scots will, of course, have to cut spending fairly dramatically. And they will have to put up taxes dramatically too. Their currency will soon become extremely weak. (There is a real risk that within a few years Scotland will go bankrupt.)

If, when the Union is broken up, and England becomes independent, the Scots choose to remain members of the EU and report to Brussels, rather than take up the far riskier course of proper independence they may be entitled to a little money from the EU. In reality, they will probably get very little – most of the

EU's available money will be spread around Eastern Europe. The voters who put the Scottish Nationalists into power will soon become restless and discontent when they look south and see England enjoying full independence outside the EU.

★★★

People talk about the 'Union' as though it is something truly 'old' and significant. It's only 'old' in the way that American buildings are 'old'. In other words, it's quite new. Just in case your history is a bit wobbly here's a potted history of the Union.

The English King, Edward I, conquered northern Wales and made it a principality in 1284. Wales was officially incorporated as part of England during the reign of Henry VIII. Scotland was independent in 1314 but was joined with England in 1603 when James VI of Scotland sat on the English throne and became James I of England. The relationship was formalised in 1707 when England and Scotland assented to the Act of Union to form the kingdom of Great Britain. (There was not, of course, much fuss about the 300 year anniversary in 2007. It is never in the EU's interests to celebrate British history.) The United Kingdom of Great Britain and Ireland was established in 1801 and broken up when Southern Ireland became the Irish Free State in 1921. In 1937, the Irish Free State adopted the name Eire and became a sovereign independent country. The rest of the Union recognised the status of Ireland in 1949 but declared that the six northern counties would not join without the consent of the people. They still haven't.

Scotland and Wales were both officially made a region of the EU in 1997, and the Scottish and Welsh regional assemblies or parliaments first met in 1999.

The simple truth is that the Union has effectively been broken up for years. The creation of the Irish Republic and the formation of the Scottish and Welsh regional assemblies ended whatever political alliance there had been. Those who cry crocodile tears over suggestions that its disappearance be formalised are, I suspect, doing so solely because they know that the best way to oppress England, and to oppose the formation of an English Parliament is to claim that an English Parliament would threaten the future of the Union. Just why should the formation of an English Parliament threaten the Union any more than the formation of Scottish and Welsh parliaments?

With great sadness I fear that the Union and Britain are finished. Things are desperate. We must now fight a rearguard action to save England. The Union simply doesn't work any more and it doesn't make any sense. England would be much better off (and the militant Scots would get what they want) if the Union was disbanded. As one observer put it 'The Union looks increasingly like one of those old-fashioned conglomerates that the business world has spent the last 20 years dismantling.' If Scotland, Wales, Northern Ireland and England weren't already joined together in an uncomfortable Union no one would ever dream of suggesting it. Unsurprisingly, a recent poll showed that a clear majority of the English would welcome giving Scotland its independence. (Scottish independence is probably more popular in England than it is in Scotland.)

Scotland, in particular, has done well out of the merger (they got access to the much larger English market and to the English colonies – most of Scotland's exports go to England) but it is now time to break up the Union and allow its constituent parts to go their own separate ways.

It is no exaggeration at all to say that the EU needs – and intends – to destroy England. It is being helped in that endeavour by all three main political parties in Britain. Curiously, the one political party which is helping England at the moment is the Scottish Nationalist Party. Their constant goading of the English, and their gloating about the amount of money they have managed to gouge out of England, is helping to build the enthusiasm for English independence and an English Parliament.

★★★

When you ask the more rabid Scots why they hate the English so vehemently those who can think of a reason will usually mention the Massacre of Glencoe.

It happened in February 1692, and resulted in the deaths of between 30 and 40 Scots but it has, for romantic rather than logical reasons, become an enduring symbol of Scottish oppression, and an everlasting reason to hate the English. Encouraged by dramatisations which are as close to history as Bambi on Ice is close to natural history the slaughter has become a symbol of the English oppression of the Scots.

The best account of what happened is recorded in the excellent book *The Massacre of Glencoe* by John Buchan.

Buchan was probably the finest, and certainly the most enduring and universally popular, Scottish writer. He is remembered today for novels such as *The Thirty Nine Steps* and *John Macnab* but he was also the author of a number of history books and biographies (among them lives of Cromwell and Sir Walter Scott). He spent his final years as Governor-General of Canada where he was known as Lord Tweedsmuir.

What made the massacre at Glencoe particularly notable was the fact that the 120 soldiers who were responsible for the killing were, prior to the Massacre, billeted in cottages belonging to the locals. They were, according to Buchan, 'mostly Highlanders and Campbells, but there were a few Lowlanders who hung together and talked their own talk, since their lack of Gaelic kept them from much intimacy with the folk of the glen.'

In fact not one Englishman was involved in the planning of the Massacre of Glencoe, and the Scots who were massacred at Glencoe weren't killed by English soldiers. The whole hideous operation was planned by Scots and the killing was done by Scots.

Buchan explains in his book that three people were responsible for planning the massacre: John Dalrymple, the Master of Stair (a lowland Scotsman), John Campbell, 1st Earl of Breadalbane and the King (King William III.)

None of these was English. (King William III was born in the Hague, Netherlands.)

'The first has the heaviest share (of the blame),' wrote Buchan. 'The last the lightest. The guilt varies with the degree of knowledge, and the intimacy of the relationship between the wronged and the wronger. In William, it was a crime against humanity in general, in the Master of Stair against his fellow Scots and in Breadalbane against those who shared with him the blood and traditions of the Gael.'

Of the three ultimately responsible men, one was Dutch and two were Scots.

The men who committed the massacre were Scotsmen too. They were, according to Buchan, 'mostly Breadalbane's own people'.

It is clear that if the Scots had studied and understood their own history, they would know that the cause of their greatest resentment towards the English is unfounded and is built entirely on an inaccurate representation of history.

Perhaps the Scots find it difficult to accept that it was Scotsmen who planned and executed the Massacre of Glencoe.

Denying the truth and rewriting history comes as easy to rabid Scottish nationalists (and their foreign supporters) as it does to run of the mill EU fascists.

★★★

The extremists in Scotland and Wales seem to believe that only the EU can offer them the independence they crave. They are deluded, of course. Membership of the EU means that the Welsh and the Scots have no chance of achieving real independence. Their dream of having their own real parliament is now further away than ever. But they don't realise this and they won't accept it as the truth. They have been misled by promises and bribed by gold from Brussels. (The supply of gold is now finished since the EU needs to distribute its takings to the East Europeans, and the Welsh and the Scots will receive nothing in the future.)

The bottom line is that there isn't much of a future for Britain or for the United Kingdom which has, let's face it, always been as loose and as uncomfortable an amalgam of nations as the USSR or indeed the EU. The UK was created only because of the physical proximity of the members and the fact of their sharing an island.

Incidentally, Welsh nationalists should be aware that when the EU recently published a map of EU countries, the eurocrats completely forgot to include Wales.

24

The Case For Leaving The EU: Why England Should Declare Independence

'In Chinese, the word 'crisis' is made up of a combination of two characters. The first signifies 'risk'. The second stands for 'opportunity'.'
JIM ROGERS

'A patriot must always be ready to defend his country against his government.'
EDWARD ABBEY

Membership of the EU brings only costs and commitments and regulations. There are no benefits. Contrary to official propaganda, membership of the EU makes England less competitive and it endangers English jobs. The EU gives us costly and damaging regulations, diminishes our ability to control immigration and reduces our freedom. Leaving the EU superstate is essential if we are to regain our freedom, privacy and independence.

It is difficult to see why any English politician could ever justify England's membership of the European Union. England has always been a massive contributor to the EU budget. It costs the English billions of pounds a year to be members of this club which, in return for our giving it money, tells us what to do and burdens us with thousands of new laws. It is much easier to see why other countries are wise to be members of this absurd club.

Spain, Greece and Ireland, for example, actually receive vast sums from the EU. What is the point of being a member of a club which has massive membership fees when you get absolutely nothing out of it that you want?

Our 30 year membership of the EU has cost England £75 billion in membership fees. A full list of the benefits the nation has obtained from the EU can be found on every sheet of toilet paper sold within the European Union.

As it has grown older the EU has, like all statist economies, acquired a life of its own. The EU is run for, not by, the bureaucratic machinery. The real needs of the people of Europe are secondary to the needs of the EU. It is because of the EU that so many Englishmen and Englishwomen now feel like visitors in their own country.

The bureaucratic economy as exemplified by the EU is utterly corrupt, out of time, out of place and irrelevant. The tumbrils are rolling towards Brussels. For the EU, if not its bureaucratic masters, the guillotine is being sharpened and oiled. The EU doesn't have a long-term future. A system which is designed for, built for and run for a bureaucracy cannot possibly be worth saving. A system which is based on wants and expectations instead of merit stifles creativity and achievement and rewards corruption and cronyism.

It is the creativity of individuals which creates and drives any economy. The EU, and its regions, will decline as individuals and entrepreneurs continue to be oppressed and continue to feel a growing sense of resentment.

Those who seem to believe that the EU offers the only way forward should, perhaps, be aware that there is a powerful movement among French politicians who have had enough of the EU, who believe that the present, over-extended would-be United States of Europe is unwieldy and of no advantage to France, who believe that 'la difference' deserves to 'vive' and who would like to dissolve the present EU and start again with a much smaller group of countries. There are, indeed, many who believe that a Franco-German union would be best. Similar feelings are commonplace in Germany where there have long been plans for the day (now recognised as an increasingly likely possibility) when the EU implodes.

The EU is doomed, as surely as the USSR was doomed, and it will eventually collapse. When the EU falls apart, destroyed by its own incompetent bureaucracy, the 'collateral' damage will be awesome. It will be as well to be as far away from it all as possible.

The EU will, like all such hubristic organisations, be destroyed by its own excessive zeal for legislation, by its own bureaucracy and by corruption. The euro will almost certainly go first. And then, as nationalist parties rise in popularity and strength, so the power of the EU itself will wane.

(There is one scary possibility. The absence of democracy (and normal democratic checks) within the EU means that a dictator could easily take control of the EU. It would be remarkably easy for an Adolf Hitler to take over the EU.)

We will be better off in every conceivable way when we leave the EU. We need to get out fast. The countries which are left in the EU at the end will suffer most from the economic and social chaos which will ensue.

★★★

'I think ...to break up the Union would be a completely regressive step, totally wrong and totally contrary to where the modern world is living, which is countries moving closer together.'

TONY BLAIR, SPEAKING IN 2006. MR BLAIR HAD CLEARLY SUCCEEDED IN SPENDING TEN YEARS AS PRIME MINISTER WITHOUT BEING AWARE OF THE BREAK-UP OF THE SOVIET UNION OR YUGOSLAVIA. BLAIR WAS, OF COURSE, TALKING ABOUT THE POSSIBLE BREAK-UP OF THE UNITED KINGDOM RATHER THAN THE EUROPEAN UNION.

★★★

Here are the advantages of remaining in the EU.

1. We get to give lots of money to other European countries without the embarrassment of them saying 'thank you'. In 2008, we will hand over a multi-billion pound cheque as our fee for membership of the EU club. (Sadly, there is no swimming pool and the tennis courts are always booked.) Over the 30 years that we have been in the EU our membership has cost us over £75 billion.

2. Former British politicians can get extremely well paid jobs in the EU – thereby taking them off the British jobs market

and providing more lavatory cleaning vacancies.

3. We get the right to plaster the blue EU flag on Government buildings, road signs, car number plates, official vehicles and everything else

4. We don't have to bother worrying about creating policies on things like trade, public spending, law making, fishing, farming or immigration because the EU does all this for us. So, instead of being dependent upon a bunch of elected MPs we are now dependent upon the whims of a small group of unelected eurocrats.

5. We can save the expense of regular elections.

6. Er...that's about it.

★★★

'But talk to foreigners, read foreign books or newspapers, and you are brought back to the same thought. Yes, there is something distinctive and recognisable in English civilisation. It is a culture as individual as that of Spain. It is somehow bound up with solid breakfasts and gloomy Sundays, smoky towns and winding roads, green fields and red pillar boxes. It has a flavour of its own. Moreover it is continuous, it stretches into the future and the past, there is something in it that persists, as in a living creature. What can the England of 1940 have in common with the England of 1840? But then, what have you in common with the child of five whose photograph your mother keeps on the mantelpiece? Nothing, except that you happen to be the same person. And above all it is your civilisation, it is you. However much you hate it or laugh at it, you will never be happy away from it for any length of time. The suet puddings and the red pillar boxes have entered into your soul. Good or evil, it is yours, you belong to it, and this side the grave you will never get away from the marks that it has given you.'

GEORGE ORWELL

★★★

Those who argue that we should simply throw in our lot with the EU and help create a powerful federal Europe which can act as a counter-weight to the power of the USA, are exhibiting great naivety and ignoring the fact that England joined the EU to please America and that our policy makers regard our major role within the EU as playing a supportive role to the USA.

Pathetically, civil servants in Whitehall, and English politicians, still regard the so-called 'special relationship' as our most important source of global power. We have, I'm afraid, become the equivalent of the under-developed teenager who hangs around with the class bully.

At the moment, the UK is in a uniquely weak position because it has tied itself to both the EU and the USA. The old saying about falling between two stools springs to mind.

We are hated by Muslims everywhere for our support of America. We have become a major target for terrorists. We spend vast amounts of money supporting American brutality and carpet-bagging. To please the class bully our Government has accepted that English citizens can be extradited to America for trial there if that is what the Americans want. (Naturally, the process does not work both ways. English courts cannot demand that Americans be extradited to the UK.)

And we are surrendering our sovereignty to the EU, and handing over billions of pounds a year for the 'privilege' because that is what the Americans want. Our industry is being wrecked by red tape, regulations and legislation imported from both Washington and Brussels. Our nation is becoming steadily poorer.

The time has come for us to say thank you and goodbye to both the USA and the EU.

England can, and should, stand proud and alone.

It is the only dignified solution. It is the only way to regain our national self-respect.

★★★

'Like all other modern people, the English are in process of being numbered, labelled, conscripted, 'coordinated'. But the pull of their impulses is in the other direction, and the kind of regimentation that can be imposed on them will be modified in consequence.'
GEORGE ORWELL

★★★

England must leave the EU and declare independence if it is to have a chance of surviving.

England is about to disappear. It already no longer exists except as a memory. England was the only team in the recent football World Cup which didn't represent a nation state. Look up England in the *Encyclopedia Britannica* and you'll find these words: 'Despite the political, economic, and cultural legacy that has perpetuated its name...England no longer officially exists as a country.'

As citizens, all that we inherit of real value is our cultural and spiritual heritage. And yet the English are now almost the only ethnic group in the world to have been deprived of their identity without a gun being fired. The denial of England, and Englishness, is turning the English into stateless persons. It is silent, bloodless ethnic cleansing. It's no exaggeration to say that it's genocide without the blood.

The basic reason for this is simple.

The EU intends to turn the United Kingdom into 12 regions. Scotland, Wales and Northern Ireland will still exist as identified regions – though their so-called Parliaments are, in reality, merely Regional Assemblies of the European Union. England, on the other hand, is being split up into nine regions. Each region already has a Regional Assembly – under the authority of Brussels. Eight of the Regional Assemblies are entirely unelected. The members are appointed by the Labour Government. The ninth Regional Assembly is better known as the London Assembly – and it's the only one of the nine which has members who have been elected.

The only way that England will be saved will be for the English to insist that England leaves the EU and reverts to being an independent nation state with its own Parliament. That's the only answer. And we can do it. If Scotland and Wales want to remain as European regions, as they seem to want to do, then we'll have to let them.

The United Kingdom is doomed and beyond help.

But England can be saved.

★★★

'For the purposes of the Race Relations Act the English are given the status of a racial group. They are deemed to be a racial group by reason of their 'national origins', which means that they are members of a community whose members share a history, culture, ancestry and communal name, and are identified with a territory, i.e. England. This was established in the case BBC Scotland v Souster, 2001.'
STEADFAST MAGAZINE

★★★

Scotland and Wales don't want to leave the EU and so their MPs (who are absurdly powerful in the Commons) will make sure that Britain doesn't leave either. So, England will have to settle for independence by herself.

As a new, sovereign state England would be far better off than she is now. For years, English taxpayers have been supporting both the Welsh and the Scottish economies with huge subsidies. If England became independent she would be far richer than she has been for decades. The Government will be able to cut taxes and improve services quite dramatically. In early 2008, it was revealed that if the South East of England were to become independent by itself it would be the world's 22nd richest nation.

It is a pity that we cannot take Britain out of the EU but, being realistic, I think we have to accept that, whatever happens, Britain, Great Britain and the United Kingdom are now nothing much more than names in old geography books.

★★★

Patriotism is all very well in its place. And the EU approves of patriotism when it's useful.

So, for example, the Welsh and the Scots are encouraged to show patriotic pride in their nations. It suits the new EU superstate for the Welsh and the Scots to regard themselves as independent (even though they are not and now never will be) because this weakens Britain and isolates England. In 2003, campaigners for the Welsh Nationalist Party in Wales claimed that they wanted Wales to be an independent country, within the EU, but outside the UK. They did not seem to realise that under the new EU constitution there will be no independent countries – all will simply be regions.

The Scots and the Welsh do not yet seem to have realised that although their countries will not disappear in name within the new EU superstate (as England will) they will be further away than ever from independence.

When the Scots and the Welsh eventually realise what is happening, they may become less enthusiastic about the EU. But by then it will be far too late.

★★★

The English should support and encourage the Scots in their battle for independence.

Here are the reasons why:

1. If Scotland becomes independent and breaks up the United Kingdom there will be an overwhelming argument for the English to be given their own Parliament. All members of the new English Parliament will represent English constituents. This means that only English MPs will be able to vote on issues affecting English citizens. (Unlike the present Parliamentary system which allows Scottish MPs, with no English constituents or English responsibilities, to vote on issues which affect the English.)

2. If Scotland has been given independence it will be possible (and crucial) for those founding the new English Parliament to insist that only citizens born in England can be elected as Members of the English Parliament. This will ensure that only people who care for the culture, history and future of England will control the nation's destiny.

3. The British Government currently spends £1,503 more per head on Scottish citizens than it spends on English citizens. Scotland has a population of around 5 million. Of these, only 163,000 are net taxpayers. In other words, of the 5 million Scots, an astonishing 4,837,000 are kept by English taxpayers.

4. An English Parliament could, and almost certainly would, vote to leave the European Union. England would once again be a strong and independent nation. Without the votes of Scottish MPs who support Britain's membership of the EU, the English would be free of European red tape and richer by many billions of pounds a year.

5. Without Scotland and the EU to support, the English could have much better schools and hospitals. And lower taxes. Even council taxes are kept much lower in Scotland thanks to English taxpayers. (In January 2008, it was revealed that council taxes in England and Wales would rise by between 4 and 5% whereas council taxes in Scotland would be kept the same.)

If Scotland becomes independent, the Scots will become a good deal poorer. But the English, who have supported Scotland for years, will become a good deal richer. Every Englishman and Englishwoman should encourage the Scots in their fight for independence.

★★★

Eurofanatics often claim that England would fall apart if we left the EU. This is nonsense. England could survive outside the EU very easily – and very successfully. Or we could establish a semi-detached relationship with the EU.

Other countries have done this.

Switzerland, for example, has succeeded in negotiating an arrangement which give the Swiss much of the upside of EU membership with none of the downside. The Swiss choose which projects to support financially (naturally, picking projects which will benefit Swiss interests) and retain their sovereignty. They can end their arrangement with the EU at any time. Having ignored the advice of their Government, and voted against joining the EU, the Swiss have negotiated for themselves an excellent trade agreement – thereby putting a lie to the utterly false claim that no European country can possibly survive unless it becomes part of the EU.

Norway is not a member of the EU and has chosen to cherry pick EU policies, opting out of the policies the Norwegians don't like, and yet remaining as a member of the European Economic Area so that they can retain access to the EU's single market. In return for this purely commercial advantage, Norway has to accept the rules relating to the single market (without having a vote to decide what they are) and must pay a small annual fee to the EU budget. It is, presumably, fairly easy for the Norwegians to decide whether or not their annual fee is value for money. If the EU tries to push their fee too high, the Norwegians can simply abandon their membership of the European Economic Area.

Norway and Switzerland chose to stay out of the EU. Both are smaller than Britain. Both have held onto their self-respect and national identity. Both still trade very well with other European countries. Both have strong economies which are unencumbered by EU regulations. Both still control their own immigration policies. Norway and Switzerland are now the two richest countries in Europe.

★★★

There has for years now been a cynical and ruthless propaganda campaign to persuade us that England has no future outside Europe. This is nonsense.

The europhiles constantly argue that England would be ruined if she left Europe.

Oh, what porkies these people do tell.

Even *The Economist* has admitted that '...the idea that leaving (the EU) would be 'economic suicide' is nonsense'.

Examine what would happen if England stopped paying subscriptions to the EU:

1. The EU would impose its external tariff on English exports to Europe. This would make very little difference to English companies – most of whose exports go outside Europe anyway. The World Trade Organisation restricts the EU to an external tariff of around 6% so the effect would, in any case, be quite small. (England would almost certainly be able to negotiate for itself a smaller tariff – in the way that Switzerland has. This would drive down the cost of leaving the EU still further.)

2. England would, inevitably, stay outside the euro. There would be an exchange rate between the pound and the euro. In the long run this could well be to England's advantage. There are already signs that the euro will soon collapse. When the euro collapses, European economies will be in chaos. Sterling will, despite the damage done to our economy by Gordon Brown survive.

3. The external tariff on England's imports from outside the EU would disappear. England would probably gain more from this than it would lose from the imposition of a tariff on English exports to Europe.

4. An England outside the EU would be able to make special trading deals with other countries – such as those in the Commonwealth. This could be hugely advantageous.

5. Europhiles claim that if England left the EU then countries from outside Europe (such as Japan and America) would invest less in England. This is nonsense. During the late part of the 20th century, and the first couple of years of the 21st century, England attracted more outside investment (known

to economists as 'Foreign Direct Investment' or FDI) than other European countries because its labour market was still relatively unregulated. If it was outside the EU, England could take advantage of its independence to reduce the number of regulations limiting foreign companies. EU regulations are already regarded as a minefield. Just ask some of the foreign companies who have had eurocrats leaping up and down all over them. Many would jump at the chance to invest in a less regulated part of Europe. Finally, even if FDI did fall, England would not necessarily lose since in an often irrational attempt to encourage foreign businesses (at the expense of British businesses) the British Government subsidises these investments. A subsidised outside investment may well not make money for the country.

If England left the EU it would leave behind an incompetent and power hungry bureaucracy which has consistently failed. And, remember, we have a trade deficit with the EU. For example, we have a deficit of over £3 billion a year trade with Germany alone. The EU countries desperately need our trade. Politicians who have supported the EU, and who have lied and deceived the British voters by signing away our rights and freedoms, have claimed that they have signed EU treaties because they wanted England to have influence in Europe. This is nonsense. England now has far less influence in Europe than ever before. Thanks to the treaties our leaders have signed (in particular the Treaty of Lisbon signed by Scotsman Gordon Brown) we have handed over control of our destiny to a bunch of unelected eurocrats.

Britain in general, and England in particular, have gained nothing from membership of the EU. Scotland and Wales have received back some of the money paid by England. But England has been a huge and consistent contributor to the EU budget. Membership has cost the English a great deal. England would survive and survive well outside the EU.

Norway and Switzerland aren't the only countries to have voted against joining the EU – and to have thrived. Greenland, once in the EU, escaped and has prospered since getting out. Iceland has 275,000 citizens and survives very well without faceless wimps in Brussels telling it what to do. If they can do it so can England. England would be richer and more powerful outside the EU. And its citizens would regain their lost independence.

In 2008, even after decades of interference from the EU, the United Kingdom still had 20% of the assets of the entire, enlarged European Union. (Most of the UK's assets are, of course, in England – the wealthiest single component of the European Union.)

If England left the EU it would regain power over its legal system, armed forces, immigration and agricultural policies. Hundreds of thousands of small businesses would be saved from stifling bureaucracy. English is the world's leading business language. English dominates the Internet. Our language means that we can trade with any other country in the world.

England would be much richer if it left the EU. We would save a fortune. And be free of over 100,000 unnecessary laws. The only people who would lose would be politicians. Countries which have stayed outside the EU have outperformed those which joined. The EU is for losers which cannot cope alone. England is not a loser.

★★★

England's manufacturing trade deficit with the EU is now well over £200 billion. The highly promoted 'single market' has removed English workers' jobs to Eastern Europe and has led to rising unemployment in England. The supporters of the EU claim that leaving the EU would lead to a loss of several million English jobs. That is a lie. Leaving the EU would lead to a massive rise in English jobs and a massive rise in profits for English companies. EU regulations affect 100% of our economy, but only 10% of our Gross National Product is exported to other regions within the EU. The regionalisation of the police force, the disbanding of long-established English regiments, the introduction of all day drinking, unlimited and uncontrolled immigration, sex education for the under 13s in schools, Sunday trading, the running down of English manufacturing industry and the costly privatisation of public services through Private Finance Initiatives are just some of the ways in which the EU is destroying our society. Since we joined the EU, taxes have doubled in real terms – but the quality of our infrastructure has collapsed.

The truth – which the Government insists on hiding – is that everyone in England – except for retiring politicians – would benefit if we left the EU tomorrow (tonight would be better).

Scotland and Wales won't leave.

So England has to leave alone.

England will survive and survive well outside the EU. We will have far more influence – and power – outside the EU.

Maybe the people of Scotland and Wales will realise that they too will benefit if their countries leave the European Union. The Scots and the Welsh who want real freedom and independence for their countries will not find it within the EU. Eventually, perhaps, the Scots and the Welsh will realise that their future lies not in being sunk without trace into a political superstate, along with Greeks, Rumanians and Poles, but in acquiring real independence and setting up a softer, less formal union with England.

Leaving the EU is simple. Parliament simply has to repeal the Acts of Parliament which hold us to the EU. We just tell the EU we want to resign and that they can have their flag back.

Simple.

England could be out of the EU in hours.

Let's go for it.

If we don't act very soon it will be too late and we will have to remain in the EU until it collapses.

If England leaves the EU now we will be the strongest and richest country in Europe within a decade.

England has excellent connections and there are still many countries where the English are respected and even admired.

Freed of the EU we could resurrect old alliances and friendships in Asia, Australasia and Africa. There is much we can learn from our old friends. Few countries are growing as fast as India, few respect individual freedom as much as Canada.

Here, to summarise, are twelve ways in which we would be better off outside the EU:

1. We would be able to decide our own foreign policy. And we

would be able to continue to maintain our own network of embassies and diplomats around the world.

2.   We would have billions of pounds a year to spend on our own nation. By 2013, we will have paid almost £300 billion to the EU. What we pay the EU is, effectively, our basic subscription cost; what it costs us to be members. The EU is estimated to cost the average family an extra £1,000 a year on food bills alone. Add your share of the saving on your food bill to the amount wasted on red tape, to the additional energy costs created by EU laws and on buying new light bulbs and light fittings to satisfy the EU and you will, I think, be surprised to see just how much your membership of the EU is costing you. But that's only the start. According to the Government's Better Regulation Task Force, complying with EU regulations now costs our economy over £100 billion a year.

Economists say that we lose another £80 to £85 billion a year because of our membership of the EU. (The loss of our fishing industry costs us around £5 billion a year.) Although I believe them to be accurate these are estimates because every Government since 1972 has refused to calculate and publish the full cost of membership of the European Union.

If England left the EU, the average family would either suddenly find themselves wealthier than they had ever dreamt possible or would find that the country's infrastructure had improved immeasurably. Or both.

3.   We would have control over our own immigration policies. We would be able to decide who had the right to live and work in our country. Since we handed over control of all our immigration policies to the EU, immigration has shot up from 30,000 a year (entirely manageable) to over a million a year. Even a million a year might be an underestimate. The Government recently admitted that in a single year, 2.6 million immigrants had applied to stay in Britain. The numbers are so huge that it's hardly surprising that the Home Office can no longer keep track of what is happening. In many British cities, the immigrant influx is such that English people make up less than 10% of the population, and the infrastructure is breaking down.

4. We would be able to say 'no' to ID cards.

5. We would regain our sovereignty. England would continue to be England and would not be replaced by nine EU regions.

6. Instead of wasting billions on EU Armed Forces, we would be able to maintain our own Armed Forces.

7. We would be able to trade with whichever countries wanted to trade with us.

8. We would lose well over 100,000 laws foisted on us by unelected EU bureaucrats.

9. We would not be forced to abandon our sensible way of dealing with our rubbish in order to satisfy EU laws.

10. We would, if we wanted to, keep England for the English. Everyone else (Romanian, Scot or German) who did not choose to take English citizenship would officially be classified as a visitor. Only English taxpayers would be entitled to vote in England. And only the English would be entitled to free health care and to access to the benefits system.

If we fight hard we can and will take back our nation from the EU. We can reclaim the England we love and respect. We can put dignity and pride back into our feelings for our nation.

We could leave the EU in just 14 hours. The abdication of King Edward VIII was passed by Parliament and signed by the Monarch in just under 14 hours. So, when we control Parliament again with independent MPs having replaced the corrupt three party system, we can repel the 1972 European Communities Act in the same sort of time span.

I hope I have by now convinced you that England's only chance of survival is to become an independent country and to leave the EU. We could sit around and wait for the EU to implode. But that will take a few years (though it will happen) and we will all be impoverished and starving by then.

We need to leave the EU not just to regain our history and our culture but also to regain our freedom, our liberty and our independence. We need to leave the EU quickly – so that we get out before the EU collapses (which it will do).

Turning back the clock will change our nation.
We may even be able to recognise it again.

The most powerful form of communication in the world is not the television, the Internet, the radio or the newspaper; it is word of mouth. Talk to your friends. Tell them what you know.

Books are the second most powerful form of communication. Books are more powerful than television, the Internet, the radio or newspapers because they are more convincing. So, please pass your copy of this book onto a friend. Regard the book as a chain letter – designed to start people thinking. Give a copy to your local library.

We at Publishing House intend to continue to do what we can to combat fascism and to fight for freedom, justice, privacy, liberty and independence. Our weapons are truth, our fraternity and our conviction that our cause is just. Please help us spread the word. This is a battle which is worth fighting. And time is running out.

If you feel shocked or horrified by what you have read and you would like to spread the truth about the EU, please tell your friends about this book. Publishing and marketing a book which tells the truth about the EU is perilous and commercially hazardous. We do need all the help you can give us. Contact Publishing House (during normal office hours) for details of the special prices we offer to those who want to help spread the word and wish to purchase several copies of this and other books.

'There comes a time in the affairs of man when he must take the bull by the tail and face the situation.'
W. C. FIELDS

I have no doubt that this book will, like its companion volumes, be banned in as many different ways as it is possible to ban a book. Newspapers and magazines won't review it. Television and radio stations won't mention it. Publications of all types will reject advertisements for it. Bookstores and libraries will refuse to stock it.

We at Publishing House rely completely on your help for this book, and its message, to reach a large audience. So please help.

We make copies of this book available for sale at the cheapest prices we can manage so that you will, we hope, lend them to other people, give them away or, if you prefer, sell them at whatever price you consider appropriate.

Appendix 1: Why This Book Doesn't Contain Any References

I will, I have no doubt, receive letters from readers wanting to know why I haven't included references for all the items in this book.

Good question.

The truth is, dear reader, that I have a room-full of papers, documents, letters, books, cuttings, journals, magazines and other research material. Much of the material was provided confidentially

If I included a full list of references at the back of the book the result would be that the book would be at least twice as thick. It would, therefore, cost a good deal more to print and to post. Very few people would buy it. And the message would remain largely unread.

I had to choose between writing a fully referenced book to be read by a very small number of people and writing a more reasonably priced, more accessible book designed to be read by as large a number of people as possible.

What do you think would be most likely to make a real difference?

That's what I thought.

Incidentally, thousands of copies of my books *England Our England*, *Saving England* and *The Truth They Won't Tell You (And*

Don't Want You to Know) About The EU have been sent to MPs, MEPs and to europhiles. I have received numerous letters from readers who have told me that these 'experts' have gone through each fact and claim in the book looking for errors. But that they have failed to find any.

Appendix 2: Biography Of The Author

Vernon Coleman was an angry young man for as long as it was decently possible. He then turned into an angry middle-aged man. And now, with no effort whatsoever, he has matured into being an angry old man. He is, he confesses, just as angry as he ever was. Indeed, he may be even angrier because, he says, the more he learns about life the more things he finds to be angry about.

Cruelty, prejudice and injustice are the three things most likely to arouse his well-developed sense of ire but he admits that, at a pinch, inefficiency, incompetence and greed will do almost as well.

The author has an innate dislike of taking orders, a pathological contempt for pomposity, hypocrisy and the sort of unthinking political correctness which attracts support from *Guardian*-reading pseudo-intellectuals. He also has a passionate loathing for those in authority who do not understand that unless their authority is tempered with compassion and a sense of responsibility the end result must always be an extremely unpleasant brand of totalitarianism.

He upsets more people than he means to but apologises only to those who are upset by accident rather than design.

Vernon Coleman is the iconoclastic author of well over a hundred books which have sold over two million copies in the

UK, been translated into 23 languages and now sell in over 50 countries. His bestselling non-fiction book *Bodypower* was voted one of the 100 most popular books of the 1980s/90s and was turned into two television series in the UK. The film of his novel *Mrs Caldicot's Cabbage War* was released early in 2003.

Vernon Coleman has written columns for numerous newspapers and magazines and has contributed over 5,000 articles, columns and reviews to hundreds of leading publications around the world. Many millions have consulted his advice lines and his website. Vernon Coleman has a medical degree, and an honorary science doctorate. He has worked for the Open University in the UK and is an honorary Professor of Holistic Medical Sciences at the Open International University based in Sri Lanka. Vernon Coleman has received lots of rather jolly awards from people he likes and respects. He worked as a GP for ten years and is still a registered medical practitioner. He has organised numerous campaigns both for people and for animals.

He likes books, cafés and writing and once won a certificate for swimming a width of the public baths in Walsall (which was, at the time, in Staffordshire but has now, apparently, been moved elsewhere). He likes cats, pens, cricket and notebooks. His favourite place is Les Invalides, his favourite author is P.G.Wodehouse and his favourite piece of music is whatever he is listening to at the time (because that's why he put it on). He can ride a bicycle and swim, though not at the same time. He likes desolate country places, small country towns and busy cities. His favourite cities in the world are London, Paris and Vienna and it is no coincidence that it was in these cities that coffee houses first appeared and it is in the last two that cafés are now still at their best.

(Some critics have sneered at his affection for the Europe on the other side of the Channel, arguing that it is absurd for someone opposed to the EU to enjoy going anywhere that isn't in Britain. What these idiots don't understand is that opposing European bureaucracy does not preclude loving European history, culture and architecture. Indeed, one of the reasons why he loathes the EU is that it wants to turn the whole of Europe into a homogenous greyness.)

OFPIS

Vernon Coleman enjoys chess, malt whisky and old films and is married and devoted to Donna Antoinette who is the kindest, sweetest, most sensitive woman a man could hope to meet and who, as an undeserved but welcome bonus, makes the very best roast potatoes on the planet. They live in Bilbury, Devon, surrounded by animals and books.

Vernon Coleman is balding rapidly and is widely disliked by members of the Establishment. He doesn't give a toss about either of these facts. Many attempts have been made to ban his books (many national publications ban all mention of them) but he insists he will keep writing them even if he has to write them out in longhand and sell them on street corners (though he hopes it doesn't come to this because he still has a doctor's handwriting).

For a catalogue of Vernon Coleman's books
please write to:

Publishing House
Trinity Place
Barnstaple
Devon EX32 9HG
England

Telephone   01271 328892
Fax   01271 328768

Outside the UK:
Telephone   +44 1271 328892
Fax   +44 1271 328768

Or visit our website:
www.vernoncoleman.com

Also by Vernon Coleman

Living In A Fascist Country
Conspiracies, peak oil, greedy politicians, endless religious wars and your disappearing freedom and privacy.

We are losing our freedom and our privacy. The world is changing so fast that it is difficult to keep up. Britain and America are now fascist states. Why? What is going on? Whatever happened to democracy? Who is behind it all? How did we come to find ourselves in what the politicians boast will be an everlasting war?

'Everybody ought to have a copy of this book.'
FOURTH WORLD REVIEW

"I suggest you buy this book, to give you perspective on what's underway and what to do about it personally."
HARRY SCHULTZ "HSL NEWSLETTER"

'... like a bedtime book of nightmares ... scary stuff indeed.'
NEXUS

'With its accounts of how the government is fooling the people ... how ID cards and under-the-skin chips will destroy personal liberty, how public infrastructure has been offloaded to the highest bidder, and how the banks and other institutions are in on the take, this book is a manifesto aimed at alerting people to the fact that they're being manipulated big-time and calling on them to rise up to assert their rights before it's too late.'
NEXUS MAGAZINE

Paperback £15.99
Published by Blue Books
Order from Publishing House • Trinity Place • Barnstaple •
Devon EX32 9HG • England
Telephone 01271 328892 • Fax 01271 328768
www.vernoncoleman.com

Also by Vernon Coleman

Oil Apocalypse

How to Survive, Protect Your Family And Profit Through The Coming Years of Crisis

Why the oil apocalypse is inevitable. How and why our dependence on oil will end in tears. And how you can prepare yourself and your family.

Also includes

- Our Unhealthy Addiction To A Gift Of Nature
- Peak Oil: The Beginning Of The End Of Civilisation
- Oil Wars: Past, Present And Future
- What Will Happen When The Oil Runs Out
- A New Energy Blueprint
- Your Personal Survival Plan
- Investing To Survive The Oil Apocalypse

The world you know is going to change dramatically and permanently. Anyone under fifty, with a normal life expectation, will live to see a world almost unrecognisable from the one they grew up in. Five billion people will die within a very short time. There will be no cars, no lorries, no buses, no aeroplanes and no supermarkets. The rich will travel by horse and cart. The middle classes will use bicycles. The poor will walk. The oil is running out and, as a result, our civilisation is reaching its end.

You will never read a more important or more alarming book than this one. The disaster inexorably heading our way will make any natural disaster, any tsunami, seem inconsequential. Forget global warming. Forget terrorism. They are trivial problems.

If you want to know the truth, and you think you can deal with it, sit down, turn to the first page and read this book now. It will change your life. Forever.

Vernon Coleman

Paperback £12.99
Published by Blue Books
Order from Publishing House • Trinity Place • Barnstaple •
Devon EX32 9HG • England
Telephone 01271 328892 • Fax 01271 328768
www.vernoncoleman.com

Also by Vernon Coleman

How To Protect And Preserve Your Freedom, Identity And Privacy

Did you know that the average person does not know that their identity has been stolen until 12 months later? Did you know that the average person believes that shredding vital documents alone will protect them from fraud? And did you know that the average person believes that identity fraud will not happen to them?

Thousands of people fall victim to identity theft every year. The consequences can be absolutely devastating and can take years to sort out. There are scores of ways that your identity can be stolen. The majority of people aren't aware of just how vulnerable they are until it's too late.

How To Protect And Preserve Your Freedom, Identity And Privacy gives advice on:

- What to do if you're a victim of identity theft (a must-have just for this advice alone).
- The type of phone you should use to protect yourself from fraud.
- The tricks fraudsters use at cash machines (a real eye opener!)
- The signs to look out for which show if you have become a victim of identity fraud.
- Why you should be wary of the 'postman' knocking at your door
- How answering your phone could leave you vulnerable to fraud
- Why you should be wary about the clothes you wear

If you should be unfortunate to find yourself a victim of identity fraud then this book will tell you what you can do. For this reason alone, you need this book. It could be a lifesaver

Paperback £9.99
Published by Blue Books
Order from Publishing House • Trinity Place • Barnstaple •
Devon EX32 9HG • England
Telephone 01271 328892 • Fax 01271 328768
www.vernoncoleman.com

Also by Vernon Coleman

How To Stop Your Doctor Killing You

Dr Coleman has been a passionate advocate of patients' rights for over thirty years, and in writing this book he has drawn together a vast amount of information which will help readers to live longer and healthier lives. It shows how patients can protect themselves against an increasingly incompetent and dangerous medical profession. To minimise the risk, says Dr Coleman, individuals should retain responsibility for their own health and not rely on outside intervention. Patients should learn to be sceptical and know how to ask the right questions. Patients should know what to watch out for when taking drugs and how to get the best out of hospitals and doctors when they are needed.

Topics covered include:

- Don't let your doctor bully you

- How to survive in hospital

- The real cause of cancer – and the solution

- How to manipulate your doctor

- Tests and investigations – are they safe?

- Should you get a second opinion?

- Questions to ask your surgeon

- Ten good reasons why you shouldn't trust
  your doctor

Paperback £12.99
Published by EMJ Books
Order from Publishing House • Trinity Place • Barnstaple •
Devon EX32 9HG • England
Telephone 01271 328892 • Fax 01271 328768
www.vernoncoleman.com

Also by Vernon Coleman

Gordon is a Moron

The Definitive And Objective Analysis Of Gordon Brown's Decade As Chancellor Of The Exchequer

In *Gordon is a Moron* Vernon Coleman examines Gordon Brown's work as Chancellor of the Exchequer, and the impact his efforts have had on the economy and on our economic future.

The dictionary defines a moron as a stupid person and it's unlikely that anyone reading this book will be left in any doubt that Gordon Brown, darling of the left wing, and widely-acclaimed by the intellectually-disadvantaged media-proponents of fascism as a heavyweight political intellectual, is a moron; a truly stupid person. Brown's term as Chancellor will, Vernon Coleman believes, be remembered for poor decisions, prejudice and Soviet quality attempts at social engineering. The book explains how Brown's stupidity and incompetence have weakened Britain for generations to come.

"If you share my horror at the lowering of quality and standards in public life you will, I suspect, also share my belief that no one exemplifies the lowering more dramatically than Gordon the Moron. I have tried to deal with Brown in an objective and academic way but I make no apologies if any of my contempt has seeped into my prose. What have we done to deserve public servants such as Brown? It must have been something pretty terrible"
TAKEN FROM THE PREFACE OF *GORDON IS A MORON*

Paperback £9.99
Published by Blue Books
Order from Publishing House • Trinity Place • Barnstaple •
Devon EX32 9HG • England
Telephone 01271 328892 • Fax 01271 328768
www.vernoncoleman.com